Terrors of the Flesh

ALSO BY DAVID HUCKVALE
AND FROM MCFARLAND

Dirk Bogarde: Matinee Idol, Art House Star (2019)

Movie Magick: The Occult in Film (2018)

*A Green and Pagan Land: Myth, Magic and Landscape
in British Film and Television* (2018)

Music for the Superman: Nietzsche and the Great Composers (2017)

*A Dark and Stormy Oeuvre: Crime, Magic and Power in
the Novels of Edward Bulwer-Lytton* (2016)

Hammer Films' Psychological Thrillers, 1950–1972 (2014)

Poe Evermore: The Legacy in Film, Music and Television (2014)

*The Occult Arts of Music: An Esoteric Survey
from Pythagoras to Pop Culture* (2013)

*James Bernard, Composer to Count Dracula: A Critical
Biography* (2006; paperback 2012)

*Ancient Egypt in the Popular Imagination: Building a
Fantasy in Film, Literature, Music and Art* (2012)

*Visconti and the German Dream: Romanticism, Wagner
and the Nazi Catastrophe in Film* (2012)

*Touchstones of Gothic Horror: A Film Genealogy
of Eleven Motifs and Images* (2010)

Hammer Film Scores and the Musical Avant-Garde (2008)

Terrors of the Flesh
The Philosophy of Body Horror in Film

David Huckvale

McFarland & Company, Inc., Publishers
Jefferson, North Carolina

LIBRARY OF CONGRESS CATALOGUING-IN-PUBLICATION DATA

Names: Huckvale, David, author.
Title: Terrors of the flesh : the philosophy of body horror in film / David Huckvale.
Description: Jefferson : McFarland & Company, Inc., Publishers, 2020. | Includes bibliographical references and index.
Identifiers: LCCN 2020027087 | ISBN 9781476682181 (paperback : acid free paper) ∞
ISBN 9781476640785 (ebook)
Subjects: LCSH: Horror films—History and criticism. | Human body in motion pictures. | Death in motion pictures. | Motion pictures—Psychological aspects. | Motion pictures—Philosophy. | Motion pictures and literature.
Classification: LCC PN1995.9.H6 H75553 2020 | DDC 791.43/6164—dc23
LC record available at https://lccn.loc.gov/2020027087

BRITISH LIBRARY CATALOGUING DATA ARE AVAILABLE

ISBN (print) 978-1-4766-8218-1
ISBN (ebook) 978-1-4766-4078-5

© 2020 David Huckvale. All rights reserved

No part of this book may be reproduced or transmitted in any form or by any means, electronic or mechanical, including photocopying or recording, or by any information storage and retrieval system, without permission in writing from the publisher.

Front cover image by Teodor Lazarev/Shutterstock

Printed in the United States of America

*McFarland & Company, Inc., Publishers
Box 611, Jefferson, North Carolina 28640
www.mcfarlandpub.com*

Table of Contents

Introduction   1

One. Copulation   15
Two. Generation   26
Three. Digestion   52
Four. Mutilation   78
Five. Infection   102
Six. Mutation   111
Seven. Disintegration   127
Eight. Extinction   140

Epilogue: Consolation   162
Chapter Notes   171
Bibliography   177
Index   181

"Let us be assured of it: that we are made of matter only, that what is immaterial is inexistent; that all we attribute to the soul is all simply the effect of matter; and this in spite of our human pride which causes us to stress the distinction between ourselves and brute beasts however it be that, like beasts, we yield up to the dust the dust whereof we are made, and when dead shall be no more punished than they for the bad deeds which the kind of organization we have received from Nature has induced us to commit, nor more rewarded for the good deeds we performed simply because we have been otherwise structured."

—Marquis de Sade, *Juliette*[1]

Introduction

> I am body entirely, and nothing beside; and soul is only a word for something in the body. The body is a great intelligence, a multiplicity with one sense, a war and a peace, a herd and a herdsman.
>
> —Friedrich Nietzsche[1]

What has become known as body horror in the cinema can be traced back to the writings of the Marquis de Sade (1740–1814). In his 1200-page novel *Juliette* (1797), Sade holds forth on the preeminence of the body:

> —Although ... everything proves to man that he feels, thinks, acquires thoughts and ideas, takes pleasure and suffers pain only by means of the sense or the organs of the body, notwithstanding he carries on with his folly and comes to the point of believing that this soul about which he knows nothing is exempt from death. But even supposing this soul to exist, tell me, if you please, how one can avoid recognizing its total dependence upon the body and the fact that it must share in all the vicissitudes of the body's fate. ... Inside and out, through and through; and once the Fates have severed the thread, the human frame is no more than an inert mass, unable to produce those movements which, collectively, constituted its life. In the dead body neither circulation nor respiration nor digestion nor locution nor intellection are any longer there; upon death, so they say, the soul quits the body; but to say that this soul, of which nothing is known, is the principle of life is to say nothing at all unless it be that an unknown force is the hidden principle of imperceptible motions. What is more natural and simpler than to believe a dead man is dead, over and done with; and what more ludicrous than to believe that when a man is dead he's still alive? ... To say that human souls will be happy or unhappy after death is tantamount to declaring that men can see without eyes, hear with fingers.[2]

Sade's 18th-century corporeal philosophy strongly anticipated that of Friedrich Nietzsche (1844–1900) in the 19th century, though Nietzsche hoped to channel his own nihilism into an optimistic framework that was not merely libertinage. His optimism was in stark contrast to the conclusions of the great philosopher of pessimism Arthur Schopenhauer (1788–1860), a thinker who nonetheless influenced Nietzsche rather more than Sade.

Neither of them believed in God, but Nietzsche believed we should all shout a resounding "Yes" to life, despite its horrors, whereas for Schopenhauer, as the following quotation makes clear, life is an unqualified disaster:

> If the act of recreation were neither the outcome of a desire nor accompanied by feelings of pleasure, but a matter to be decided on the basis of purely rational considerations, is it likely the human race would still exist? Would each of us not rather have felt so much pity for the coming generation as to prefer to spare it the burden of existence, or at least not wish to take it upon himself to impose that burden upon it in cold blood?[3]

Schopenhauer may well have a point, but the fact remains that we are here, and in the brave new world of the modern age, horror films have been the most influential way we have negotiated both the many uncertainties of existence and its only absolute certainty of death. David Cronenberg, one of the most famous exponents of body horror in the cinema, is a true follower of Nietzsche and Sade:

> For me, the human body is the first fact of human existence. I do feel that death is the end, there is no afterlife, and therefore the existence of the body is the existence of the individual; and therefore the focus of the films on the body, as a way of exploring the various aspects of life as a human, seems obvious. ... I'm saying that there is no morality or ethics than is other than what we create; there are no absolutes that come from outer space or from God or religion, or whatever—that in fact we create them and therefore they are very changeable, and very malleable.[4]

In an earlier interview, Cronenberg confessed:

> The true subject of horror films is death and anticipation of death, and that leads to the question of Man as body as opposed to Man as spirit. All my films have a strong physical consciousness. Being a mind in a body is a conundrum especially as, as happened to my father, the body starts to go and the mind has not.[5]

Cronenberg wrote the screenplay of *Shivers* (1975) while his father was dying, "and we were very close. It was a quite horrible death. No reason for it. It was just bad. Catharsis: that's what the films can do. It's a release of inner tension to get involved with a film like that and have it end the way it does."[6]

One of Cronenberg's most memorable images actually makes the means by which his films were most widely disseminated in the 1980s, the video cassette, into a thing of flesh and blood itself: In *Videodrome* (1983), not only does a VHS cassette squirm, bulge and bleed, thanks to the hallucinatory premise of the story, but in its fleshy state it is actually inserted into the stomach of the hero Max Renn (James Woods) through a bloody slot that appears in his stomach. He is thus made into a human VCR, a condition that wittily, if gruesomely, epitomizes the fate of many a couch-bound film fanatic.

Introduction 3

What follows is therefore a kind of autopsy of those films that explore the profound anxieties we have about our own bodies and consequently of our very existence. As such, they are philosophical films. We are, after all, so vulnerable, so fragile, so *penetrable*, that it is not overstating the case to say that we retire to bed each night the victor of a battle in a war unwon. "With cautious step and anxious glance around he pursues his path," Schopenhauer once wrote, "for a thousand accidents and a thousand enemies lie in wait for him. Thus he went in the savage state, and thus he goes in civilized life; there is no security for him."[7] Without God, the body becomes our *only reality*, and because our understanding of reality is entirely the product of our own fleshly brains, our understanding of that reality becomes increasingly uncertain the more we think about it. We often speak of "my body" as though it were a thing we own—a kind of robot, as opposed to our consciousness, which is the "real" us. Religion teaches the doctrine of the soul in this respect. We like to see ourselves as the commanders of our bodies, using them as vehicles of the will, but in fact we are entirely the servants of our bodies. Everything about destiny is inevitably dependent upon our inescapable physicality. The whole edifice of civilization rests upon the constitution of the body, a point grasped by Scrooge in Dickens' *A Christmas Carol* in which he condenses the vast superstructure of human metaphysics with the comment addressed to the Ghost of Jacob Marley as having "more of gravy than of grave" about it. "You may be an undigested bit of beef," he argues, "a blot of mustard, a crumb of cheese, a fragment of an underdone potato."[8] And he is right, even though the story in which he finds himself playing so central a role disagrees with him. Similarly, society has often chosen to disagree with—and punish—those of who have rejected its institutionalized supernatural convictions.

Nietzsche writes of the hidden causes of our illnesses, which may lie "in a sickening of the *nervus sympathicus*, or in excessive secretion from the gall-bladder, in a deficiency of sulphuric or phosphoric potash in the blood, or in poor circulation in the lower body, or in the degeneration of the ovaries or the like."[9] The reason Nietzsche indulges in such a long list of malfunctions is to emphasize his new approach to human destiny: that is it not dependent upon the metaphysical but the entirely physical. We must, of course, care for our bodies, as a good servant cares for his master, but we can never leave their service, until death makes us all unemployed.

Uncertainty regarding the nature of reality was famously proposed by Immanuel Kant (1724–1804), who argued that it is impossible to know its essence. What he called the "Ding an sich," or the "thing-in-itself," is forever far beyond our unreliable perception of it, a perception that is entirely dependent upon our bodily organs. Schopenhauer, much influenced by and indeed dependent upon Kant, summed up this dilemma:

> Time, space, and casualty are not determinations of the thing-in-itself, but belong only to its phenomenon, since they are nothing but forms of our knowledge. Now as all plurality and all arising and passing away are possible only through time, space, and causality, it follows that they too adhere only to the phenomenon, and by no means to the thing-in-itself. But since our knowledge is conditioned by these forms, the whole of experience is only knowledge of the phenomenon, not of the thing-in-itself; hence also its laws cannot be made valid for the thing-in-itself. What has been said extends even to our own ego, and we know that only as phenomenon, not according to what it may be in itself.[10]

G.W.F. Hegel (1770–1831) went further and dispensed with the thing-in-itself altogether, arguing that what we know is in fact all there is, and that, as Peter Singer has explained, "the only thing that is ultimately real is the absolute idea, which is Mind, knowing itself as reality."[11]

Cronenberg actually reflects this view of reality in *Videodrome* (1983) in which the character Professor Brian O'Blivion (Jack Creley) insists, "After all, there is nothing real outside our perception of reality." Cronenberg also suggests that his chosen medium is, like the videodrome itself, "a massive hallucination machine." The imagery of the glowing hallucination recorder, which is placed on Max's head, recapitulates the less elaborate helmet worn by Peter Gilmore's scientist Charles Aitken in *Warlords of Atlantis* (dir. Kevin Connor, 1976). The helmet treats Aitken to an overview of humanity's historical development, all apparently manipulated by the Martians who inhabit the subaqueous kingdom of Atlantis in which Aitken and his friends find themselves. Cronenberg's helmet, however, glows with anatomical undertones, providing a powerful symbol of his main point in this film that it is the brain that creates our understanding of reality—perhaps even reality itself.

Extending the metaphor, O'Blivion even goes so far as to suggest that "television is reality and reality is less than television." Such a view is no more than a re-phrasing of Oscar Wilde's famous dictum that it is Nature that imitates Art and not vice versa: *Videodrome* is primarily concerned with the power of the "realities" of television (or "art" in general) to influence the way in which we behave and understand the world, not to mention the hallucinations experienced by the protagonist Max Renn, which are as real for him as anything else. If "mind" is our only reality, there is no proof that everything is not a hallucination, even the body itself; it is certainly an unstable reality, subject as it is to sudden mutilation or gradual mutation. The body is so fluid and so impermanent that nothing in our existence, other than death, can be relied upon.

Following Cronenberg's example, this book was originally inspired by the deaths of my own parents, whose terminal decline I, like so many other people, both observed and cared for over a considerable period of time. This process, with all its attendant horrors, brought home to me the grim truths of the horror films I have spent so much of my life watching and thinking about, and my experiences of the sick room led me even further afield into the more obscure territory that Sigmund Freud had tentatively begun to chart in his late essay "Beyond the Pleasure Principle" (1920). As I watched the bodies of my parents literally collapse before my eyes, almost like vampires in daylight or Egyptian mummies deprived of Tana leaves, Freud's so-called death-instinct appeared to me as a merciful aspect of the psyche, which, if indeed part of Nature's plan, seemed to counterbalance its appalling cruelty. Indeed, Freud appropriately brings Schopenhauer to his aid when discussing his still controversial theory:

> There is something else, at any rate, that we cannot be blind to. We have unwittingly steered our court into the harbor of Schopenhauer's philosophy. For him death is the "true result and to that extent the purpose of life," while the sexual instinct is the embodiment of the will to live.[12]

One of the first historians of the horror film genre, Carlos Clarens, appears to have agreed with Freud here: "Fantastic art, of which horror films and science fiction are the popular champions," he writes in his *Illustrated Survey of Horror Films*, "makes us realize that man carries in himself an instinct for destruction, but also the will to curb this instinct."[13]

The instinct to perpetuate the species is indeed a very powerful one, but body horror films often expose our ambivalence about the idea of reproduction. This contentious view has recently been repackaged by the contemporary anti-natalist philosopher David Benatar, who believes that having children is, quite simply and in every respect, a mistake: "It is curious that while good people go to great lengths to spare their children from suffering, few of them seem to notice that the one (and only) guaranteed way to prevent all the suffering of their children is not to bring those children into existence in the first place."[14] Some horror films do indeed promote a horror of giving birth along with a positive fear of children, and this apparent contradiction requires, it seems to me, some careful investigation.

The horror and psychological denial we have of our mortality, along with the corruptibility of our flesh, are persistent themes in all drama, which body horror films have, of course, intensified in increasingly graphic terms over the years. One might say that such films articulate the horror we have of ourselves, particularly as the capability we have of inflicting harm on each other has grown with advances in technology across the military, marketing and social media worlds. The feminist writer Anne Elizabeth Moore has, for example, used the genre of body horror to identify the misogyny inherent in contemporary capitalist society, equating the exploitation of women's bodies in the name of profit with what happens to so many female bodies in body horror films. She argues that "the most terrifying aspects of your average body horror narrative might actually be so common among folks who experience the world as women that the stories are no longer scary." She also equates capitalism and body horror in terms of the physical illnesses actually caused by capitalism, which in turn transform us all into monsters. Her own physical ill health made the connection:

> Body horror describes storytelling media, including literature, film, TV, video games, and comics. Originally it applied to any horror story that dealt with the body, but now it's come to refer to something more specific, a focus on bodily changes—particularly stories that offer a visceral sense of the body changing. So having a monster in a horror film doesn't make it body horror, but when the story is told from the point of view of the monster it often is body horror, because the monster is going, like, "Aaah, my arm (or whatever)! There are horrible things going on with me and here is how they feel inside me and it also looks disgusting!"
>
> I've always watched a lot of horror films, but as I started to get sick I connected more deeply to the monster narrative. So I'll watch a body horror film now and evaluate it more on my experience of what is being portrayed than on how disgusting it is or how awesome it is or how well done the makeup is. ...
>
> This may sound weird and awful but I am often treated as if I were becoming a monster.[15]

Terrors of the Flesh is by no means an exhaustive survey of every body horror film ever made; rather I have selected titles that seem to me to epitomize our many corporeal anxieties, which I have divided into seven broad themes: not so much the seven ages man as the seven *stages* of the human body. Chapter One penetrates the ambivalent world of sex and reproduction, which Mary Shelley, in *Frankenstein*, called "the filthy workshop of creation." Chapter Two explores the bodily horrors of birth and our often-ambivalent responses to children, which many films have presented as being particularly monstrous. In Chapter Three we journey into the very core of what it means to be human: our digestive system, the source of a great deal of the horror we have of ourselves. Chapters Four and Five are devoted, respectively, to various aspects of mutilation and mutation, which embrace a variety of symbolic uses both sociological and psychological. Chapter Six is devoted to that other corruptibility of the body that leads to insanity before we head toward the final section on death itself, which is perhaps the least terrifying of all seven categories. Having observed its arrival on several occasions, along with the release it brings, it has always appeared to me as far less terrifying than life.

Drama in general has always had a cathartic function, as Aristotle made clear in his *Poetics*, where he described tragedy as "effecting, through pity and fear, the purification of such emotions."[16] Horror and fantasy films are, similarly, responses to life's adversities, particularly the disturbing destiny of our own flesh and blood. What the film historian Lotte H. Eisner called the "face of death on the battlefields"[17] during the First World War went on to inspire the classic German horror films of the 1920s, and later body horror movies have addressed the overwhelming carnage and mutilation of the 20th century's subsequent military conflicts. By bravely facing the horrors of the body, fantasy films have helped us negotiate those horrors by, to some extent, immunizing us against them. Like braving a vindaloo curry, there is a certain machismo in engaging with cinematic gore. How much can you take? And, anyway, it's all make-believe, but if we can laugh at horror on screen, we find it easier to pretend that we might be able to laugh at the real thing if it should happen to us—which, of course, it will. Nietzsche, even though he became insane before the cinema was born, would have agreed with the process entirely:

> Here, when the danger to his will is greatest, *art* approaches as a saving sorceress, expert at healing. She alone knows how to turn these nauseous thoughts about the horror or absurdity of existence into notions with which one can live: these are the *sublime* as the artistic taming of the horrible, and the *comic* as the artistic discharge of the nausea of absurdity.[18]

The absurd horror of our fleshly destiny can indeed be transmuted into nourishing fantasy. Because we are all conscious of the inevitability of death, because we know that we will inevitably suffer somehow while we are alive, horror films provide us with a magic mirror that reflects our anxieties back at ourselves. As Carlos Clarens puts it, "there seems to be inside us a constant, ever-present yearning for the fantastic, for the darkly mysterious, for the choked terror of the dark."

> This demand is orthodoxly satisfied by religion or, surreptitiously, by superstition. Unfortunately, the enemies of the surviving religions have not survived with them: in recent times, witches and demons have lost their hold on us. Everything horrible has been swallowed up by the unconscious—that swamp of self-dread from which there emerge many ambiguous manifestations of itself. And these are the black arts of the day.[19]

Horror serves much the same function, therefore, as the traditional consolations of philosophy we find in writers of the Stoic school, such as Marcus Aurelius:

> Consider that before long thou wilt be nobody and nowhere, nor will any of the things exist which thou now seest, nor any of those who are now living. For all things are formed by nature to change and be turned and to perish in order that other things in continuous succession may exist.[20]

To this we may add the closing comments of the Chorus in Sophocles' *King Oedipus*.

> Then learn that mortal man must always look to his ending,
> And none can be called happy until that day when he carries
> His happiness down to the grave in peace.[21]

These lines are the seed of so much later drama, particularly those Elizabethan and Jacobean tragedies that were in so many ways the precursors of 20th-century horror films. In Act III of Shakespeare's *Measure for Measure*, for example, Duke Vincentio counsels the condemned Claudio with advice that has much in common with what Schopenhauer and Benatar put forth in their respective philosophies:

> Be absolute for death; either death or life
> Shall thereby be the sweeter. Reason thus with life:
> If I do lose thee, I do lose a thing
> That none but fools would keep: a breath thou art,
> Servile to all the skyey influences,
> That dost this habitation, where thou keep'st,
> Hourly afflict: merely, thou art death's fool;
> For him thou labour'st by thy flight to shun
> And yet runn'st toward him still. Thou art not noble;
> For all the accommodations that thou bear'st
> Are nursed by baseness. Thou'rt by no means valiant;
> For thou dost fear the soft and tender fork
> Of a poor worm. Thy best of rest is sleep,
> And that thou oft provokest; yet grossly fear'st
> Thy death, which is no more. Thou art not thyself;
> For thou exist'st on many a thousand grains
> That issue out of dust. Happy thou art not;
> For what thou hast not, still thou strivest to get,
> And what thou hast, forget'st. Thou art not certain;
> For thy complexion shifts to strange effects,
> After the moon. If thou art rich, thou'rt poor;
> For, like an ass whose back with ingots bows,
> Thou bear's thy heavy riches but a journey,
> And death unloads thee. Friend hast thou none;
> For thine own bowels, which do call thee sire,
> The mere effusion of thy proper loins,
> Do curse the gout, serpigo, and the rheum,
> For ending thee no sooner. Thou hast nor youth nor age,
> But, as it were, an after-dinner's sleep,
> Dreaming on both; for all thy blessed youth
> Becomes as aged, and doth beg the alms
> Of palsied eld; and when thou art old and rich,
> Thou hast neither heat, affection, limb, nor beauty,
> To make thy riches pleasant. What's yet in this
> That bears the name of life? Yet in this life
> Lie hid one thousand deaths: yet death we fear,
> That makes these odds all even.[22]

Similarly, Macbeth concludes his bloody career with appropriately nihilistic view that "all our yesterdays have lighted fools/The way to dusty death."

Introduction

> Life's but a walking shadow, a poor player
> That struts and frets his hour upon the stage
> And then is heard no more. It is a tale
> Told by an idiot, full of sound and fury
> Signifying nothing.[23]

Shakespeare, however, was always sure to frame his tragedies within a wider social context. After his tragedies reach their culminations, other characters ensure that the social world will pick up the pieces and continue the project. After the general slaughter at the end of *Hamlet*, for example, Fortinbras arrives to restore order and meaning to the meaningless chaos he discovers at the court of Elsinore, but in his earlier "To be or not to be" soliloquy, Hamlet has so strongly undermined the possibility of any restoration of "common sense" or triumph of everyday expedience that Fortinbras' arrival on the scene seems redundant. Hamlet has acknowledged the desire "to die: to sleep."

> No more; and by a sleep to say we end
> The heart-ache and the thousand natural shocks
> That flesh is heir to, 'tis a consummation
> Devoutly to be wish'd.

Only Hamlet's Christian upbringing prevents him acting on this insight:

> For who would bear the whips and scorns of time,
> The oppressor's wrong, the proud man's contumely,
> The pangs of despised love, the law's delay,
> The insolence of office and the spurns
> That patient merit of the unworthy takes,
> When he himself might his quietus make
> With a bare bodkin? who would fardels bear,
> To grunt and sweat under a weary life,
> But that the dread of something after death,
> The undiscover'd country from whose bourn
> No traveller returns, puzzles the will.[24]

This ultimate soliloquy was nobly recited by Vincent Price in the black comedy *Theatre of Blood* (dir. Douglas Hickox, 1973), a film that delightfully cements the connection between the bodily horrors of Shakespeare and the horror films for which Price had by that time become so well known. *Theatre of Blood* revels in a compendium of bodily mutilations perpetrated by Price's disgruntled actor manager Edward Lionheart. Overlooked and derided by the committee of London Critics' Circle Awards, he stages his own death before returning to avenge himself on those very critics by Shakespearean means. The murder of the first (played by Michael Hordern) resembles that of Caesar in *Julius Caesar*, whose body is violently stabbed to death. The death of the second critic (Dennis Price) recapitulates Hector's murder in

Troilus & Cressida, as he is dragged behind a galloping horse and mutilated into a bloody pulp. The third (Arthur Lowe) has his head severed like Cloton's in *Cymbeline*. For the fourth (Harry Andrews), Lionheart rewrites *The Merchant of Venice*, removing what he calls Shakespeare's "pettifogging piece of legal trickery" from the text and thus allowing him to cut out his adversary's heart, which Shylock is prevented, at the last minute, from so doing to Antonio in the original play. The fifth critic (Robert Coote) is drowned in a butt of Malmsey, as is the Duke of Clarence in *Richard III*. The sixth critic (Jack Hawkins) is persuaded to strangle his own wife like Othello, hence ensuring his life imprisonment, while the seventh (Coral Browne, who, having encountered Price while performing in this film, went on to marry him) is electrocuted under a hair dryer, imitating the fiery execution of Joan of Arc in *Henry VI: Part One*. We will encounter the eighth critic (Robert Morley) and his particularly grotesque fate in a later chapter, and the ninth (Ian Hendry) is subjected to a duel à la *Romeo and Juliet* before being threatened with blindness as is Gloucester in *King Lear*.

Theatre of Blood juxtaposes black comedy with extreme visceral body horror fully in the spirit of the approach of Shakespeare himself, and though

Pound of flesh. Harry Andrews as Trevor Dickman (middle foreground) playing his part in the Edward Lionheart production of "The Merchant of Venice" with Vincent Price (second from right) and Diana Rigg (right) in *Theatre of Blood* (dir. Douglas Hickox, 1973).

Lionheart is not allowed to get away with his crimes, his own demise is the only really tragic death in the whole piece. His heroic rejection of a world and value system with which he is so at odds resembles not only the grotesquely disfigured Dr. Anton Phibes, which Price also played in *The Abominable Dr. Phibes* (dir. Robert Fuest, 1971) and *Dr. Phibes Rises Again* (dir. Robert Fuest, 1972), but also that of Erik, the Phantom of the Opera in Gaston Leroux's famous novel (and its subsequent cinematic adaptations, which we will be exploring in more detail later on). Both Erik's and Phibes' facial disfigurements symbolize their alienation from society with its philosophical, moral and esthetic assumptions. The everyday, common sense world does indeed restore order at the end of *Theatre of Blood*, but not without considerable regret for the audience, for Lionheart, despite his madness, represents a more Romantic and indeed meaningful approach to life than the lifeless values upheld by the Critics' Circle, who assemble amid the significantly very modern (for the 1970s) décor of the chairman's flat. And it is there that Lionheart does indeed put Hamlet's "To be or not to be" into practice. Before reciting, with superb panache, the famous lines and hurling himself into the river Thames, he accuses the critics of indulging in "overweening malice" against him by having given that year's award to a "twitching mumbling boy who can barely grunt his way through an incomprehensible performance." The vocabulary is telling, reminding us of Hamlet's reference to the way in which we "grunt and sweat under a weary life."

Unlike Shakespeare (or *Theatre of Blood*), Shakespeare's contemporary Christopher Marlowe offers little sense of a restoration of order at the end of *Doctor Faustus*, in which the restless, and what we would now call existential alienation of Hamlet, is recast in the character of the famous magician, who concludes his earthly journey with the line "Curs'd be the parents that engendered me!" before thinking twice and instead cursing himself and his pact with Lucifer. The context of all this is obviously Christian, and Faustus envies the natural, "unconscious" state of animals— "All beasts are happy,/For when they die/Their souls are soon dissolved in elements,/But mine must live still to be plagued in hell"—but as E.D. Pendry suggests in his introduction to the play,

> The last speech is moving not because it springs from fear of death or fear of punishment, but because, in marked contrast to Faustus's early speeches in the play, it springs from fear of life. It is the utterance of someone who would rather dissolve, be no one, nothing. The vast prospect of eternity is appalling, but the consciousness of time passing and of the present moment in its intensity is no less so. In short, any human being, atheist or not, responds to such a speech, since it defines the anguish of what it is to be a soul poised for a span on the brink of infinity.[25]

Pendry also points out, "Marlowe does not know why man is put here. But he is sure the arrangement does not work. Every one of his heroes has high hopes of making something of himself and his life, but comes to find that the world is not for him, nor he for the world."

> This may seem well within the tradition of classical tragedy, which affirms that the greatness of men and richness of their experience lie as much in their agonies and defeats as in their triumphs. But Marlowe's tragedy is not like that. We think less well of his heroes at their ending, and the world is a smaller and grimmer place. Nor are there Christian consolations. Marlowe is nothing more unchristian than in flatly denying the oath of failure. To his eye his heroes die in vain. They do not learn, we do not learn, from their mistakes; there is nothing to compensate for loss either here or hereafter.[26]

Faust's fear of hell is a physical one—the ultimate bodily horror of torment unending—but the most obvious Jacobean precursor to the body horror and Grand Guignol of later films is surely John Webster's *The Duchess of Malfi* with its graphic violence and atmosphere of nightmare anxiety, its frightening wax effigies (which would later inspire the horrors behind the veil in Ann Radcliffe's famous Gothic novel *The Mysteries of Udolpho*), the sinister incorporation of an echo that anticipates the "Nevermore" of Poe's "The Raven," and its madmen who are paraded before the condemned Duchess to terrify and unnerve her. (Hammer's ubiquitous composer James Bernard began his career with incidental music for a BBC radio production of this play in 1954, and later recast the motif with which he accompanied the madmen's lines "O let us how, some heavy note,/Some deadly-dogged howl" as the theme for *The Curse of Frankenstein* [dir. Terence Fisher, 1958].) *The Duchess of Malfi* also makes reference to werewolves with regard to the villain of the piece, the crazed and vengeful brother of the Duchess, Ferdinand. A doctor explains that lycanthropy is a "melancholy humor," causing those who suffer from the delusion to

> steal forth to churchyards in the dead of night,
> And dig dead bodies up: as two nights since
> One met the Duke, 'bout midnight in a lane
> Behind St. Mark's church, with a leg of a man
> Upon his shoulder; and he howled fearfully—
> Said he was a wolf; only the difference
> Was a wolf's skin was hairy on the outside,
> His on the inside.[27]

(We will be returning to the subject of werewolves, an important manifestation of bodily horror, in a later chapter.) It is left to the soldier, informant and arranger of Ferdinand's grotesque schemes, Bosola, to express Webster's pessimistic view of the human body. This occurs during the play's most macabre moment, when a coffin is brought into the Duchess' chamber and two executioners appear with the cord that is to strangle her. In response to the Duchess' "Who am I?" Bosola replies:

Thou art a box of worm seed, at best but a salutatory of green mummy. What's this flesh? a little cruded milk, fantastical puff paste: our bodies are weaker than those paper prisons boy use to keep flies in, more contemptible—since ours is to preserve earthworms. Didn't thou ever see a lark in a cage? such is the soul in the body: this world is like her little tuft of grass and the heaven o'er our heads, like her looking glass, only gives us a miserable knowledge of the small compass of our prison.[28]

He concludes:

> Of what is't fools make such vain keeping?
> Sin their conception, their birth, weeping:
> Their life, a general mist of error,
> Their death, a hideous storm of terror.[29]

Are we then imprisoned in our bodies, which confine our dreams, or are our bodies chained to and therefore constrained by our imaginations? For Nietzsche the answer was both simple and complex:

> You say "I" and you are proud of this word. But greater than this—although you will not believe in it—is your body and its great intelligence, which does not say "I" but performs "I."
> What the sense feels, what the spirit perceives, is never an end in itself. But sense and spirit would like to persuade you that they are the end of all things: they are as vain as that.
> Sense and spirit are instruments and toys: behind them still lies the Self. The Self seeks with the eyes of the sense, it listens too with the ear of the spirit.
> The Self is always listening and seeking: it compares, subdues, conquers, destroys. It rules and is also the Ego's ruler.
> Behind your thoughts and feelings, my brother, stands a mighty commander, an unknown sage—he is called Self. He lives indoor body, he is your body.[30]

In Nietzsche's view, the imagination (and what is religion if not something *imaginary*?) is a part of the body, which is our only frame of reference. When we imagine angels, we depict them as having bodies. Gods have bodies too, sometimes animal, sometimes composite. Aliens are usually humanoid. Everything that we imagine as being *beyond* this world can only be imagined using what we know of this world, and what we know best of all is the body that is our sole instrument for comprehending it.

"I sing the body electric," sang the great American poet of physicality Walt Whitman:

> The lung-sponges, the stomach-sac, the bowels sweet and clean,
> The brain in its folds inside the skull-frame,
> Sympathies, heart-valves, palate-valves, sexuality, maternity,
> Womanhood, and all that is a woman, and the man that comes from woman,
> The womb, the teats, nipples, breast-milk, tears, laughter, weeping, love-looks,
>   love-perturbations and risings,
> The voice, articulation, language, whispering, shouting aloud,
> Food, drink, pulse, digestion, sweat, sleep, walking, swimming,

> Poise on the hips, leaping, reclining, embracing, arm-curving and tightening,
> The continual changes of the flex of the mouth, and around the eyes,
> The skin, the sunburnt shade, freckles, hair,
> The curious sympathy one feels when feeling with the hand the naked meat of the body,
> The circling rivers the breath, and breathing it in and out,
> The beauty of the waist, and thence of the hips, and thence downward toward the knees,
> The thin red jellies within you or within me, the bones and the marrow in the bones.[31]

This book is about all that, our complete and inescapable dependence upon the body, its pains and pleasures, and most of all, our anxiety over and horror of its perishable *vulnerability*.

One

Copulation

"Sex is very similar to torture or surgery."
—Charles Baudelaire[1]

Mary Shelley referred to the laboratory in her famous *Frankenstein* as a "workshop of filthy creation."[2] Superficially, this refers to its similarity to a "dissecting room and the slaughterhouse,"[3] but in Mary's subconscious, sex was quite horrific enough on its own to qualify such a designation. Accordingly, Kenneth Branagh, in his unsuccessfully glossy 1994 adaptation of the novel (*Mary Shelley's Frankenstein*), emphasizes the womb-like nature of Frankenstein's laboratory. His Frankenstein is erotically stripped to the waist, drenched in sweat and later in what is obviously intended to suggest amniotic fluid. After his chemical and electrical copulation, so to speak, he wrestles his creation to the floor in a sticky deluge of broken waters, the horror of his situation is fully encapsulated in his *sotto voce* exclamation, "What have I done?" This "birth" is obviously interpreted as a crime and very much against the libertinism of Sade, who argued, "Nature's single precept is *to enjoy oneself, at the expense of no matter whom.*" It is patently not the case here that "there is no wrong in doing anything we may well please," as Sade would have us believe.[4]

Curiously, Schopenhauer's *World as Will and Representation* was published in the same year as *Frankenstein* (1818) and Schopenhauer arrived at an astonishingly similar conclusion to Shelley. Both texts are in fact highly critical of intercourse and reproduction, and when Frankenstein's creation threatens his maker with the line, "I shall be with you on your wedding night,"[5] Shelley is really suggesting her own revulsion at the issue, not to mention the actual act of marital congress itself. The implication is that all babies are not only all potential monsters but are also themselves inevitably subject to all manner of bodily horrors. The guilt Frankenstein feels over his unnatural act is comparable to the guilt Schopenhauer ascribes to the "natural act" of sexual intercourse. Schopenhauer considers the woman's part in procreation "in a certain sense more innocent than the man's, inasmuch as the man gives to the child *will*, which is the prime sin and thus the source of all wickedness and evil, while the woman gives it *knowledge*, which opens the road to salvation."

> The act of generation is the node of the universe; it declares: "The will to live is once more affirmed." Conception and pregnancy, on the other hand, declare: "To the will there is once more joined the light of knowledge"—by means of which it can find its way out of the world again.
>
> It is this that explains the notable fact that every woman, while she would be ready to die of shame if surprised in the act of generation, nonetheless carries her pregnancy without a trace of shame and indeed with a kind of pride. The reason is that *pregnancy is in a certain sense a cancellation of the guilt incurred by coitus* [my italics]; thus coitus bears all the shame and disgrace of the affair, while pregnancy, which is so intimately associated with it, stays pure and innocent, and is to some extent sacred.[6]

Schopenhauer is nonetheless fully aware, from his own personal experience, of the immense power and determination of the sex drive:

> The sexual impulse is the most vehement of cravings, the desire of desires, the concentration of all our willing. Accordingly, its satisfaction, corresponding exactly to the individual desire of anyone, thus to a desire directed to a definite individual, is the summit and crown of his happiness, the ultimate goal of his natural endeavors, with whose attainment everything seems to him to be attained, and with the missing of which everything seems to have been missed. In just the same way we find, as the physiological correlative of all this, in the objectified will, and thus in the human organism, the sperm or semen as the secretion of secretions, the quintessence of all humours, the final result of all organic functions.[7]

Similarly, during the dreary night in November when the accomplishment of his toils is fulfilled, Frankenstein is "oppressed by a slow fever" and is "nervous to a most painful degree." This is a man who is tormented by sexual shame: "I shunned my fellow-creatures as if I had been guilty of a crime,"[8] he confesses, which is exactly the word used by Schopenhauer when discussing sex and "the crime of being born."[9]

> The story of the Fall is consequently the only things which reconciles me to the Old Testament; I even regard it as the sole metaphysical truth contained in that book, even though it does not appear clothed in allegory. For our existence resembles nothing so much as the consequence of a misdeed, punishment for a forbidden desire.[10]

The 20th-century philosopher E.M. Cioran followed this interpretation by describing birth as an abyss, "a gulf into which we do not fall but from which, instead, we emerge to our universal chagrin."[11]

But what if the crime of procreation is compounded by being committed by a couple of homosexual men? For the gay film director James Whale, who created the most lasting and powerful cinematic incarnation of Shelley's originally rather vaguely described Creature, Frankenstein is as gay as he and his leading actors were. Colin Clive's Frankenstein may have a fiancé in the original film of 1930 and may be about to get married in the sequel, but the real

Bride of Frankenstein is surely Frankenstein's mentor and collaborator Dr. Pretorius (played by the equally gay Ernest Thesiger). It is also highly significant that Elsa Lanchester's necrophilous Nefertiti-style "mate" in *The Bride of Frankenstein* (1935) rejects Boris Karloff's lumbering male groom with all the revulsion of a press-ganged lesbian. The relationship between Pretorius and Henry Frankenstein reflects the implied love affair between Henry Clerval and Victor Frankenstein in Shelley's novel. It is *they* who create the creature together. Frankenstein is the active participant, Clerval the passive. Frankenstein describes Clerval in amorous terms: "He was a being formed in the 'very poetry of nature.'" "His soul overflowed with ardent affections." He is "gentle and lovely," and "beaming with beauty."[12] Whale was quite aware of Frankenstein's latent homosexuality in this regard, as the conflation of Clerval's Christian name with Frankenstein's surname in both films demonstrates. Whale's Monster is the nightmare of a narcissistic homosexual who is more interested in his own imagination than in reality. The consequence is his own destruction and the misery of the creature he creates. In *The Bride of Frankenstein,* the ghost of Clerval inhabits the grotesque Pretorius.

"My God," Thesiger says in Christopher Bram's novel *Father of Frankenstein,* when Lanchester is brought on set, "is the audience to presume that Colin and I have done her hair? I thought we were scientists, not hairdressers."[13] These lines are retained in the film adaptation *Gods and Monsters* (dir. Bill Condon, 1999). "What a couple of queens we are, Colin," Thesiger continues.

> —"Yes, a couple of flaming queens," [Whale] declares, mincingly, knowing how Clive hates effeminacy. "And Pretorius *is* a little in love with Frankenstein, you know."[14]

In Whale's interpretation, the Creature is unnatural for obvious reasons and unwanted because its parents are homosexuals who have no interest in raising a family. Leonard Whiting's Frankenstein in *Frankenstein: The True Story* (dir. Jack Smight, 1973) is similarly narcissistic. The film is not "true" in the sense that it faithfully follows Shelley's text, though it is closer than most, and the relationship between Clerval and the Baron is moved to a more central position by the homosexual screenwriter Christopher Isherwood. His Frankenstein is at first infatuated by his beautiful Creation (Michael Sarrazin), but when the Creature starts to grow ugly, Frankenstein realizes that "the process is reversing itself," as Clerval always knew it would, but whose premature death prevented him from passing on this vital information to his protégé. Like all exploitative narcissists, gay or straight, Isherwood's Frankenstein loses interest in the Creature when it ceases to titillate his own vanity. Whiting does a splendid job in conveying the distaste of this esthetic Frankenstein. More of a bored lover than a disappointed father, he tries to destroy his creation, but discovers that it will not be erased like an unsightly smudge.

The Creature may have offended Frankenstein's esthetic sensibility, but he is even more offended by Frankenstein's rejection of him.

The heterosexual Peter Cushing, who had no children of his own, presented Frankenstein as a ruthlessly ambitious father. He is never revolted by the creatures he creates, merely frustrated by their failures and infuriated by the censoriousness of society with regard to his experiments. The creations of Cushing's Baron are merely demonstrations of his own genius. His Frankenstein has no particular interest in what his "children" look like and certainly doesn't really care about their feelings. In this respect his Frankenstein is the worse parent of all, ready to sacrifice all human feelings in the name of his own intellectual pride.

Sex and birth are central concerns of the horror film precisely because this is where the horrors of the body begin. Larry Cohen's *It's Alive* (1974) is another study of parental guilt. Frank Davis plays John Ryan, whose wife gives very bloody birth to a mutant baby (the ironic consequence of having previously taken a new form of contraceptive). The baby then attacks everyone that threatens it. Referring to Boris Karloff's monster, Ryan says, "I thought he was Frankenstein. Then I went to high school and I read the book. I realized Frankenstein was the doctor who created him. Somehow the identities get all mixed up, don't they?" Horrified by the violence of his hideous progeny (whose screen time Cohen sensibly restricts to a minimum), Ryan

Teething trouble. The demonic baby in *It's Alive* (dir. Larry Cohen, 1974).

tries to disown it. "It's no relation to me!" he shouts, before shouldering his responsibility and understanding that the baby is as frightened of the world as the word is frightened of him. Indeed, Cohen suggests this, his principle theme, from the opening title sequence, in which police flashlights form constellations in the dark, and recur toward the end of the film during the final pursuit of Ryan and his monstrous baby. Cohen thus suggests that society, as represented by the trigger-happy Los Angeles Police Department, is in fact far more terrifying than any killer baby. One scene is particularly telling, in which two cops draw their guns and aim directly at an innocent toddler, whom they suspect might have been responsible for the murders. The infant stares in mild bewilderment as the police hesitate and change their minds, but if babies are in some senses innocent, they are also far too much in thrall to the demands of their own monstrous egos to be entirely so. Cohen seems to be suggesting that all babies would happily kill anyone who posed a threat to their own safety if they had the physical strength to do so. No film better illustrates the old Roman adage, later adopted by Schopenhauer, "Illico post coitum cachinnus auditur Diaboli" ("directly after copulation the devil's laughter is heard").[15] Can one claim that children are completely innocent? Cohen leaves his audience to ponder this, and meanwhile developed the despotic tendencies of the LAPD in his New York–based *Maniac Cop* (1988).

The complex subject of children and innocence was also examined in David Keating's *Wakewood* in 2009. Here, Kenneth Branagh's *Frankenstein* imagery is made all the more explicit by placing it a contemporary and rural setting. The story concerns a pagan ritual that brings a girl back to life after having been fatally savaged by a dog. Unfortunately, the process has the unfortunate effect of morally corrupting the young girl; or was the evil there all along? Timothy Spall's cattle farmer Arthur presides at this unnatural birthing, replete, as it is, with fluids, fire and flesh, but not before we have been subjected to a great deal of natural farmyard horrors—slurry, sick cattle and the accidental death of a farmhand during a routine veterinary procedure in a cattle shed. All this blood, bovine horror and implied stench prepare us for the grotesque birthing scene, which is very much a 21st-century workshop of filthy re-creation, and as messy, liquid, and primordial as Keating can make it.

Vampire films often face the problem of sex symbolically, following the example of Bram Stoker in *Dracula*. Stoker's description of Dracula lying in his coffin in effect presents him as a man-sized penis, still tumescent, but post-coital. The prudish and consequently hypocritical Jonathan Harker describes his terrifying host accordingly: "It seemed as if the whole awful creature were simply gorged with blood. He lay like a filthy leech, exhausted with his repletion."[16] Such a state is deemed "awful" and "filthy" while simultaneously encouraging our fascinating and identification with it. Ironically, Stoker would go on to attack pornography and the overt representation of the sexual act in his article "The Censorship of Fiction," first published in 1908, in which he wrote, specifically with regard to stage drama, "A close analysis will show that the only emotions which in the long run harm are those arising from the sex impulse, and when we have realized this we have put a finger on the actual point of danger."[17] Despite such views, he was, nonetheless, one of the Victorian era's most persuasive purveyors of soft porn within the covers of his most famous novel. When Jonathan Harker is visited by Dracula's three "brides," in the early part of the novel, Stoker leaves little to the imagination:

> I was afraid to raise my eyelids, but looked out and saw perfectly under the lashes. The girl went on her knees, and bent over me, simply gloating. There was a deliberate voluptuousness which was both thrilling and repulsive, and as she arched her neck she actually licked her lips like an animal, till I could see in the moonlight the moisture shining on the scarlet lips and on the red tongue as it lapped the white sharp teeth. Lower and lower went her head as the lips went below the range of my mouth and chin and seemed about to fasten on my throat. Then she paused, and I could hear the churning sound of her tongue as it licked her teeth and lips, and could feel the hot breath on my neck. Then the skin of my throat began to tingle as one's flesh does when the hand that is to tickle it approaches nearer—nearer. I could feel the soft, shivering touch of the lips on the super-sensitive skin of my throat, and the hard dents of two sharp teeth, just touching and pausing there. I closed my eyes in a languorous ecstasy and waited—waited with beating heart.[18]

Vampires must be staked, a phallic censoriousness made only more obvious when the vampire being staked is a woman. The idea of men staking male vampires raises more complex interpretations, but the censorial sexual symbolism remains. It is not so much the pleasure of sex that is under attack here as its consequences. When a vampire drinks blood, his victim is reborn as a monster like himself, implying that the issue of human intercourse is also at least potentially monstrous.

To be "undead" is to be immoral. Vampires can do what they want with whoever they want, the only restriction upon them being the time of day at which to do it, for biting and sucking must take place after dark, when reason sleeps. Vampires are sexually liberating, but also terrifying and compelling, like sex itself. As Maurice Lever said of Sade's writings, "the sexual instinct is anarchic and uncontrollable. After Sade, we no longer think of sex as something light, playful and superficial."[19] The vampire's gaze, like that of the Mona Lisa (whom Walter Pater appropriately compared to one of these mythical beings), is irresistible, even though one knows the price. ("She is older than the rocks among which she sits; like the vampire, she has been dead many times, and learned the secrets of the grave."[20])

The allegory for humans here is not merely *la petite mort* of orgasm, but also that the new life, which orgasm is designed to bring about, has death built into it. (Nicolas Roeg's *Don't Look Now* [1973] makes the connection explicitly, interpolating extremely realistic depictions of intercourse between its stars Donald Sutherland and Julie Christie, in a story that is really all about the protagonist's premonition of his own death at the hands of a monstrous "baby"—a hideous psychopathic dwarf in a red raincoat, who wields an immensely phallic knife.)

Werewolves are persecuted for similar reasons. Larry Talbot, as portrayed in successive incarnations by Lon Chaney, Jr., in the Universal Studios films, is the most tragic of all movie monsters. Imprisoned by his own sexual impulses, which he in unable to control, he forfeits every woman whom he might have made his bride, and the reason for the suffering of vampires and werewolves is not so much because they are evil, but more because they are *sexual.* Sex ensnares us all in the vortex of desire, which Buddhism has always identified as the source of all unhappiness. If fangs and blood are metaphors of phallus and semen, what these films are really describing are forms of rape. Science fiction and stories of the occult are often more overt, in this respect, than Gothic horror.

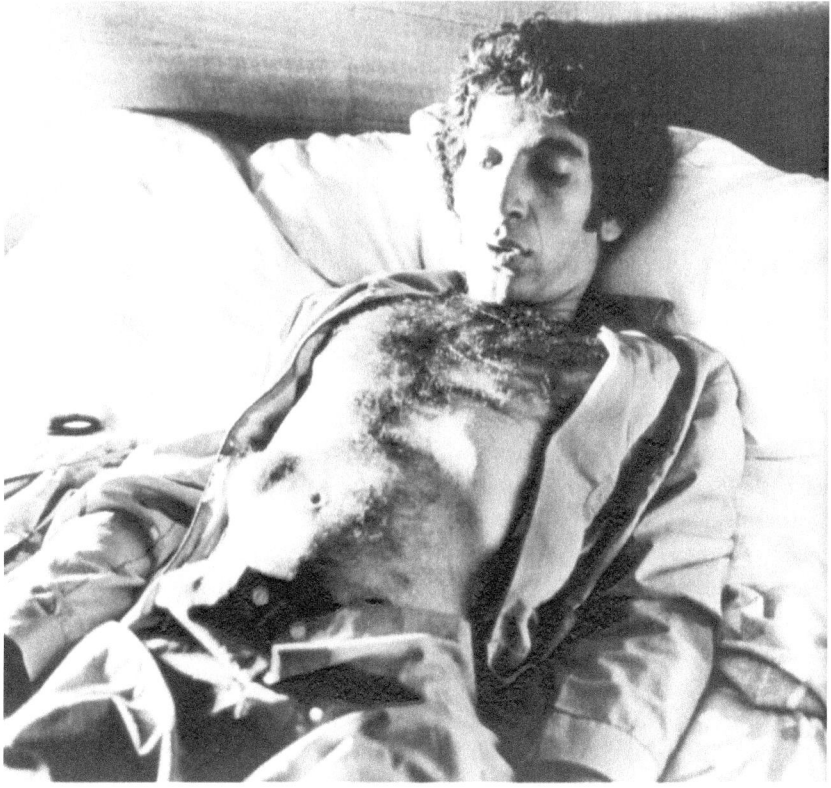

Upset tummy. Paul Hampton as Roger St. Luc in *Shivers* (dir. David Cronenberg, 1975).

Cronenberg's *Shivers* (1975) is a rumination on the medical consequences of promiscuous sex, thus foreshadowing the AIDS epidemic that was soon to follow the film's release, but the horror of having an alien organism moving around inside one's body is also part of the unease here and is surely a reflection of Cronenberg's disquiet about pregnancy itself. A parasite created by a scientist as "a combination of aphrodisiac and venereal disease that will hopefully turn the world into one beautiful mindless orgy" takes the form of a raw, bloody penis, which is also a metaphor of disease and of the human embryo itself. (Sade had previously floated this idea, of course, notably in *Juliette*, where he advocates "a girl, a woman, and a boy, granting their favors to the first comer, prostituting themselves with effrontery and in every sense, everywhere, all the time."[21])

After we have perceived this parasite pulsating beneath the skin of Nicholas Tudor (Alan Migicovsky), it eventually pops up through the plughole of the bath in which Barbara Steele's lesbian, Betts, is relaxing. Then, it inevitably rapes her, turning the bathwater a distinctly menstrual shade of magenta. This moment is obviously indebted to the shower scene of Hitchcock's *Psycho*, in that half the unease derives from the setting itself: Bathrooms are where we are most vulnerable and where our fleshly reality is at its most exposed. (In *Rabid*, Cronenberg's follow-up to *Shivers*, an attack in a jacuzzi offers a variation on the same theme, which grimly echoes Ingrid Pitt's Countess Dracula in Peter Sasdy's 1971 Hammer film of that name in which she dabs herself with virgin's blood beside a bath in which a murdered prostitute has been bled to death. Similarly, the body of a murdered housemaid is discovered in the bath in Sasdy's *Hands of the Ripper* (1972) and even the vampire Johnny Alucard in Alan Gibson's *Dracula A.D. 1972* is dispatched by the corrosively clear running water from a shower in his presumably unfrequented bathroom. These and countless other examples demonstrate that whenever a character finds his or herself in a bathroom in a horror film, harm is imminent.)

The parasite of *Shivers* is now ready to be transferred to other hosts in various ways. An elderly woman is attacked by the parasite while loading clothes into a washing machine. Attacking her face, it prefigures the preferred mode of attack in Ridley Scott's *Alien* (1979). Betts transfers the parasite orally when indulging in a French kiss with Janine (Susan Petrie). Eventually, the residents of the entire apartment block in which the action so claustrophobically takes place, are transformed into nymphomaniac zombies. That many of them are elderly only increases the horror of the situation for Cronenberg's intended teenage audience, as nothing sends shivers down the spine of an adolescent quite like the idea of intercourse among old age pensioners.

In *Demon Seed* (dir. Donald Cammell, 1977), Julie Christie plays Susan Harries, a child psychologist who finds herself being raped by a super-intelligent computer called Proteus. Proteus is indeed a Nietzschean philosopher gone wrong. "What is, is natural," it quite logically argues. Therefore, it reasons, a computer capable of inseminating a human woman is also natural. The film, however, asks us to refute this. "I'm frightened," Susan whimpers during childbirth, rightly so, even though under "normal" circumstances, childbirth is usually regarded as a reason to be joyful. As a child psychologist, Susan has dedicated her life to helping children negotiate the uncertainties of the world, but here she is, about to give birth to another child, and she is terrified by the prospect. This is yet another version of Shelley's "filthy workshop of creation," for Proteus has created for himself a telescopic stainless steel penis. Graphics, which anticipate the later effects of CGI, create a "techno-delic" equivalent of conventional erotic imagery. Proteus' penis is supposedly more frightening than the human equivalent, but the implication is that all penises are potentially violating instruments of domination, engendering life, which, as Proteus explains is "more terrifying and more mysterious" than death. *Inseminoid* (dir. Norman J. Warren, 1981) set its rape imagery on an alien planet, where Judy Geeson's human character, Sandy, is artificially inseminated by an extraterrestrial insect with cliché goggle eyes. This latter looms over her as a glass tube is inserted into her vagina, through which green semen is pumped. Understandably, Sandy is as terrified by what is happening to her as was Susan. A feminist deconstruction of all this would quite rightly focus on the rape, but the green fluid suggests a deeper unease with bodily fluids and their consequence, no matter the circumstances in which they are exchanged.

Some women in horror films don't in fact want to have sex in the first place, and this aversion forms the basis of Roman Polanski's *Repulsion* (1965), in which Catherine Deneuve plays what Polanski himself described as "a homicidal schizophrenic running amok in her sister's deserted London apartment."[22]

Based on a seemingly innocent and demure girl Polanski had once known, who had been "simultaneously attracted to and repelled by sex, as well as prone to sudden, unpredictable bouts of violence,"[23] Deneuve's Carol was so accurately conceived that Polanski was "embarrassed to have to admit that we'd simply used our imagination"[24] when a psychiatrist complimented him on his accuracy in depicting a homicidal schizophrenic. As Carol's sanity collapses around her, sex becomes increasingly equated—even replaced—by death, as the various men who attempt to interest her in the former discover to their cost. Carol loathes being touched by men, and a dead rabbit, which was originally intended as a supper dish but which remains uneaten, becomes a symbol of the fetus she will never allow herself to bear in her womb. (It does indeed resemble a monstrous fetus.) She protects this rotting corpse half with desire, half with disgust, and with regard to the successive murders she commits, Ivan Butler perceptively observes that "Carol is not, to her, killing human beings at all, but rather destroying some threatening obscenity as one might stamp repeatedly on a loathsome insect."[25]

The horror of sex has never been quite so powerfully expressed as it is in Polanski's film, and Carol's personality problems are explained at the very end of the film when we are shown a photograph of her as a child recoiling in revulsion and hatred from her presumably sexually abusive father. Sex becomes death in this film.

Though not a horror film in the traditional sense of the term, *Picnic at Hanging Rock* (dir. Peter Weir, 1975) employs sexual tension as the implied "cause" of the unsolved mystery that forms the action of the film. When a party of pubescent, virginal school girls, resplendent in white muslin, voyage out to Hanging Rock for the eponymous picnic under a blazing Australian sun, three them mysteriously vanish, never to be seen again, along with their strict and mathematically-inclined schoolmistress, who is seen by one of the other girls climbing up the rocks without her skirt. The phallic rocks pierce the sultry heat of the primeval outback, and seem themselves to be guilty of raping their victims—all of whom are the product of a European civilization that has been incongruously imposed upon this wild and an alien landscape with which they have nothing in common. The rocks seem both to intimidate and liberate the girls, simultaneously absorbing them into their own sexual mystery and annihilating them in the process. The terror of sex is palpable throughout this film in the constrained atmosphere of Appleyard College where the girls are educated along conventionally prudish lines and which is presided over by the increasingly alcoholic headmistress (Rachel Roberts), whose past in England may well have been far less respectable than she would have people believe. (Australia was, after all, the terminus for exiles who had offended the moral strictures of the old country.) Sex education, as one would expect, is rigorously excluded from the syllabus of Appleyard College, where it would have been regarded as disruptive, immoral and even disastrous. Indeed, life itself is regarded by Miss Appleyard as an abhorrence, and when the scandal of the picnic threatens financial ruin on her academy, suicide becomes her only recourse. Joan Lindsay's novel on which all this is based, concludes with a final image of the triumphal rocks, on which Miss Appleyard is phallically "impaled upon a jutting crag."[26] Weir omits this graphic image of body horror, perhaps feeling to might have suggested the more melodramatic impalement of Christopher Lee's Dracula on a crucifix at the end of *Dracula Has Risen from the Grave* (dir. Freddie Francis, 1968), but it would nonetheless have helped explain to baffled audiences at the time what the film is really all about.

Ken Russell, unique in so many ways, was also one of the few filmmakers of the 1970s to describe a homosexual's horror of heterosexual congress in *The Music Lovers* (1971). The famous scene on board a train in which Glenda

Jackson plays Tchaikovsky's ill-fated bride, Antonina Milyukova, is one of the cinema's most disturbing scenes, even though this film is, again, not a horror film in the conventional sense. Confined to their compartment on the return trip to Moscow, Tchaikovsky (Richard Chamberlain) drinks champagne and attempts relations with his bride. She is all for it; he is aghast. If any imagery could explain the anguish that inspired the opening movement of Tchaikovsky's Sixth Symphony (which he called *Pathètique,* while refusing to explain exactly why), it is surely this nightmare of heterosex on a train. The composer gazes in terror down the red rib-cage of his wife's corset, which strongly resembles the devouring passage of her vagina, and rarely has the female form been photographed less erotically in an erotic situation than it is in this representation of a homosexual's horror of female flesh. Swaying to the rhythm of both the train and the music, Jackson's body is reduced to a piece of meat on a butcher's slab, as Russell's camera focuses on her pubic hair from Tchaikovsky's point of view with an intensity of horror that foreshadowed John Hurt's reaction to the eruption of the phallic monster in *Alien* eight years later. It is highly disturbing example of cinematic body horror without the need for any of the prosthetics and gore we find in conventional horror films.

Tchaikovsky's life was indeed a horror tale of homosexual repression and suicidal tendencies, the resulting neurosis of which informed his famous ballet *Swan Lake.* Significantly, the most neurotic music of that ballet was frequently employed by Universal Studios to introduce their early horror "sex" films *Dracula* (dir. Tod Browning, 1931) and *Murders in the Rue Morgue* (dir. Robert Florey, 1932). The sexual nature of the former would be elaborated upon for the remainder of the century in which it first appeared, that of the later is conceivably more disturbing, being, as it is, a Darwinian version of *King Kong,* in which Bela Lugosi's sinister Dr. Mirakle injects the blood of his sideshow ape Erik (a name he shares with the Phantom of the Opera) into the veins of various young women with the aim of providing Erik with a mate. Mirakle's belief in humanity's kinship with apes was still sufficiently disturbing to grip audiences 60 years after Darwin had first published his revolutionary theories, and the idea of mixing ape blood with the human variety was perhaps felt to have been even more troubling than being bitten by vampire. Certainly, the shots of Erik's primeval shadow looming over the sleeping Camille (Sidney Fox) are far more frightening in their expressionist manner than that of Lugosi looming over his victims in *Dracula.*

Two

Generation

"And now, once again, I bid my hideous progeny go forth."
—Mary Shelley[1]

Childbirth is, naturally, often painful and, until relatively recently, frequently fatal as well. A host of babies have, like monstrous intruders, killed their mothers on arrival, and this irony is, of course, a central aspect of *Frankenstein,* in which the monster attacks its creator. It is a theme that also occurs in other types of horror film. In Hammer's *Blood from the Mummy's Tomb* (dir. Seth Holt, 1971), for example, which is based on Bram Stoker's novel *The Jewel of Seven Stars,* the mother of the infant Margaret Fuchs dies in childbirth, the implication being that the ancient Egyptian Queen Tera, intent on substituting Margaret's spirit with her own, is responsible. "She died giving me life," Margaret later explains. "Not exactly," replies her boyfriend (the oddly named Tod Browning), before explaining what he thinks has really happened. In the later adaptation of this novel, *The Awakening* (dir. Mike Newell, 1980), Margaret's mother does not die, but her violent birth pangs are accompanied by intercut shots of Charlton Heston as her husband forcing his way into the tomb of the Egyptian queen, emphasizing not only the violence of sex, which here suggests rape rather than consensual intercourse, but also making quite clear that Margaret's destiny is to be distinctly incestuous: In the original novel, and Hammer's adaptation, the professor seems not to have been too distressed by Tera's "murder" of his wife. The reason for this is that the Egyptologist in Stoker's story is indeed infatuated with his own daughter.

The opposite thing happens in the "Morella" section of Roger Corman's Poe triptych *Tales of Terror* (1962). Here, Vincent Price plays a father who loathes his own daughter for having caused the death of his wife in childbirth. Like a male Miss Havisham, he wanders around his decaying mansion in a decadently purple dressing gown, a prey to alcohol, grief and self-pity.

"You understand nothing!" he shouts at her. "When she died I died with her. All that remained of me was this … this walking corpse, this shell, this ghost of flesh. She was my life."

"And I killed her?" his daughter enquires. "That's it, isn't it?"

"Yes!" he snaps, but then relents. "Oh, no. She thought you did. She said so on her death bed. She was so young, so alive. To die just a few months after giving birth to you; I couldn't accept it. I hated you. Oh dear God how I *hated* you. I wanted to kill you. I went into your nursery and I took you from your cradle and I almost hurled you out of the window!"

One might usefully compare this moment with a scene in Gabrielle D'Annunzio's sumptuously decadent 1892 novel *L'innocente*, in which an unwanted baby is deliberately left out in the snow to catch a fatal chill. "The future looked appalling, hopeless," D'Annunzio's hero, Tulio, confesses. "The indeterminate image of the creature that should be born grew and dilated like one of those horrible shapeless things we see in nightmares, and occupied my whole field of vision. There was no question here of regret, remorse, of an indelible memory, of any mental burden however heavy, but of a living baby. My future was linked with a creature imbued with a tenacious and malignant life; was fettered to a stranger, an interloper, an abhorrent creature against whom nor only my spirit, but my flesh, every drop of blood, every fibre of my body, rose up in loathing—brutal, fierce, implacable, till death, yea, and even beyond that."[2] The key vocabulary here is "horrible," "shapeless," "nightmares," "creature," "malignant" and "abhorrent," which demonstrate that, for Tulio, a perfectly normal baby becomes a thing of horror as monstrous as Frankenstein's creature or Larry Cohen's razor-toothed terror. The extremes of physical body horror in film are, after all, usually only representations of *inner* psychological anxieties. In his film adaptation of the novel Luchino Visconti carefully dramatizes the moment when Tulio leaves the child out in the snow to catch its death:

> I retreated, approached the cradle, overcoming by a violent effort my extreme repugnance, lifted the baby very very gently, and holding it away from my side where my heart beat like a sledge-hammer, I carried it to the open window and exposed it to the death-dealing air.[3]

The director's biographer, Laurence Schiffano, describes this last film of the great realist master, filmed with "voluptuously mournful red and black lighting" as "the final ritual before Visconti's descent into death and his origins. This was an ultimate family tragedy, in which a mother and father momentarily join in their desire to rid themselves of a bastard child, an intruder."[4]

Rosemary's Baby (dir. Roman Polanski, 1968) explored the idea of babies as intruders along demonic lines, combining it with birthing anxiety and post-natal depression. Half the fun of Polanski's approach is created by the structure of the story, but the central anxiety is not so much the disturbing demonic rape, which Rosemary only half recalls in her drugged state, as the discovery of who and what her offspring really is. Her reaction to this knowledge resembles Frankenstein's horror of the monstrous "child" he has created. ("His yellow skin scarcely covered the work of muscles and arteries beneath; his hair was a lustrous black, and flowing; his teeth of a pearly whiteness; but these luxuriances only formed a more horrid contrast with his watery eyes ... his shriveled complexion and straight black lips."[5]) It is the eyes of Rosemary's baby that indicate what is wrong, even though Polanski sensibly refrains from showing them to us. "He has his father's eyes," explains the chief Satanist, Roman Castavet (Sidney Blackmer).

It is also the eyes of the children in *Village of the Damned* (dir. Wolf Rilla, 1960) that convey their alien quality and which are also the lethal weapons of their formidable will power. While we admire maturity in adults, we remain suspicious of it in children. Intelligence, seriousness, humorlessness, neatness, capability, independence—the Midwich cuckoos all share these qualities, along with a malevolence, which, to them, is merely a necessity. Human beings find themselves in the awkward position of being part of nature but also alienated from it by consciousness and the inevitable morality that springs from it. When Nietzsche observed that there is no morality in nature, only necessity, he isolated the problem, which films like *Village of the Damned* explore, and which cause audiences such disquiet. These children are motivated entirely by necessity, and therein lies their monstrosity. Just as bodily horror exposes us to the mutability and vulnerability of our physical reality, these alien children expose the powerful natural instincts we attempt to restrain in ourselves. Unconcerned with such moral niceties, the Midwich cuckoos have far more power. The film undermines our preconceptions about the innocence of children, for innocence is often really only powerlessness.

Village of the Damned succinctly reveals that the fear we have of ourselves is very real, and explains why it is necessary to constrain children through schooling. It is because of the cloak of "innocence" we force children to wear that we are so particularly shocked when real children commit acts of bodily horror. Infamously, this happened in the UK in 1993, when toddler Jamie Bulgar was murdered by two young boys in Merseyside, but there is no reason whatsoever why children under the age of 10 should not be as violent or depraved as any similarly inclined adult. Cronenberg's *The Brood* (1979) presented an astonishing premonition of the imagery of the Bulgar case. The director's habitually chilly esthetic once more prevails with snow, leafless trees, soulless architecture and characters who have trouble communicating. The hero, Frank Carveth (Art Hindle), is separated from his psychologically disturbed wife, Nola (Samantha Eggar), who is tormented by rage with her parents, her husband and her own child Candice (Cindy Hines). (Frank explains that he got involved with a woman who married him for his sanity, hoping it would rub off.) Nola's rage is externalized in the form of a murderous "brood" of children, who emerge from an external womb sac on

The eyes have it. The alien children of *Village of the Damned* (dir. Wolf Rilla, 1960).

her thigh. The first one we encounter, who attacks Nola's own mother, wears a red jacket, reminiscent of the psychopathic knife-wielding dwarf in Roeg's *Don't Look Now*. The murderous children in *The Brood* have no navels, having "never really been born," which helps us to differentiate them from "normal" children, who are not meant to have such dangerous impulses. They are also freakish in feature. The ultimate inversion of childhood innocence occurs when two of the brood children infiltrate an infant school room. They bludgeon the schoolteacher to death in front of her traumatized charges before abducting Candice. A later shot of her, flanked by her murderous kidnappers as they walk along a road, is astonishingly like the CCTV imagery of the Bulgar boy flanked by Robert Thompson and Jon Venables in 1993.

So these brood children have "never been born," they are not innocent, and they abduct a child whose mother wants to murder her. Not only do we have perverted children but a perverted mother, who licks her monstrous babies clean like some dreadful cat. Like the Midwich Cuckoos, the brood are totally malevolent, killing everything their mother wills, including Oliver Reed's psychiatrist, who has rather misjudged the situation. The film did not come from nowhere: Cronenberg was inspired to write the screenplay after an acrimonious divorce from his own wife, and his concomitant struggle for the custody of their child, but it also taps a deeper level of anxiety about children themselves. Children, after all, are merely undeveloped adults. If we fear ourselves, we must inevitably fear children as well. My own first day in a school playground demonstrated to me quite clearly how wars begin.

Blood on Satan's Claw (dir. Piers Haggard, 1971) filtered this dilemma though an earlier historical context: A group of children are corrupted by the appearance of Satan in a remote rural community. Chief among them is the ironically named Angel Blake (Linda Hayden), whose name not only suggests the fallen angel Lucifer, but also the connotations of William Blake's 1789 poetic cycle juxtaposing *Songs of Innocence and Experience.* Angel indeed becomes a handmaiden of her Satanic Lord, luring village children to the secluded ruins of a chapel in the woods, where rape, murder and devil worship threaten to destroy the entire community. Haggard's presentation of this conspiracy of children against their elders and even against other children, is one of the most compelling of its kind in film, and it also foreshadowed, within a traditionally Christian context, the much more "meaningless" horror of the Bulgar case, along with the Internet-inspired "Slender Man" atrocity of 2014, in which a 12-year-old girl, Peyton Lautner, was stabbed 19 times by her two 12-year-old "friends," Morgan Geyser and Anissa Weier. Inspired by the fictional Slender Man created in 2009 by Eric Knudsen, known as "Victor Surge" in his online incarnation, Slender Man, a long-armed, faceless, abnormally tall alien being who kidnaps children, is in direct line of descent from E.T.A. Hoffmann's Sandman (1817) or the Scissorman of Heinrich Hoffman's *Strewelpeter* (1854) and, of course, the Satanic creature that appears at Angel Blake's woodland rituals. The moment in *Blood on Satan's Claw*, in which two nubile girls appear outside the cottage of the boy Mark Vespers (Robin Davies), is almost a prototype of the Slender Man case. After glancing knowingly at each other, these creepy girls ask, "Wilt thou come and play with us, Mark? Please!"

"I don't play girls' games," Mark replies, contemptuously biting on his apple.

"Angel has taught us some new games," one of the girls replies with an expressionless face. "Please come," adds her companion. Mark hesitates. "Angel wants thee," she adds. Finishing his apple, rather as Eve might have done in the garden of Eden, Mark is unable to resist the temptation, and follows them to his doom.

"There is growing amongst you all, an insolent ungodliness, which I will not tolerate," the disturbed priest (Anthony Ainley) later shouts at his disrespectful charges in the schoolroom, but he is powerless to stop the corruption from spreading. Indeed, Angel later appears to him and lets fall her robe revealing her body for him to enjoy if he would. "Do you like what you see?" she asks. When he rejects her (not without an effort of will), she hisses, "Would you like to know what becomes of your precious pupils? One of them is dead already. Little Mark has the devil in him, so we cut it out."

Stanley Kubrick may well have had little Mark's seduction in mind when directing one of *The Shining*'s most famous scenes in 1980. "Hello, Danny," say the two terrifying Grady twins whom young Danny (Danny Lloyd) encounters in the disturbingly negative spaces of the Overlook Hotel's labyrinthine corridors. "Come and play with us for ever and ever and ever," they chant. Although these creepy sisters are actually the ghosts of murdered children, they are no less eloquent manifestations of child malevolence. Their doll-like features, lit in such a way as to emphasize the skulls beneath their skin, along with their matching blue dresses and pink ribbons entirely invert the time-honored clichés of childhood, and particularly *feminine* innocence. Their stillness is the same as that of the girls in *Blood on Satan's Claw*.

In some horror films, while the couples are more than content to engage in sexual relations, the babies, when they come, do not want to be born. One of these reluctant infants inspired the title of the film in which it appears. *I Don't Want to Be Born* (dir. Peter Sasdy, 1975) begins with the kind of birthing scene later to be satirized in *Monty Python's Meaning of Life* (dir. Terry Jones, 1983). In the Python sketch (which is actually very similar to birthing scene in Cohen's *It's Alive)*, a mother is surrounded by a myriad of medical machines, her legs hoisted high above her while her baby is unceremoniously plucked out by Graham Chapman's doctor, peremptorily rubbed down with a towel and then dangled briefly in front of the mother by John Clease. "Is it a boy or a girl?" the mother inquires. "Now, I think it's a little early to start to impose roles on it, don't you?" replies Chapman's doctor. In *I Don't Want to Be Born*, Joan Collins' Lucy Carlesi writhes and screams in her own birthing agony, while Donald Pleasence's Dr. Finch observes, "This one doesn't want to be born." Throughout the main title sequence, we focus on the mother's discomfort, while Ron Grainer's electric guitar score appropriately (though perhaps not intentionally) seems to be referencing Paul McCartney's 1973 song "Band on the Run," specifically the melody that introduces the second verse, which refers to escaping from a confined space.

When husband Gino (Ralph Bates with an unconvincing Italian accent) visits Lucy, he discovers her distraught after having been scratched by her demon baby, which is drooling a gobbet of blood like an infant vampire. A few scenes later the baby bites the housekeeper Mrs. Hyde (Hilary Mason, who had usefully appeared in *Don't Look Now* two years earlier). Sasdy chose a baby with wide, black, expressionless eyes to suggest its "otherness," much as the eyes of the Midwich Cuckoos in Rilla's *Village of the Damned* indicate that the infant prodigies are not "normal." What both films are concerned to convey, of course, is the fact that there is nothing particularly innocent about children, who are capable of intense cruelty; even the innocent are subject to corruption, both physical and moral, and I will be addressing this aspect in more detail in the next chapter. Here, though, it is instructive to compare such infant evil with what one of Sade's characters has to say about God's relation to his creations (not that Sade believed in God himself):

> I raise up my eyes to the universe: I see *evil, disorder, crime*, reigning as despots everywhere. My gaze descends, and it bends upon that most interesting of this universe's creatures: I behold him likewise devoured by vices, by contradictions, by infamies; what ideas result from this examination? That what we improperly call evil is really not evil at all, and that this mode is of such high necessity to the designs of the being who had created us that he would cease to be the master of his own creation were *evil* not to exist universally upon the earth. Well persuaded that this is so, I tell myself: there exists a God; some hand or other has necessarily created all that I see, but has not created it save for *evil*, is not pleased but by *evil*; *evil* is his essence, and all that he causes us to suffer from the *evil*, provided it be advantageous to him? Does it not seem I am his favorite child? If the misfortunes that afflict me from the day I am born until the day I die prove his indifference to me, I may very well be mistaken upon what I call *evil*. What I thus characterize relative to myself seems indeed to be a very great good relative to the being who has brought me into the world; and if I receive *evil* from others, I enjoy the right to pay them back in kind, to be the first to cast the stone: so, henceforth, *evil* is good, just as it is for the author of my existence: the *evil* I do others makes me happy, as God is rendered happy by the *evil* he does me.[6]

Gino is not, in fact, the father of the baby in *I Don't Want to Be Born*, as its hefty weight and size suggests. It apparently trashes its nursery and decapitates dolls. "He frightens me," Lucy confesses. "It's been like a nightmare since he's been born. I feel he hates me—*loathes* me!" As a former nightclub dancer, Lucy's partner in a double-act was a dwarf called Hercules, played by George Claydon. One night, Hercules attempted to seduce her, but was rejected, a rejection that had disastrous consequences, for Hercules cursed her: "You will have a baby—a monster—an evil monster conceived in your womb, as big as I am small and possessed by the devil himself."

Gino's sister Albana (Eileen Atkins providing another unconvincing Italian accent) is a nun in full habit. She suggests that the baby's violence is not only due to the fact that he is possessed by the devil but is also exacting his revenge against having been born in the first place: a truly Miltonic fury, which reminds us of the quotation from *Paradise Lost* with which Shelley began *Frankenstein:* "Did I request thee, Maker, from my clay / To mould me Man, did I solicit thee / From darkness to promote me?"[7]

When Albana forms the sign of the cross over the child, it causes a terrifying tantrum. This reaction is amplified during a later baptism scene, which also looks forward to Damien's visit to Guildford Cathedral in *The Omen* (dir. Richard Donner, 1976) as well as back to baby Leon's baptism in Terence Fisher's *The Curse of the Werewolf* (1961), in which the very baptismal waters themselves ripple with disquiet.

I Don't Want to Be Born can more prosaically be deconstructed as a study of postnatal depression, even though here it is the baby that rejects its mother rather than the other way around. The doctor admits that this particular infant is "a remarkable child. He's astonishingly strong and well developed for his age. I had to sedate him." Baby smashes his feeding bottle, pushes his nanny (Janet Key) into the lake at Black Park (Key had previously encountered demonic forces in *Dracula A.D. 1972*), drops a dead mouse in Mrs. Hyde's morning coffee, kills Gino, murders Dr. Finch and ultimately stabs his mother to death. Once again, we revisit the territory Mary Shelley had charted in *Frankenstein* so many years before. Predictably, it is left to the nun to exorcise the monster, which also brings about the death of the dwarf, who is still working at the nightclub and dies on stage. At last, it seems as though the baby has been released from its spell, though Sasdy leaves us in some doubt at the end. The whole premise is confused, but nonetheless rooted in an ambivalence about babies, which might usefully be clarified by the simple statement, "Hitler was an infant once."

The main idea of *I Don't Want to Be Born* would be handled much more convincingly the following year in *The Omen*, where it is given rather more of an interesting theological justification than mere petulant revenge, but three months before *The Omen* was released Hammer came up with its own demon baby story with a very loose but highly imaginative adaptation of Dennis Wheatley's *To the Devil a Daughter* (dir. Peter Sykes, 1976). This film places its sexual activity within a ritualistic context, again as a form of rape, with birth itself being represented as its monstrous consequence. The birthing ordeal of baby Astaroth's mother (played by Isabella Telezynska) is appropriately gruesome for her role as an anti-Madonna: her legs are tied together, so that the creature is forced to burst its way through her stomach, much as the voracious monster in *Alien* chomps its way through John Hurt's stomach on its own way out into the world. (H. R. Giger's design for the Alien, incidentally, also evokes a monstrous penis with two sets of teeth.)

Catherine Beddows (Nastassja Kinski) later has a dream in which she imagines herself being born as baby Astharoth, using similar methods to escape the confines of the womb:

> I had a horrible dream. I dreamt I was being born. I was clawing my way out. I was hideous, inhuman. They were sick and revolted when they saw me.

John Verney (Richard Widmark), the occult writer who is looking after her, admits, "It's a little worrisome when she sees herself born as some hideous creature."

"That's just a Freudian nightmare," scoffs Honor Blackman's Anna Fountain, and she is both right and wrong—wrong in terms of the film's story but also quite right with regard to the birth we all endure, which is presumably so terrifying none of us can remember it, but for residual echoes of the event in the deepest layers of the sub-conscious.

Peter Sykes considered Wheatley's original novel "basically unfilmable,"[8] and the story was indeed radically altered, retaining, however, its basic elements. Wheatley's vision was of grotesque homunculi rather than of demons as such; one of those horrors is to be fertilized with the blood of the novel's virginal heroine by the sinister Canon Copley-Style (a character loosely based on Wheatley's own personal encounter with Montague Summers, with whom he did not get on). Whatever one thinks of the general style of the rest of the book Wheatley's description of the embryo homunculus is an astonishingly arresting, indeed surreal expression of embryo body horror:

> In the clear liquid that filled the giant bottle was a naked female monster. She was about the height of a child of eight, yet far broader, having big breasts and thick thighs; but from the crutch downwards her legs were tied, and ended in tiny tapering feet, so that she resembled a squat and hideous mermaid. Her flesh was entirely bald. As she stared at her she slowly opened a pair of red-rimmed lashes eyes and blinked at him.[9]

Another homunculus in Copley-Style's little collection opens and shuts its mouth "in the same manner as a fish. When the cover was first removed from her jar she appeared to be asleep, but almost instantly she woke and became imbued with horrid life, grimacing at them and clawing furiously at the glass as though she would rend and devour them if she could."[10]

Oddly, given the novel's explicit biological horrors, Christopher Lee regarded the crawling, deformity created by Les Bowie for the infant Astharoth as "totally obscene and totally unnecessary ... revolting."[11] So too did the distraught and disappointed Wheatley, but Bowie's highly effective creation was mild compared to the repulsive horror of the monstrous human fetus in David Lynch's *Eraserhead*, made the following year. The *non plus ultra* of parental anxiety films, *Eraserhead*, with its nightmare aesthetic of monochrome expressionism and urban anomie, accompanied by the perpetual wheezings, humming and hissings of machinery, is also a study of existential anxiety. It begins with a sperm emerging from the mouth of the hero, Henry (Jack Nance). He seems also to be screaming, or is this merely orgasmic release? Perhaps both. The sperm then plunges into oceanic amniotic fluids, and the horror begins.

When Henry visits his girlfriend's home for dinner, he is confronted by the sight and sound of a bitch feeding its brood from her teat, an unfortunate meal-time reminder of the fatherhood Henry is now so reluctant to embark upon. On being informed that his son has been born prematurely, Henry promptly suffers a nose bleed before he is introduced to the tadpole-like spawn of his conjugation—a hideous thing. (Lynch's view is very obviously that babies are quite literally a bloody nuisance, bringing in their wake the horrifying prospect of sleepless nights, marriage to a hysterical female and a life in which the future resembles the brick wall that blocks out the view from Henry's bedroom window.) The wailing of the "baby" forms a cacophonous counterpoint to the soul-destroying rumbling of the industrial nightmare, which is made all the more lugubrious by a distinctly Gothic thunderstorm.

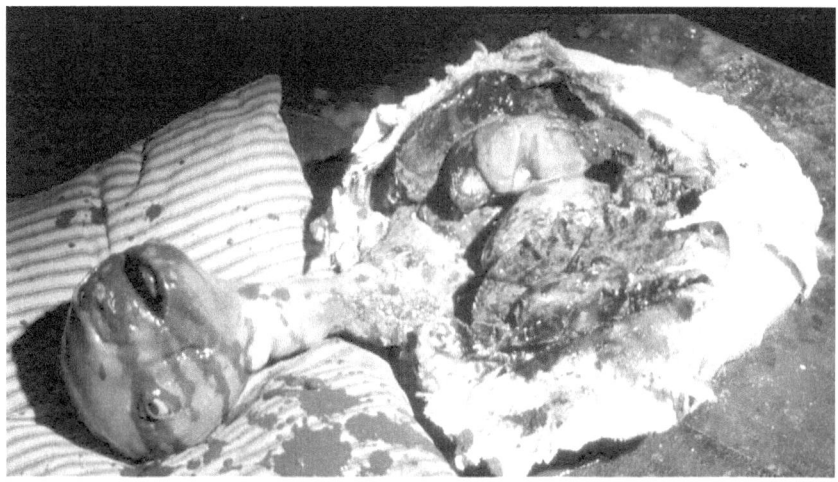

Embryorgans. The "baby" in *Eraserhead* (dir. David Lynch, 1977).

Father and son soon find themselves abandoned. "Shut up!" the mother shouts at her wailing offspring, before walking out, and Henry is left to care for his little monster by himself. He does his best, and is indeed dutiful. He takes baby's temperature and observes it covered in spots. "You *are* ill, aren't you?" he observes, but in the end, he cuts open its bandages and the body of the creature literally falls apart, engulfed in its own porridgy puss. A more graphic example of the bodily horror we all carry around within ourselves would be had to imagine, but the "baby" nonetheless has its revenge and grows to monstrous proportions, suggesting, no doubt, the horrors of dealing with adolescence. No wonder the film ends with Henry locked in an expression of catatonic horror.

Meanwhile, *The Omen* had been breaking box-office records, and redefining what horror films could be. Damien, the devil child of Richard Donner's new cinematic vision, is born of a jackal and brought into the world by a group of decidedly dedicated Satanists. Damien, of course, definitely wants to be born, unlike Sasdy's reluctant cot monster, but *The Omen* in general shares the "Catholic" contexts of both *I Don't Want to Be Born* and *To the Devil a Daughter*. As humanity's technological capacity to destroy itself grows ever greater, popular culture increasingly attempts to exorcise the fear we have of ourselves. *The Omen* is really little more than a series of grisly murders, but the motivation behind them is significant: the devil is in charge of American politics and is hell-bent on his age-old desire to destroy humanity. The ultimate horror of nuclear war is never mentioned but that is what this film is all about. A poem created by the screenwriter David Seltzer implies this subtext:

> From the eternal sea he rises,
> Raising armies on either shore,
> Setting man against his brother
> Till man exists no more.

The photographer played by David Warner analyses the poem by explaining: "In 'Revelations' it says 'he shall rise from the eternal sea.' ... And theologians have already interpreted the eternal sea as meaning the world of politics, the sea that constantly rages with turmoil and revolution; so the Devil's child will rise from the world of politics."

Any hope that we will be able to stop our imminent nuclear destruction at the hands of Damien, the Devil's child, when he grows up, are quashed at the end of the film, when Gregory Peck's Senator Thorn is shot by the police while attempting to destroy this demonic cuckoo in the nest. The moment is a pivotal one in the horror genre for it shows that audiences no longer believed in their own salvation. The moral ending dies with Thorn, for the devil has won, and humanity, it would appear, is rendered either powerless to save itself, or no longer even sufficiently interested so to do.

As the Omen sequels progressed, their audiences were taken ever closer to this ultimate goal. With the arrival of President Reagan and his adoption of *Star Wars* mythology to define his nuclear defense policy, followed by President Trump's even more irrational approach to governance, the *Omen* films now seem positively prophetic, but we might more usefully compare such apocalyptic anxieties to the mediaeval era. *The Omen* franchise is in some way the late 20th century's equivalent of St. Augustine, Albrecht Dürer and Hieronymus Bosch, but stripped of their Christian certainties. Ironically, sales of the Bible soared after the release of *The Omen,* reacquainting people with a text that had hitherto been relatively neglected.

The Omen would therefore appear to provide a very negative critique of children, which successive films would develop with increasingly grizzly imagery. In Mary Lambert's 1989 adaptation of Stephen King's *Pet Sematary,* the cutest of little boys, Miko Hughes, plays Gage Creed, who is killed in a road accident and is later resurrected as an infant zombie with a taste for blood. Hughes was only three years old when he sank his fangs into Fred "Hermann Munster" Gwynne's Judd Crandall, by which time the cinema had been flooded with demonic children (*The Exorcist* and *The Omen*), not to mention demonic dolls (such as Chucky), suggesting that there was something of a crisis in late 20th century's relationship with the realities of childhood—a crisis that has since grown ever more alarming. The imbalance between the violence of 20th-century current affairs, beamed with increasing pervasiveness into middle–American living rooms, and the desire for the good life seems to have been one of the main cause of this obsession; also an increasing infantilization of society in general, in which children have become more privileged than ever before in human history. There seems to have been and still is a desire on the part of parents to protect their children from a world for which those same parents are ultimately responsible, which does indeed make one wonder why parents have children in the first place if they are so terrified of what the world might do to them. As David Benatar suggests, "Nor is the harm produced by the creation of a child usually restricted to that child. The child soon finds itself motivated to procreate, producing children who, in turn, develop the same desire. Thus any pair of procreators can view themselves as occupying the tip of a generational iceberg of suffering."[12]

The pervasive influence of the internet, together with technology's ability to make such characters as Slender Man seem so much more real than any fictional character before them, no doubt played its part in the transference of fantasy, via the copycat actions of two teenage girls, into bloody reality. Ironically, this fictionally-inspired murder has itself inspired a *Slender Man* film, directed by Sylvain White in 2018, but the film is in effect more concerned with anxieties about the internet, which first disseminated the meme (though I will be returning to it when we come to consider the bodily horror of eating, as the girls in *Slender Man* are indeed *consumed*). In this respect, the film merely updated Cronenberg's earlier *Videodrome,* which responded to anxieties about the effect of what, in the 1980s were called "video nasties" and the genuine death and torture in "snuff" movies. In *Videodrome,* Max accidentally discovers, via a pirate satellite dish, a "snuff" channel called Videodrome. (In fact, he has been the victim of a political organization and an arms company, which jointly aim to control the minds of North Americans in a forthcoming struggle for supremacy over the rest of the world. It plans to achieve this by sending a television signal that induces a brain tumor in its viewers, thus creating hallucinations.) Similarly, the Slender Man enters the minds of the girls who accidentally discover him on the internet, and apparently hallucinate as a result, ultimately being absorbed by him, just Max is forced to kill himself by the Videodrome at the end of Cronenberg's film.

Both films are largely concerned with how far morality can be corrupted by the experience of technology, but other films have explored our ambivalence over children in more traditional contexts. In Keating's *Wakewood,* the "reborn" nine-year-old Alice, who is played with astonishing virtuosity by Ella Connolly, becomes increasingly malevolent because Louise and Patrick have broken the rules of the village ritual that facilitated her resurrection. (Alice has been dead for over a year, and it is specified that the spell will only work properly if she has been dead for no longer than a year.) Louise pays the price when Alice drags her quite literally down to hell, much as Frankenstein's creation ultimately destroys his own creator, but before that happens, one member of the community, Peggy O'Shea (Ruth McCabe), senses that all is not as it should be with Alice. Their scene together is Connolly's greatest acting triumph, combining doe-eyed charm with sullen malice. "Alice, are you a normal little girl?" Peggy asks her, at which Alice storms off, hissing, "I don't like *that woman!*" Connolly demonstrates by her impressive performance that children don't have to be resurrected from the dead to be frightening. Alice is malevolent, certainly, but so many "normal" children are too, especially when they cannot have their own way. What Connolly achieves so brilliantly is to suggest the supernatural by only slightly heightening the quite natural petulance and determination of many a normal little girl, who has been adored by her doting parents. Like so many contemporary parents, Patrick and Louise (Aiden Gillen and Eva Birthistle) are psychologically compartmentalized. The "adult" and "mature" approach they have to their rather dull working lives (Patrick is a somewhat dour vet, Louise is a somewhat matter-of-fact pharmacist) is contrasted with their child-like spontaneity, creativity and fun, which are channeled entirely through their daughter. This is, of course, the main reason why people have children—to recapture what they have been foolish or unfortunate enough to have lost in themselves, and it is why the corruption of childhood innocence in horror films is so powerful a symbol of the psychological loss of so many adults.

Wakewood has much in thematically, if not stylistically in common with *The Innocents,* Jack Clayton's 1961 adaptation of Henry James' "The Turn of the Screw." Though *The Innocents* eschews the graphic body horror of *Wakewood,* both films concern adults who wish the children in their care to be entirely "good," and yet end up investing them with their own sins. Both films are also deeply rooted in an ambiguity about sex. *Wakewood* explores this in a highly physical way, *The Innocents* by suggestion, but it is constructive to compare the two. The very title of Clayton's film is, of course, an ironic comment on what is going on, which is far from innocent. Because we are predisposed to imagine that children are born innocent and remain so until adolescence, the gradual revelation that this might not in fact be the case is deeply disturbing, undermining, as I have already suggested, one of the prime justifications for reproduction. Preferring to sever "evil" from conception, attributing it to the vicissitudes of experience, it seems we are still reluctant to believe in the concept of original sin, in both a theological and psychological sense. Are Miles and Flora pure or corrupt? We can never know for sure, but by casting Martin Stevens, fresh from his success as a malevolent alien child in *Village of the Damned,* we are encouraged to believe the latter, until the end, that is, when he seems utterly perplexed by the accusations of his governess (Deborah Kerr). When she kisses him directly on the lips, just before the end titles role to the disturbing sound of a nightingale ("Now more than ever seems it rich to die,/To cease upon the midnight with no pain," as Keats put it) our suspicions fall more heavily upon her.

A Freudian analysis, at least of Henry James' story, was certainly considered possible by Edmund Wilson in his famous essay "The Ambiguity of Henry James." Is this repressed young woman, the daughter of a vicar, secretly in lust with her unresponsive employer? (The narrator of James' tale refers to the interview between the employer and the governess as a "seduction excised by the splendid young man. She succumbed to it."[13] He is a man of "high fashion, of good looks, of expensive habits, of charming ways with women."[14]) Is the governess emotionally unstable to the point of insanity? Are all her anxieties and fears really the result of being terrified of herself? Wilson observes that the ghosts of Peter Quint and Miss Jessel, whom she believes corrupted the innocence of her two charges, Miles and Flora, occur on a tower (Quint) and beside a lake (Jessel), which are, respectively, convenient symbols of the phallus and the vulva. Just before the ghost of Miss Jessel appears, Flora "had picked up a small flat piece of wood, which happened to have in it a little hole that had evidently suggested to her the idea of sticking in another fragment that might figure as a mast and make the thing a boat"[15] and, of course, sticking a piece of wood into a hole in another piece of wood is another convenient sexual symbol, should one wish to interpret it as such. This Wilson does, arguing that sexual hysteria lies behind the visions. There is no hard evidence that anybody but the governess sees them; she may believe the children see them too, but James avoids providing us with any proof that this is the case. Clayton masterfully maintains this ambiguity until the very end of the film when Miles dies, apparently bewildered by the Governess' accusations that Peter Quint is responsible for the decline in his morals. He shouts: "You're insane! Peter Quint? Where? Where, you devil?" We are shown fleeting glimpses of Quint (Peter Wyngard), whom the Governess seems to see, but Miles seems not to see, before, staring into the middle distance, he collapses and dies.

The ambiguity of the children is, of course, the most compelling aspect of the film. Are they really evil, or in fact as angelic as they seem? They certainly misbehave and often appear to be very knowing and secretive, not to mention cynical and cruel, but is the real evil, rather, the way in which the Governess interprets the behavior of the children, acting as she does *in loco parentis*. Caring for children is inevitably related to sexual desire because children are the *result* of sexual desire, and yet taboos decree that our relations with children should remain devoid of sexual feeling, and that the children themselves should have also have no sexual feelings of their own. As Miles and Flora are not the Governess' own children there is all the more reason for her to impose her own guilty feelings upon them. The "sins" of the children are more likely to be the "sins" the Governess has thought about but never acted upon in her life.

In Truman Capote's screen adaptation for the Jack Clayton film, the very title of the film begs the question, "who are the innocents?" The children may not be in league with corrupting ghosts, but neither are they entirely innocent; no children ever are. The Governess is far more culpable than James allows in the tale, and her potentially pedophiliac nature subtly emphasized. "More than anything I love children!" she states from the outset, which is technically what the term pedophile means. She is certainly not a pedophobe, but this again raises the question of what kind of love is most appropriate for a parent or surrogate mother to have. When does love become oppressive, intrusive, or downright destructive as it does in *The Innocents*? "They need affection, love, someone who will belong to them," she continues, in fact voicing her *own* needs.

"Do you have an imagination?" asks Michael Redgrave, who plays the children's distant uncle. The governess certainly does have an imagination—far too much imagination for her own and everyone else's good. Whereas the uncle believes that only people with imagination can attain the truth, the governess' imagination creates fantasies, which ultimately destroy Miles. The uncle realizes that his own life in London, with its presumably sexual amusements, is "not the sort of amusement that one could suitably share with children." No pedophile he, but the governess confuses her own sexual needs with those of the children—indeed imposes them upon the children. She is also attracted to the uncle, and later confesses as much when saying that she will not write to him about her fears for Miles and Flora because he might think it "some sort of stupid trick *to get him to notice me,*" which is exactly what she wants him to do.

Consequently, the uncle's country estate of Bly becomes a corrupted Garden of Eden, the corruption symbolized by the white rose petals that continually fall from their stems in the manner of Gabriele D'Annunzio, a decadent writer incidentally much admired by James, who described the Italian's prose style as resembling "a mantle of voluminous folds, stiff with elaborate embroidery."[16] Indeed, a line from D'Annunzio's *Il Piacere* (*The Child of Pleasure*), we find similar imagery: "On the mantelpiece a great white rose in one of the vases as dropping its petals softly, languidly, one by one, giving an impression of something subtly feminine and sensuous. The cup-like petals rested delicately on the marble, like flakes of snow."[17]

"It's a heaven for children here," says the housekeeper Mrs. Gross (Megs Jenkins), and Miles and Flora are indeed a kind of Adam and Eve, with the role of the serpent being far more likely to be that of the governess than the ghosts of Quint and Miss Jessel. Out of conversational fragments and hinted mysteries, the governess constructs a mighty conspiracy theory. Because Flora likes to go off on her own, she must, therefore, be up to no good. Because Mrs. Gross mentions that Peter Quint had "the devil's own eye," regarding pretty women, the governess makes a demon out of him. When Flora wonders out loud if she might not be good, and that God might therefore leave her spirit on earth "to walk around," the governess regards this as proof that the ghosts exist. That Flora is not entirely good (she can quite happily watch a spider eat a butterfly), does not make her thoroughly corrupt, merely human. The audience of the film is manipulated into being as guilty as the governess in jumping to conclusions. Smiles, whispers, private jokes, ambivalent expressions, even the fact that Flora seems to expect Miles to be sent home from school, all suggest a knowingness and a corruptibility that are not really there at all. Mrs. Gross knows exactly what the governess is doing. "Are you afraid he'll corrupt you?" she asks, regarding Miles, but like Dorian Gray, we are never told exactly what evil acts Miles is supposed to have committed at school. He himself says he was expelled merely because he was different and "made things up," but that hardly seems worthy of such drastic punishment. Indeed, Flora also makes things up, but what else is there for them to do in their isolated paradise? These lonely children are far more sinned against than sinning. "It's a bit sad, though, people not having time for you," Miles confesses.

The governess is also lonely, and with far too much time on her hands her imagination creates all sorts of imaginary monsters. Soon after she finds a portrait of Quint, whom she now significantly regards as "handsome and obscene" (an interesting juxtaposition), she thinks she sees his ghost. Her horror at the vision mingles with an attraction she cannot admit to herself. Quint has therefore to become totally evil, just as she wishes the children to be totally good. Mrs. Gross says that Miles doted on Quint only because he had no father of his own, but the governess, in her quest to redeem Miles for herself, places all the blame on Quint, interpreting Miles' recitation of the ambiguous lines "What shall I say when my Lord comes a-calling" as referring to his ghostly nemesis, when they might very well be no more than an innocent dramatic recitation. She reaches the crazed conclusion that Quint and Miss Jessel can "only reach each other by entering the souls of the children and possessing them."

The governess is often tired. Sleep eludes her and she also often feels hot (no doubt due to naturally unmentioned hormonal "flushes"). In this exhausted and sexually agitated state, Quint and Miss Jessel become devils of sex—embodiments of the sexual urge the governess fears within herself. For her, sex is always "indecent." The ghosts are always "indecent, obscene horrors." Mrs. Gross eventually explains that Quint abused Miss Jessel, who masochistically accepts his violence, and when Miles hurts the governess by holding rather tightly on around her neck, we wonder if the governess is enjoying being hurt in a similar manner, imagining that Miles is in fact her demon lover. Mrs. Gross observes that Miss Jessel "grieved till there was something crazy in her eyes," at which point Clayton focuses on the governess' face with her similarly crazy eyes.

There are two kisses between the governess and Miles. "Kiss me good-night, Miss Giddons," Miles asks. They do so, and there is a tense frisson afterwards as Miles smiles ambivalently back at her. When at the end of the film, the governess kisses Miles on the lips, she finally seems to realize that she is reenacting Jessel and Quint making love, and her guilt at this realization explains why the films opens and ends with a shot of her hands clasped fervently in prayer. Miles knows what has been going on, calling her a "damned hussy—a dirty-minded hag." Mrs. Gross accuses the governess of wakening the "bad memory" of Miss Jessel's suicide and Quints violent death, which has caused Miles and Flora to misbehave. It is not the ghosts, merely the governess' hysteria that has set everything out of joint. In her pursuit to purge herself of sexual feelings while simultaneously longing for them to be consummated, and in using the children as symbols of this inner psychological drama of her own, she has brought about their destruction.

Clayton and Capote worked allusively, but by far the most graphic deconstruction of childhood innocence is undoubtedly William Golding's 1954 novel *Lord of the Flies*, which was deliberately conceived as an antidote to the romantic fantasy of R.M. Ballantyne's adventure novel *The Coral Island* of 1858. Golding was very much aware that if a group of children were actually stranded on a desert island, they would soon turn into savages. To underline his irony, he borrows the names of Ballantyne's boy heroes, who encounter danger from the island's "savages" but do not become savages themselves. Indeed, for Ballantyne, being stranded on a desert island is more like a tropical beach holiday than a disaster:

> What a joyful thing it is to awaken, on a fresh glorious morning, and find the rising sun staring into your face with dazzling brilliancy! to see the birds twittering in the bushes, and to hear the murmuring of a rill, or the soft hissing ripples as they fall upon the sea-shore! At any time and in any place such sights and sounds are most charming, but more especially are they so when one awakens to them, for the first time, in a novel and romantic situation, with the soft sweet air of a tropical climate mingling with the fresh smell of the sea, and stirring the strange leaves that overhead and around one, or ruffling the plumage of the stranger birds that fly inquiringly around, as if to demand what business we have to intrude uninvited on their domains. When I awoke on the morning after our shipwreck, I found myself in this most delightful condition.[18]

Golding has none of this. He describes his island in much more troubling terms. Ralph stands "among the skull-like coco-nuts with green shadows from the palms and the forest sliding over his skin. He undid the snake-clasp of his belt, lugged off his shorts and pants, and stood there naked, looking at the dazzling beach and the water."[19] "Skull-like," "green," "sliding," "snake-clasp," "dazzling"—there is nothing "fresh" or "romantic" about these images, and neither would Ballantyne's boys go around naked. Golding's view is obviously that the majority of British public-school boys, if not boys in general, are potential little devils, and in a curious way, are indeed encouraged so to be by the institutions that nurture them.

Lord of the Flies is indeed a nightmare vision of what used to be called the British public-school system. Golding merely removes the school and leaves the boys to be boys on their own terms. In fact, this revelation of the barbarism that lurks beneath the surface veneer of social rules had been brilliantly described in the nightmare vision of Hans Castorp in Thomas Mann's novel *The Magic Mountain*. (Within a serene classical temple, Castorp observes two hags dismembering a child. "In dreadful silence they tore it apart with their bare hands—Hans Castorp saw the bright hair blood-smeared—and cracked the tender bones between their jaws, their dreadful lips dripped blood."[20])

"*Kill the pig! Cut his throat! Kill the pig! Bash him in!*" the boys shout during their celebrated pig hunt, and, appropriately, Ralph responds to the comment "That was a good game" with the line "I got jolly badly hurt at rugger once."[21]

One of the book's most hauntingly horrifying images is that of the airman who has parachuted from his plane and fallen to his death on the island:

> Here the breeze was fitful and allowed the strings of the parachute to tangle and festoon; and the figure sat, its helmeted head between its knees, held by a complication of lines. When the breeze blew the lines would strain taut and some accident of this pull lifted the head and chest upright so that the figure seemed to peer across the brow of the mountain.[22]

The beast. *Lord of the Flies* (dir. Peter Brook, 1963).

Stanley Kubrick seems to have paraphrased this image in *Full Metal Jacket* (1987) when the grown up little boys who have been sent out to Vietnam encounter old buddies, one of whom reveals the corpse of a Vietcong soldier and addresses it disconcertingly as "my bro," rather as Ralph in *Lord of the Flies* addresses the slaughtered pig. Peter Brook's film adaptation of Golding's novel spends less time on the ghostly vision of the dead airman, but the descent of British school boys into painted savages is brilliantly transcribed into visual terms, especially in the closing frames, when the disturbing image of Ralph appears before the British naval officer who eventually comes to the rescue. In the book, the officer says, "I should have thought that a pack of British boys—you're all British are you?—would have been able to put up a better show than that," before relenting and nodding more sympathetically. "Jolly good show," he adds. "Like Coral Island," unaware that this is precisely what it is *not* like. Ralph is left weeping for "the darkness of man's heart,"[23] echoing the title of Joseph Conrad's famous short story. In the film, the officer is much more visibly disturbed by what he finds, reflecting the unease of the audience itself. Again, we are left with the horror we all share of our own reality.

The film opens with still photographs of a typically Victorian prep school, accompanied by a tolling bell and group photos of schoolboys in uniform gathered around their masters. We then hear them at their desks and in the refectory, with Latin being construed and hymns being sung in chapel. Polite applause at a cricket match is eerily juxtaposed with the sound of timpani, photos of warplanes and the sounds of aerial combat, summing up in only a few moments the hideous connection between public schools and the military, society and savagery, even civilization itself and barbarism. The playing fields of Eton, so to speak, were very much the incubator of the British Empire and its wars.

A group of highly patrician choirboys have also been stranded on the island, and Brook introduces them to us walking along the beach in their long gowns, incongruously singing "Kyrie eleison." But there is, of course, no Lord to have mercy on any of them. The head chorister proudly claims: "Got to have rules and obey them; after all we're not savages. We're English and the English are the best at everything." Ironically, it is this very upper-crust head chorister who transforms his choirboys into a group of hunters, and it is not long before, stripped to the waist, they trap and slaughter a pig, which the boys tuck into like the wild animals they are rapidly becoming. It is the choirboys who most enthusiastically take to painting their bodies in the most un-Christian manner, ultimately dispatching one of the other boys while shouting, "Kill! Kill! Kill!"

The composer, Raymond Leppard, comments on this transformation by accompanying shots of the boy's corpse with "Kyrie eleison" once more. Decent Ralph, still "civilized," is troubled by this and voices his disquiet with

Piggy, the porcine boy whose glasses have been broken by the chief chorister, but Piggy argues that it wasn't murder. "It was dark. There was that bloody dance. There was thunder and lightning and rain. We were scared. It wasn't what ... you said. It was an accident."

"Oh God," Ralph moans, "I want to go home," but there is no going home in the psychological sense. He has seen too much and will forever more remain a stranger to civilization, even after he has been rescued, for no amount of civilization can veil the abyss into which he has peered. Ralph takes on the head chorister and a fight ensues. Piggy intervenes: "Which is it better to be?" he asks. "A pack of painted savages like you are, or sensible like Ralph?" But a rock crushes Piggy, and simultaneously flattens his argument. By the time the shining white beacon of the Royal Navy officer comes to the rescue it is really all too late, all of Ralph's ideals of civilization having been well and truly demolished.

The Lord of the Flies itself is in fact the severed head of a pig. It of course attracts the flies, especially when it is mounted on a stick. In the book, Ralph has imaginary conversations with it:

> "Fancy thinking the Beast was something you could hunt and kill!" said the head. For a moment or two the forest and all the other dimly appreciated places echoed with the parody of laughter. "You knew, didn't you? I'm part of you? Close, close, close! I'm the reason why it's no go? Why things are what they are?"...
>
> Simon found he was looking into a vast mouth. There was blackness within, a blackness that spread....
>
> Simon was inside the mouth. He fell down and lost consciousness.[24]

This is the core of the novel's meaning, connecting, of course, the devil within with Beelzebub (the devil without), who is also known as the Lord of the Flies. (We should be mindful, however, that this is in fact a corruption of "Lord of the Flyers"—as Beelzebub was an excellent flier, but it is also possible that Judaism used the image of flies to refer to his followers, implying that they were like flies attracted to dung.) In the novel, "the pile of guts was a black blob of flies that buzzed like a saw. After a while these flies found Simon. Gorged, they alighted by his runnels of sweat and drank. They tickled his nostrils and played leap-frog on his thighs. They were black and iridescent green and without number; and in front of Simon, the Lord of the Flies hung on his stick and grinned."[25]

But when one of the boys in the film suggests, "Maybe there is a beast ... what I mean is, maybe it's only us," he is ridiculed by the others. "Nuts!" one of them shouts. Fear, of course, is what unites them, as it did in a different way at school. Schoolmasters rule by fear, as does society, but here the fear is born of itself. There is no more compelling document or film that demonstrates more disquietingly the latent savageries of children and the horror humanity has of itself.

In the same year, 1963, Hammer Films released a rather different approach to the subject of children and innocence. *The Damned* was directed by Joseph Losey in his only film for the company. It concerns a group of children incarcerated in a secret government facility, who have all been irradiated in preparation for the "inevitable" nuclear war that lies before them. Having been inured to the consequences of atomic fall-out, they will be able to inherit the world and thus rebuild civilization, at least in theory. Here, the terrible secret of the children, which even they do not understand, is a powerful symbol for the beast within. These children not only bear the sin but also the guilt of their fathers, who have created the grotesque possibility of nuclear war. They are the ultimate scapegoats, segregated from society in their underground bunker, cared for and educated by remote control. Their surrogate father, Bernard, played by Alexander Knox, has every confidence that what he is doing is right, but when his girlfriend, Freya (Viveca Lindfors), finds out what is really happening, she asks him exactly what kind of world he expects these children will inhabit. He has no answer, of course, and once Freya learns of the secret operation, she is liquidated. Are these damned children innocent victims or themselves carriers of the ultimate plague—the ultimate sin? Their cries for help at the end of the film suggest a cry for help from the whole of humanity to be released from its collective guilt.

Hammer went on to explore the problem of children in films such as *The Nanny* (dir. Seth Holt, 1965), which is really a study in child psychopathology rather than any kind of metaphysical or inherent evil. William Dix's young Joey has fun terrorizing adults by pretending to hang himself, and causes a great deal of trouble in his misunderstood battle with Bette Davis' deranged Nanny. It is adolescents rather than children who featured in *The Witches* (dir. Cyril Frankel, 1966), as was the case with all their subsequent juvenile leads in such delights as *Taste the Blood of Dracula* (dir. Peter Sasdy, 1970), *The Vampire Lovers* (dir. Roy Ward Baker, 1970), Sasdy's *Hands of the Ripper* and Gibson's *Dracula A.D. 1972*. More pertinent to our theme, in Fisher's *The Curse of the Werewolf*, the young Léon (Justin Walters, whose adult incarnation is later to be played by Oliver Reed) provided one of cinema's most truly disturbing images of child malevolence. Having been taken hunting with Warren Mitchell's Pepé, Léon, disturbed by the killing of a squirrel, attempts to comfort it and accidentally tastes its blood. He then explains the effect this experience has upon him:

> It tasted sweet. I wanted to keep on tasting it, but Pepe took it away. ... Ever since then, I've had bad dreams, uncle. I dream that I'm a wolf, like in a picture book. I dream I'm a wolf drinking blood. Help me, uncle! Please help me!

But this is merely a prelude to what is perhaps the film's most frightening image, as Léon in his nightshirt, with incipient fangs bared, pulls violently against the bars at his bedroom window by the light of the full moon. This is in fact more troubling than the visceral horror of our first glimpse of Reed's mature werewolf in full make-up because a child is popularly assumed to be free of those disturbing sexual impulses that lie behind the werewolf myth as a whole.

To watch a child in the grips of sexual excitement can really only be depicted in the fantasy context of Gothic horror. The smiling, fanged vampire child (Lance Kerwin) who floats outside the bedroom window of Brad Savage's Danny Glick in *Salem's Lot* (dir. Tobe Hooper, 1979) updated Fisher's vision, and is even more disturbing. Whereas werewolf Léon is trying to get out, vampire Mark is trying to get in, but both boys negotiate their entrance into maturity through similar windows of opportunity. Hammer would return to the disquieting equation of werewolves with children in the "Children of the Full Moon" episode (dir. Tom Clegg, 1980) from the television series *Hammer House of Horror*. These angelic children, cared for by the charmingly sinister Diana Dors, are all werewolves with a taste for blood.

Vampire and werewolf children are rare precisely because they offend the innocence taboo. One of the rare examples of a cinematic vampire child is Claudia, played by Kirsten Dunst, in Neil Jordan's 1994 adaptation of Anne Rice's novel *Interview with the Vampire*. Claudia becomes undead at the age of five, though Dunst was 11 when she took the role. "I want some more!" she complains, after Lestat (Tom Cruise) cautions her against drinking too much blood on the first occasion. "Look at you!" he compliments her, like a proud father. "Not a drop spilled. Very good!" And to compound the violation of social rules, Claudia then becomes the "daughter" of this pseudo-gay vampire couple of Lestat and Louis (Brad Pitt). "A little child she was," Louis reminisces, "but also a fierce killer, now capable of the ruthless pursuit of blood with all a child's demanding. She slept in my coffin at first, curling her little fingers around my hair, till the day came when she wanted one other own, but still whenever she awoke she would crawl into mine." She slaughters toyshop owners and piano teachers. "To me, she was a child," Louis explains, "but to Lestat, a pupil, and infant prodigy with a lust for killing that matched his own. Together they finished off whole families." Rice spares the reader none of Claudia's ferocity in her original novel, as in this early scene in which Claudia, described as a Botticelli angel, attacks the vampire Lestat, during which she suddenly "flashed at me a virulency I'd never seen in her face, and as I stood there paralyzed, she gashed his throat, and he let out a sharp, choking cry."[26] Much blood follows, as one would expect.

Perhaps more genuinely disturbing, because so much less melodramatically underplayed, is the angelic Chloe Franks in the "Sweets to the Sweet" episode of *The House That Dripped Blood* (dir. Peter Duffell, 1971). Taking a quotation from *Hamlet*, which refers to the funeral bouquet that Queen Gertrude throws into the grave of the dead Ophelia, "Sweets to the Sweet" similarly concerns the death of innocence, except that what seems so innocent (Frank's Jane Reid) has never actually been innocent at all. Duffell wanted to call the whole film "Death and the Maiden" after the subtitle of Schubert's famous D minor String Quartet, which itself quotes a melody from Schubert's song "Das Tod und das Mädchen" ("Give me thy hand, oh! maiden fair to see,/For I'm a friend, hath ne'er distress'd thee./Take courage now, and very soon/Within mine arms shalt softly rest thee!"). Peter Cushing's character Philip, plays a recording of this quartet in the "Waxworks" segment of the film, but in "Sweets to the Sweet" Death and the Maiden are combined in the character of Jane. We first see her follow her father John Reid (Christopher Lee) into the eponymous house, with cheerful birdsong fluting in the garden and bright morning light filtering the gloomy interior. She herself continues this false impression by looking neat, innocent and delightful. "What a very lovely child she is," observes the estate agent, Mr. Stoker (John Bryans). "Yes," Reid replies, without conviction.

Jane is terrified of fire because her mother was witch, who was presumably somehow burnt at the stake, despite this being 1971. Appearing to be withdrawn, lonely and sad, Jane has been kept in virtual quarantine by her terrified father, who forbids her toys and contact with other children. Jane is "the living image" of her mother, and Mr. Reid, who appears at first to be a tyrant, is in fact a victim; at least this is one way of looking at the affair. A different perspective is to see the story from Jane's point of view. If her father hadn't been so terrified of her, thrown her doll on the fire and allowed her to brood in her isolation, she may not have become so interested in witchcraft, and her desire to dispose of her father by sympathetic magic may well not have arisen. The film thus spans the categories of the "evil child" and the "bad parent." And, of course, there remains the possibility that Mr. Reid is himself a fantasist whose judgment cannot be relied upon. (He is, after all, discovered reading a paperback copy of Lee's own favorite bedtime reading, *The Lord of the Rings*.) When Reid challenges Jane over some missing candles during a suitably Gothic thunderstorm, Duffell juxtaposes Lee's already well-established demonic features with Frank's seemingly angelic ones to magnificent effect. Lee also writhes and screams much like his incarnations as Dracula when Jane skewers her wax figure of him with a hatpin, again suggesting the tyranny he has exerted over his daughter. No wonder Jane smiles like a fallen angel when the wax melts in the flames at the end, accompanied by her father's death agony.

Does the desire of adults to raise children suggest a deeper psychological desire to revert to an infantile fantasy state, as though by having a child, we might purify and idealize the ambivalent memories of our own lost but mistily remembered infancies? Some might say that this process has ultimately led to the creation of the over-entitled adolescents—the so-called millennial "snowflakes" of our own time. Capitalism, of course, has also played its part, focusing its commercial attention on childish desires and the desire of adults to gratify and further fuel them. Our desire to maintain the innocence of children—to construct it indeed—may well be the result of our own despair at having created the opposite in our voracious consumer culture.

A 20th-century manifestation of this dilemma can be seen in Fritz Kiersch's adaptation of Stephen King's *Children of the Corn* (1984) in which a group of children in the American Midwest murder their own parents as sacrifices to a supernatural entity that dwells in the corn rows surrounding their now deserted town. (These seem to echo the cane plantation in Val Lewton's *I Walked with a Zombie* of just over 40 years earlier.) In fact, the film filters the basic idea of *Lord of the Flies* through the prism of Sir James Frazer's *The Golden Bough*. Along with all sinister corn dollies and rural folk horror, the children are shown to be murderous savages, under thrall of John Franklin's demented *Führerkind*, Issac, whose dirty work is mostly executed by the more thuggish (and somewhat older) Malachai of Courtney Gains, who is also a rather better actor. Even the most "angelic" of the children, Anne Marie McEnvoy's clairvoyant little Sarah, smiles sweetly when showing Linda Hamilton's Vicky a drawing she has made, which predicts her murder. Does she understand what she has drawn, or is she truly innocent? The ambivalence here is reminiscent of "Sweets to the Sweet." There is even a nod to the dead airman of *Lord of the Flies* in the striking image of a crucified, long-dead policeman, killed earlier by the children and referred to by them as "the blue man." The whole thing might thus be fairly judged as somewhat derivative (the music score is obviously inspired by Jerry Goldsmith's satanic chanting for *The Omen*), but it is nonetheless a useful corrective to the idea that children are necessarily more innocent and less violent than adults.

All these sexual and infant horrors reached their culmination in Nadine Labaki's *Capernaum* (2018) in which a child sues his parents for the crime of giving him life and bringing him into a war-torn world of their creation. "What do you want from your parents?" the judge asks. "I want to stop them having children!" the boy replies, but Guillermo del Toro's much-acclaimed *Pan's Labyrinth* (2007) suggests that despite life's horrors—indeed *because* of them—children should still be born, and that it is through them that life is made worth living. In his unflinching portrayal of General Franco's fascist will-to-power that led to so much violence and bloodshed in war-torn Spain, del Toro spares no feelings in his graphic obsession with bodily horror: There are shootings, knifings, beatings, euthanasia, amputation and tortures galore, all of which should prove beyond a shadow of a doubt that, as one of the characters herself says, "life is not like your fairy tales. The world is a cruel place…. Magic does not exist." However, del Toro's Goya-esque vision of horror is deeply rooted in Spanish Catholic tradition, a key element of which is actually spoken during a funeral service in the film: "it is in pain that we find the meaning of life." An atheist might well disagree with this, but del Toro is not an atheist. The imaginative fantasies of the young girl Ofelia (Ivana Baquero), who finds herself at the mercy not only of the Spanish civil war in general and her appallingly sadistic stepfather, General Vidal (Sergi López) in particular, are really the teachings of the Catholic Church in disguise. A film as bloody and brutal as this one should really have no redeeming moral at all, but even though the fascist Captain shoots Ofelia before meeting his own end at the hands of partisans, del Toro bathes his bruised and battered audience with glittering CGI visions of what amount to the triumph of the imagination over reality, thus cancelling out the real world he is at such pains to present in all its ghastliness.

Set in 1944, when Franco's regime was triumphant and merely mopping up resistance, del Toro relishes, with a kind of outraged fascination, the brutalities of Captain Vidal who bludgeons a farmer's son with a wine bottle and then casually shoots the farmer himself at point blank range. This would be all very well if the film confined itself to such atrocities, but side by side with these graphic indulgences (reminiscent of a Catholic fanatic scourging himself) his message, via Ofelia's fantasies, is that the imagination can redeem any amount of horror in reality, regardless of the fact that Franco won the war, as the Captain at one stage eloquently points out. Ofelia descends a winding staircase down a large hole (like the one in *Alice in Wonderland*). This presumably symbolizes her subconscious, and there she escapes from reality, despite the fact that there is in reality no escape; del Toro however keeps trying to imply that there is. Ofelia has the makings of a good anti-natalist when the Captain's housekeeper Mercedes (Maribel Verdú), who is in league with the partisans, says, "Having a baby is complicated." "Then I'll never have one," Ofelia replies. Her mother does, however, and Ofelia protects it. Indeed, by allowing her own blood to be shed rather than that of her infant brother at the end of the film, she gains her imaginative reward, which has absolutely nothing to do with the world in which she dies. She is transformed into a magical Princess in posthumous underground kingdom where there are no lies or pain; del Toro's Catholic context is both confusing and illogical. Ofelia knows full well that "things out here aren't too good." She whispers this to her unborn brother, whose fetus we see gently bobbing around in the amniotic fluid, listening. "But soon you'll come out," she adds. This is surely not good either—but, at the end of the film, del Toro tells us that it is: Life is a good thing, apparently, despite the catalogue of horrors accompanying it, and the fairytale that runs alongside the war narrative insists that peace and harmony will one day reign, which they unfortunately never have and probably never will. Only once in the film does a character adopt a logical response to the horror of the world in which the film takes place: A tortured, mutilated partisan fighter asks the doctor played by Álex Angulo to kill him with a lethal injection.

Three

Digestion

> "Ah kidneys—delicious!"
>
> —Peter Cushing
> as Baron Frankenstein[1]

Eating is also a complex process, and *how* we eat lies at the root of civilization itself: "the raw or the cooked," as Claude Levi-Strauss once put it, is a basic question of all societies, but raw or cooked *what*? How do we cope with the idea of ingesting nutrients from other lifeforms, including our own species? And what of the digestive consequences?

Eating disorders such as anorexia are now very well-publicized, especially after the exposure of high-profile sufferers from the complaint such as Princess Diana, but the process of eating among the rest of us has always been both socially and psychologically problematic. Table manners are, after all, primarily designed to disguise the unappealing facts of eating: mastication, swallowing, excess wind, undesirable aromas, to say nothing of defecation. The Marquis de Sade was well aware that table manners are a kind of hypocrisy shared by sexual prudery. "It is as ridiculous to pretend that chastity is a virtue as it would be to assert that it is a virtue to deprive oneself of food," he wrote, adding in a footnote:

> Solitary, man blushes at nothing; modesty grips him only when he is surprised in the act, which proves that modesty is a ridiculous prejudice, absolutely unrecognized by, absolutely alien to, Nature. Man is impudicious born, his impudicity he has from Nature; civilization may tamper with her laws, but never shall civilization extirpate them from the philosopher's soul. "Hominem planto," said Diogenes, as he fucked by the side of the road; and why be more eager to conceal oneself when planting a man than a cabbage?[2]

This is probably why David Cronenberg so often shows us characters eating messily and talking with their mouths full. In *Shivers*, for example, Joe Silver's Rollo Linsky explains the premise of the film while eating a somewhat phallic gherkin and swilling it down with a soft drink, wiping his ample, greasy lips mid-sentence. We have no real need to know that Linsky is a messy eater, but as Cronenberg's focus is always on the body, this detail fits well into the overall perspective, preparing us for the corporeal shocks that follow. Indeed, Cronenberg is fascinated by mouths in general. In *Videodrome*, characters also talk with their mouths full, Peter Dvorsky's Harlan chews on his screwdriver and Max hallucinates himself through a bulging television screen where he is devoured by Debbie Harry's much magnified lips and titanium white teeth. Much of the horror of more conventional vampire films is also oral, of course, perhaps the most disturbing of all Hammer's efforts in this direction being the gaping orifice, fangs at the ready, of Noel Willman's Dr. Ravna in Don Sharp's *Kiss of the Vampire* (1963), as he descends upon Jennifer Daniels. In fact, Willman was required to devour the camera itself when filming this famous close-up, which provides one of cinema's most amusing personifications of the phrase "hungry for fame."

Vegetarianism and veganism, for all their ethics regarding animal welfare, are also responses to a physical distaste at certain types of food, which does not necessarily have anything to do with morality. That infamous vegetarian, Adolf Hitler, once said of the ham that was served to him for breakfast on the morning that his niece Geli was found shot in his Munich apartment, "It's like eating a corpse."[3] Loving animals considerably more than human beings, Hitler hoped that his favorite dog, Blondi, would eventually become a "confirmed vegetarian,"[4] and his confused moral stance reached its peak during an interminable lunchtime monologue on 20 August 1942:

> As it is a poacher kills a hare and goes to prison for three months! I myself should have taken the fellow and put him into one of the guerrilla companies of the SS. I am no admirer of the poacher, particularly as I am a vegetarian; but in him I see the sole element of romance in the so-called sport of shooting. Incidentally, there is no doubt that we number quite a few poachers among the most stalwart adherents of the Party. When I say this, do not imagine that I condone the wholesale depredations of poachers among the wild life of the forests. On the contrary, my sympathies are entirely with the gamekeepers.[5]

Vegetarianism is just as much a matter of taste as of morality and ethics. During its long history, stretching back to Pythagoras, it has had many eloquent supporters in the arts. Dryden's translation of the fifteenth book of Ovid's *Metamorphoses* is almost entirely concerned with vegetarian ethics.

> O Mortals from your Fellow's Blood abstain,
> Not taint your Bodies with a Food profane.[6]

But mingled with this moral censure there is also an esthetic revulsion:

> We, by destroying Life, our Life sustain;
> And gorge th' ungodly Maw with Meats obscene,
> Not so the Golden Age, who fed on Fruit,
> And durst with bloody Meals their Mouths pollute.[7]

Ovid's distaste finds a graphic manifestation in Cronenberg's *Rabid* in which Marilyn Chambers' Rose feasts on a cow's blood, embracing the animal like a vampire bat before the voracious skin graft on her arm begins to suck. She then vomits the bovine blood, but the imagery of a woman embracing the cow is perhaps more disturbing, particularly for those who enjoy eating raw steak. Who would wish to embrace the cow one is later to find served on a plate for one's evening meal?

As the invention of table manners demonstrates, an underlying disgust with food, or at least a troubling or repressed attitude to eating and digestion, is to some extent common to us all. In *La Grande bouffes* (dir. Marco Ferreri, 1973) disgust results not from any particular food but rather from its quantity. Excess is the cause of our revulsion in this story about a group of people who intend to commit suicide by over-indulgence. Various digestive consequences cause the demise of the film's four protagonists. The first, infuriated by his sexual impotence, causes the sewage system of the house in which this dubious banquet takes place to burst. He then drives off in a snowstorm and freezes to death. The bowels of the second erupt whilst he is playing the piano. The third suffers a seizure while masturbating at the same time as being fed three different types of liver *paté* that have been served up in the shape of the dome of St. Peter's in Rome. The fourth dies after eating a cake modeled into the shape of a pair of breasts. The connection between culinary and sexual appetite is thus made explicit, as it is in Cronenberg's *Shivers,* in which a waiter who has been infected by the vampire parasite, attacks two women in an elevator. He announces himself to his horrified victims with a face full of food, stuffing lettuce and tomato ketchup into his mouth as he advances.

Similarly, in *Eraserhead*, the mealtime scene is combined with the news that Henry's fiancé has given birth to a child: "We've got chicken tonight. Strangest damn things," exclaims the emaciated father who presides at the head of the table. "They're man-made." The horror of eating and the parental tyranny of mealtime combine here, everyone resembling not so much the walking as the sitting dead. Henry is asked to carve, but the chicken begins to move as blood emerges from its back passage, reminding us of a reality that the rituals of cooking attempt to disguise. The mother has a seizure on realizing that what she is about to eat was once alive like her, even though she is half-dead herself. She runs from the table followed by her mewing daughter. "Well, Henry, what do you know?" the grinning gargoyle of a father asks, inanely.

Stephen King inverted the premise of *La Grande bouffes* in his novel, *Thinner,* the 1996 film adaptation of which was directed by Tom Holland. This has Raymond John Burke as the morbidly obese lawyer Billy Halleck. He has always eaten greedily, prompting his wife's insistence on a reformatory diet: "I want you to stop digging your grave with a spoon and fork," she insists, while simultaneously attempting to distract his thoughts from the larder by encouraging him into the bedroom, but one evening, Billy kills the wife of a gypsy (Michael Constantine) in a road accident, while driving under the influence of his wife's fellatio. Being a well-connected lawyer, he is acquitted, much to the gypsy's wrath. In revenge, the gypsy meets him outside the courthouse, touches his face and with the single utterance of "thinner" places him under a wasting curse. Accordingly, Billy starts to lose weight quite drastically no matter how much he eats. This unexpected development causes even more anxiety: "If I gain weight I have a heart attack. If I lose weight I've got cancer. I can't win," he complains. Against the grim reaper, none of us can, of course, but Billy aims to extend his chances by using his criminal contacts to force the gypsy to lift the curse. (Billy has successfully acquitted a mafia crook, who owes him a favor.) The circus environment in which the gypsies live remotely echoes that of *Freaks* (dir. Tod Browning, 1932), where body horror is a stock in trade, and the body horror on offer in *Thinner* is equally grotesque, not merely the transformation of Billy's legal colleagues into reptilian and ulcerating monstrosities, but also in the emaciation of Billy himself.

Thinner presents eating as a metaphor of social inequality. The lawyers in the film call the gypsies "filthy" and "thieving." "They bring disease, crime and prostitution," but the gypsy who curses Billy calls him "the white man from town," accusing him of not having watched the road ahead when the accident happened. "You never see us," he adds, implying a somewhat socially wider meaning: Stephen King thus uses culinary greed and sexual appetite as metaphors of the corruptions of consumer capitalism on the one hand, and the injustices of social inequality on the other, but Billy learns none of these lessons. Thinking his wife is being unfaithful to him, he presents her with a strawberry pie, which the gypsy has also cursed, with the information that his own curse will be lifted if he passes it onto another via a portion of the now magically poisoned pudding. The wife cannot resist her favorite dish, but unfortunately neither can Billy's daughter. Billy has had his revenge on an unfaithful wife, but loses his daughter in the process. The last images of the film suggest that even this tragedy hasn't taught Billy the social message of the film, for when his suspicions that his wife has indeed been having an affair are confirmed, he merely smiles with vindictive triumph.

Even food we normally enjoy can be disgusting when we have no appetite for it. (Donald Pleasence amusingly demonstrates this when playing Dr. Seward in John Badham's *Dracula* [1979] when shoveling runny fried eggs into his bearded orifice after the death of his own daughter, a healthy appetite his fellow diners find appalling under the circumstances.) What has been slaughtered and is even rotting is often appetizing to those with a taste for it, and the predilection of one person or species for a particular food source can provide ample horror to those who do not share it. In this respect, vampirism is a food-related issue, its culinary ramifications being made clear in the black comedy of the "Midnight Mess" episode from *The Vault of Horror* (dir. Roy Ward Baker, 1973), in which Daniel Massey finds himself dining at an exclusively "vampires only" restaurant. "How would you like your roast clots, sir?" asks the waiter. "Medium? Rare?" When Massey's character realizes what his soup is really made from, he spits it out, unmasking himself as a mortal interloper. Trussed up by the vampires after this exposure, a tap is inserted into his neck and his blood provides the diners with a witty little nightcap—"much better than the frozen stuff." In an inversion of this vampire restaurant, *Blood for Dracula* (dir. Paul Morrissey, 1974) has Udo Kier's vampire throwing up the blood he has drunk into a bidet, having imbibed an incompatible blood type, very much in the manner of someone who has drunk too much cider.

Blood, as Roland Barthes points out, is really what eating meat is all about, at least from a cultural (and hence semiotic) point of view:

> The prestige of steak evidently derives from its quasi-rawness. In it, blood is visible, natural, dense, at once compact and sectile. One can well imagine the ambrosia of the Ancients as this kind of heavy substance which dwindles under one's teeth in such a way as to make one keenly aware at the same time of its original strength and of its aptitude to flow into the very blood of man. Full-bloodedness is the raison d'être of steak; the degrees to which it is cooked are expressed not in calorific units but in images of blood; rare steak is said to be *saignant* (when it recalls the material flow from the cut in the animal's throat), or *blue* (and it is now the heavy, plethoric, blood of the veins which is suggested by the purplish color—the superlative of redness).[8]

This is not exactly cannibalism, but close to it, and the understandable horror we have at the thought of eating our own species has provided horror films with considerable mileage. Early in the history horror movies, cannibalism featured in *Doctor X* (dir. Michael Curtiz, 1932), in which John Wray's Dr. Haines is suspected of cannibalism. As Lionel Atwill's Doctor Xavier himself puts it, "Dr. Haines and two other scientists were shipwrecked off Tahiti about a year ago while making a study of the coral reefs for the Killary Foundation.... They were adrift for twenty fours days. Their supplies were exhausted. When they were picked up, Haines and one other were delirious. The third had vanished. There was no explanation at the time. Haines later claimed at the time the man had died and he had been thrown overboard." Appropriately, Haines is first presented to us in silhouette, his goatee beard and topknot suggesting a devilish image. What is hinted at here would eventually be fully "fleshed out," so to speak, in Hammer's TV thriller "The Thirteenth Reunion" (see below).

Jimmy Sangster added a taste for human flesh to the monster of *The Revenge of Frankenstein* (dir. Terence Fisher, 1958), explaining in 1987 that he had tried "think of something which really frightened me—upset me personally—revolted me, actually, and that's the business I wrote about the monster they'd created ate people, because I have a horror of being eaten by anybody."[9] We don't actually see the monster rip anyone's flesh, but Fisher did dwell on salivation, which was to return in *The Curse of the Werewolf,* when the imprisoned beggar played by Richard Wordsworth, whose sexual rather than cannibalistic appetites have been aroused by the Werewolf's future mother, similarly salivates. "Have you got the white of egg?" Fisher asked as they were about to start filming the scene. Wordsworth didn't know what he was talking about. "I asked, 'er, what's this white of egg for?' 'Oh, this is something we always do,' he said. 'You have a mouthful of egg white and when you see the girl you slobber a little of it. But keep it tasteful.'"[10]

Cannibalism is usually considered to be beyond the pale, but Werner Herzog is of the opinion that "cannibalism is certainly within human nature, and it is a phenomenon that has always interested me because it has a direct link with a part of ourselves that is very ancient and buried deep with us."[11] Curiously, the legend of Sweeney Todd, surely the most famous urban myth regarding cannibalism, has inspired relatively few films. The first, directed by George King in 1936 and based on Frederick Hazleton's stage version of the original 1846 novel by Edward Lloyd, starred the suitably named Tod Slaughter as the demon barber who "polishes off" his victims, thereafter dispatching their corpses to Mrs. Lovett's famous pie shop next door. One of Slaughter's most famous lines, "You have a beautiful throat for a razor," has much in common with the preferred area of entry for Bram Stoker's vampire in *Dracula,* a novel that owes much to Lloyd's original penny-dreadful. When we are shown Mrs. Lovett's customers tucking into their pies, they discuss the murders that have been happening all around them, the consequences of which are now filling their stomachs. "What does he do with them?" one man asks of the unknown murderer. "How do I know?" replies another as he takes another lusty bite. The connection between oral eroticism and eating is a perhaps obvious but nonetheless powerful one, and is made explicit in Thames Television's adaptation of the story directed by Reginald Collin for the *Mystery and Imagination* series in 1970, which stars Freddie Jones in the title role. "If I cannot have a pie, Mistress Lovett," says one of the customers, "I shall have a kiss. Without a pie, my mouth is vacant for other work." By emphasizing the crude manners of these pie-chomping cannibals, as Tod accurately calls them, the disturbing aspects of mastication and consumption, to say nothing of the origins of the actual product, are magnified to enhance our discomfort. Edward Lloyd was keen to highlight this erotic connection between eating human flesh and human sexuality in his novel. To begin with, the customers are mostly "young bloods" and hence sexually active:

> There was a Mistress Lovett; but possibly our readers have guessed as much, for what but a female hand, and that female buxom, young and good-looking, could have ventured upon the production of those pies. Yes, Mrs Lovett was all that; and every enamored young scion of the laws, as he devoured his pie, pleased himself with the idea that the charming Mrs Lovett had made the pie especially for him.[12]

Like an animal attracted to the smell of carrion, Mrs. Lovett's customers are attracted by "the savory steam of the hot pies [that] went out in fragrant clouds into Bell Yard, being sniffed up by many a poor wretch passing by who lacks the means of making one in the throng that were devouring the dainty morsels within."[13]

In Tim Burton's 2008 film adaptation of the Stephen Sondheim stage musical based on the subject, Johnny Depp's Tod is given a great deal of psychological and political motivation for his actions. Whereas Freddie Jones' Tod is revealed (more subtly) to have been the victim of child abuse, Depp's reasons are more traditionally based on revenge. Indeed, it is perhaps not merely a coincidence that Sondheim's musical and Claude Michel Schönberg's *Les Misérables* appeared within a year of each other (the former in 1979, the latter in 1980), both being critiques of capitalism and social injustice at the beginning of Margaret Thatcher and Ronald Reagan's neoliberal political revolutions in the UK and the United States. The cannibalism of Sondheim's version is presented as an allegory of capitalism itself, which minces up humanity in the name of power for the ruling elite. (The capitalist, Karl Marx pointed out, "proceeds to consume the commodity, the labour-power the he has just bought, by causing the labourer, the impersonation of that labour-power, to consume the means of production by his labour."[14])

Poverty is indeed the Sondheim's main issue, a subject rarely touched by horror films, which are more concerned with exposing the taboos of sex and death. Whereas the Tod Slaughter version disguises it with a veneer of Dickensian grotesquery, Tim Burton sidelines Sondheim's concern by Gothicizing what should really have remained a tale of grimy, proletarian horror. Only the Freddie Jones incarnation inhabits the appropriate milieu, and even that is romanticized to some extent. Poverty exposes the horror of life for what it is, and the result is so depressing that horror films, which prefer to titillate and entertain rather than proselytize, leave this job to political film makers such as Ken Loach or Mike Leigh. These latter want to persuade us to take action and put an end to poverty, whereas horror films use poverty as yet another factor in their overall aim to make us question the point of existing in the first place. Loach's *I, Daniel Blake* (2016) is far closer to the horror of poverty than *Sweeney Todd*, but it is hardly a horror film. Similarly, Leigh's first film, *Bleak Moments* (1971), is one of the cinema's most unflinching examinations of the horror of poverty, with nothing Gothic about it, but in David Lynch's *Eraserhead*, in which nightmare visions take place in ruinous Kafkaesque cityscapes, decay and poverty are essential elements in a story that is fundamentally about the horror of birth and the terror of being responsible for it.

The main titles of Burton's *Sweeney Todd* make much of human meat being passed through a mincing machine, emerging not unlike a series of turds, but to eat human meat is not materially any different from eating cows, horses or dogs, each of which are forbidden in some cultures while being perfectly acceptable in others. Nothing is more upsetting for the British, for example, than the idea of eating their dogs, which is quite acceptable to the Chinese. Apropos of this, Robert Morley's character Meredith Merridew, one of the several theater critics who meet violent ends in *Theatre of Blood*, is fed pies made from his beloved poodles in a parody of Shakespeare's *Titus Andronicus*, in which the Empress Tamora is fed a pie made from her own slaughtered sons, before being killed herself by the eponymous chef:

> Hark, villains! I will grind your bones to dust
> And with your blood and it I'll make a paste,
> And of the paste a coffin I will rear
> And make two pasties of your shameful heads,
> And bid that strumpet, your unhallow'd dam,
> Like to the earth swallow her own increase.
> This is the feast that I have bid her to,
> And this the banquet she shall surfeit on.[15]

Titus Andronicus is, indeed, a forerunner of what used to be called "video nasties" and what has now become body horror. The critic S. Clarke Hulse identifies "14 killings, 9 of them on stage, 6 severed members, 1 rape (or 2 or 3, depending on how you count), 1 live burial, 1 case of insanity and 1 of cannibalism—an average of 5.2 atrocities per act, or one for every 97 lines."[16] Just as horror films used to be, *Titus* has consequently been Shakespeare's most unjustly derided play, its horror seeming bad taste to conventional Bardolaters.

Initially, the highly camp Merridew in *Theatre of Blood* finds his own dish of minced poodle delicious before being informed of the ingredients by Vincent Price's Edward Lionheart (Price was himself an accomplished amateur cook), who proceeds to force-feed the now horrified critic, just as Hamlet forces poison into the mouth of King Claudius at the end of Sir Laurence Olivier's 1948 film of *Hamlet*. Such a transgression against table manners serves to emphasize what table manners are designed to disguise—the ghastliness of ingestion, no matter what is being consumed. This is why Dracula and other assorted movie vampires are so often shown with blood dripping from their mouths. The table manners normally associated with aristocrats are suspended in horror movies in their bid to expose the truth. Horror films

Poodle pie. Robert Morley as Meredith Merridew (right) and Vincent Price as Edward Lionheart in *Theatre of Blood* (dir. Douglas Hickox, 1973).

are all about truth! Indeed, Stoker's description of the bloated vampire king in his famous novel uses significant adjectives to undermine the decorous we seek in our own act of consumption:

> on the lips were gouts of fresh blood, which trickled from the corners of the mouth and ran over the chin and neck. Even the deep, burning eyes seemed set amongst stolen flesh, for the lids and pouches underneath were bloated. It seemed as if the awful creature were simply gorged with blood; he lay like a filthy leach exhausted with his repletion. I shuddered as I bent over to touch him, and every sense in me revolted at the contact.[17]

This masterly description of the messy eater, the greedy gorger, not to mention the kind of post-prandial, snoring oblivion induced in majority by overindulgence on Christmas Day is in fact very human, but distanced from humanity by being transferred to a mythical monster. It is rather like calling those we fight in war "the enemy," which immediately strips the opposition of the humanity we share with them. Efficient housekeeper that Dracula is (he is even seen making Jonathan Harker's bed at one point in Stoker's novel) Dracula also swiftly consumes what is necessary to keep him going, with the advantage that there are no dirty dishes to wash up afterwards. It helps that Dracula is a solitary drinker, but such a state of affairs in not always possible with family dining, where power structures, of course, dictate events. Meal times are far more than being merely about the consumption of nutrients; it is around the dinner table that one learns obedience and self-denial. Meal times are indeed a form of tyranny, as Visconti demonstrated in *The Damned* (1970), where paterfamilias Joachim von Essenbeck (Albrecht Schoenhals) authoritatively raps the table with the flat of his hand to make important announcements. This ritual was later imitated by Dirk Bogarde's Friedrich Bruckmann, when he becomes head of the family through marriage.

Though Bruckmann has murdered his way to the top, cannibalism is not technically involved. This, however, would hardly be inappropriate in this Nazi fable (despite Hitler's famous vegetarianism). The taboo of cannibalism forms the basis of *Soylent Green* (dir. Richard Fleischer, 1973), which is mixed with a prescient ecological agenda founded on Thomas Robert Malthus' observation that the world's human population will eventually outreach its resources, and that humanity will inevitably fall into a horrifying "Malthusian trap" of famine and disease. Charlton Heston's policeman, Robert Thorn, discovers this only when it is too late for him:

> The ocean's dying. Plankton's dying. It's people. Soylent Green is made out of people. They're making our food out of people. The next thing, they'll be breeding us like cattle for food. You've gotta tell 'em. You gotta tell 'em!

The ironic use of Beethoven's Pastoral Symphony after these words emphasizes the disjuncture between our acceptance of farming animals in a "green and pleasant land" with the distinctly unpleasant reality of Soylent Green. Indeed, the film as a whole exposes what the animal rights philosopher Peter Singer has identified as "Speciesism." When Thorn is given a taste of beef stew by Sol Roth (Edward G. Robinson) he finds it good, both in a culinary and a moral sense, but *Soylent Green* in general suggests that eating human meat is really no different from eating cattle. There is no material difference between the film's conveyor belt of human corpses on their way to a giant mixing machine, and an abattoir in which animals are "humanely" killed for human consumption.

Tobe Hooper's *Texas Chain Saw Massacre* (1974) similarly exposes speciesism for what it is, by focusing on the terrified eyes of Sally (Marilyn Burns) as Leatherface prepares to carve her up for his dinner. The close-ups of Sally's eyes strip them of their specific humanity. These eyes could just as well be those of a sheep or a cow about to be slaughtered. As Hooper has explained, this film is "about meat" and the unnecessary slaughter of sentient beings to provide sustenance for human beings. As such, it is, perhaps unexpectedly, a horror film that promotes the vegetarian cause. Indeed, this entire dinner scene can instructively be viewed as a satire on the American nuclear family, so often portrayed in television situation comedies around the dinner table, consuming their daily meat. Hooper's film also articulates what James Orbesen had to say after reading Anne Elizabeth Moore's book on *Body Horror*: "We all inhabit meat."[18]

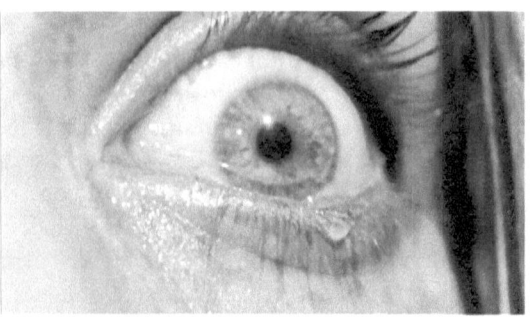

Animal eye. Marilyn Burns as Sally in *The Texas Chain Saw Massacre* (dir. Tobe Hooper, 1974).

This subject forms the basis of two interesting British horror films. The first, directed by the American Gary Sherman in 1971, is known as *Death Line* in the UK and the somewhat more visceral *Raw Meat* in America. After an accident at the end of the 19th century, several people had been trapped in the tunnels of the London Underground. Their descendants have lived on into the 1970s, surviving on human flesh, which they abduct from the platforms of Great Russell Street Underground station. The blood and gore were considered shocking for the time, but despite the presence of Christopher Lee, who only agreed to appear in it because he wanted to work with his co-star Donald Pleasence, the most interesting thing about this film is the way in which Sherman presents the Underground tunnels themselves as an immense urban gastrointestinal tract, the trains that run through them suggesting the movements of the city's bowels deep below the streets. Human beings are, in this sense, the excrement of the capitalist system, and it is therefore appropriate that the student (David Ladd) who becomes involved in the police's missing persons enquiry should be reading economics at university. Capitalism is presented here not so much as vampirism (Karl Marx's preferred metaphor in *Capital* in which capitalism "lives only by sucking living labor, and lives the more, the more labor it sucks"[19]), but as a vast digestive system. To this, Sherman adds some interesting contrasts between other private and public activities. The senior Civil Servant played by James Cossins, for example, who forms one of the cannibals' victims, has a taste for sex shows and prostitutes despite his respectable bowler-hatted appearance (trains entering underground tunnels also lend their phallic symbolism here), and the imagery of human corpses lined up in the cannibal's underground larder should, but apparently do not make us question our patronage of butchers' shops where animal corpses similarly hang on bloody hooks.

The other notable British cannibal story is the aforementioned television episode of *Hammer House of Horror*. "The Thirteenth Reunion" concerns a group of people who managed to stay alive after an air crash in the Atlas Mountains by eating the bodies of their fellow passengers. The episode begins with two morticians examining a body before one of them raises a meat cleaver to butcher it. The story itself unfolds against the backdrop of a draconian slimming club, which gets results by humiliating the overweight, presumably with the intention of causing some kind of therapeutic anorexia. A similar kind of cover-up to what we find on a more ambitious scale in *Soylent Green* also provides the dramatic tension, and this leads to the dénouement around an elegantly laid table, which, like all elegantly laid tables, civilizes the necessary daily ritual we all perform, but not with the same cuisine. "It's extraordinary how canny people can be when they're up against it—the things they can bring themselves to do," explains one of the ghoulish diners (Paula Jacobs). Manners maketh man, but if any film drama demonstrates my contention that table manners disguiseth what man's meal times are really all about, this is surely it, as the camera pans down from an elegant chandelier in a room whose walls are painted an appalling shade of cerise and illuminated by blood red candles. Attired in black tie formality and elegant gowns, the diners are served on the best china by an obsequious waiter. "I doubt if anyone could share [my habits…] who hasn't had to make a virtue out of necessity," explains the leader of this charming little group, played by Richard Pearson, and after soup, in comes the main course under a silver cover. A carving knife is sharpened. The guests lick their lips in anticipation.

All these ideas reached their ironic, fleshly pinnacle in Brian Yuzna's *Society* (1989), in which the rich quite literally feed on the poor. Taking cannibalism to extremes, Yuzna mixes with it the paranoia of Brian Forbes *The Stepford Wives* (1975) and turns what could have political allegory into a nihilistic body horror romp in which one of the characters serves a cup of tea, first offering milk and sugar before suggesting she pees in it, someone else eats an apple filled with worms, we seem to see a back-to-front body behind the frosted glass of a shower door and, in the culminating so-called "shunting" orgy scene, wealthy socialites (hence the title) literally consume their less well-off guests. Rich flesh osmoses poor flesh, bodies merge and meld, and abnormally extended rich tongues lick off and swallow down poor sweat. None of these ideas was particularly new but the graphic intensity of the imagery was shocking enough at the time to seem novel.

A similar situation occurs in *Delicatessen* (dir. Marc Caro and Jean-Pierre Jeunet, 1991) in which a butcher (Jean-Claude Deyfus) overcomes the food shortage in the film's post-apocalyptic society (which has much in common with the nightmare world envisioned by David Lynch in *Eraserhead*, though with rather more obvious humor). The butcher murders his employees and chops them up for meat, but a group of underground vegetarian rebels eventually take on this cannibalistic enterprise, nicely articulating the Pythagorean dichotomy that underlies the whole question of human survival. As with "The Thirteenth Reunion," much is made of the sinister sharpening of knives and meat-cleavers, which surely serve as symbols of our subconscious guilt at eating our fellow creatures.

Hannibal Lechter, as portrayed by Anthony Hopkins, is surely the connoisseur of cannibals, famous for combining human liver with fava beans and a nice Chianti. In what is rather too interesting to remain as a mere footnote, Colin Spencer writes in his history of vegetarianism that the humble fava bean was prohibited by Pythagoras because these particular beans, "squinted at sideways, bear a resemblance to female pudenda."[20] When buried in the earth for 40 days "it would be found shortly afterwards to be giving off the smell of human semen or of blood shed in a murder." Hence eating beans was at some level tantamount to murder; as Pythagoras says: "to eat beans is a crime equal to eating the heads of one's parents,"[21] which perhaps explains why Hannibal's penchant for using them as a side-dish to the acquired taste of his main course.

Nowhere is the hypocrisy of elegant dining exposed to more sensational effect than in the brain-eating scene in *Hannibal* (dir. Ridley Scott, 2001) in which Ray Liotta's Paul Krendall is actually fed morsels of his own brain, which is carefully exposed as he sits at another elegantly laid table. The scene is, in effect, a reworking of the one in *Frankenstein Must Be Destroyed* (dir. Terence Fisher, 1969) in which a scalped brain is similarly revealed by Peter Cushing's Baron, though in that instance for operative cure rather than consumption. In *Hannibal*, Lechter fries a morsel of prefrontal cortex in the best tradition of table-side *flambé*. It's important "always to try new things," he later insists to an unsuspecting schoolboy, whom he encounters on a plane. We are horrified—or meant to be—but if we are, why are we not similarly horrified by a plate of sardines on toast? Some of us are, of course.

Hannibal is more disturbing than the more traditional brain-eating zombies of countless earlier films because he is still alive, and therefore more recognizably human. A brain-eating zombie may well be disturbing but is easily dealt with; Hannibal, however, is less easily dispatched. Hopkins has described him as "the bogeyman," but his appeal is in fact far more straightforward: he is merely the rest of us in heightened form. When cannibalism returned in in John Hillcoat's 2009 *The Road* the context had changed to reflect our environmental anxieties. Here, in a post-apocalyptic world, cannibal rednecks imprison human "livestock" after global warming has destroyed civilization, suggesting in the process that Werner Herzog was, in fact, quite right.

Three. Digestion

If we have a horror of eating other people, we are even more distressed by the thought of actually being eaten ourselves, and the imagery of ingestion is a recurrent preoccupation in horror films. In the Brothers Grimm story, Hansel and Gretel are just too expensive for their parents to keep feeding. Abandoned in the forest, the orphans soon find a surrogate sugar-mother who wants to eat them. Dorothy Blotch's 1977 study, *So the Witch Won't Eat Me*, explores this archetype from the point of view of clinical, specifically Freudian psychology, and demonstrates that there is far more to "Hansel and Gretel" than merely a frightening story. Indeed, the Grimms' tale was updated in one of Hammer's best psychological thrillers, *The Nanny*, in which Bette Davis plays an incarnation of "medicine and duty" who is turned into a potential child killer by a careless accident. There is no biological horror in this film, but the issues it raises are similar to those of much bloodier content that deal with this particular issue. The story, claustrophobic and intense, is set almost entirely in the Vane's flat—the epitome of familial constraint, in which Joey is almost imprisoned much as Hansel in the witch's kitchen.

Not realizing that the little girl in her charge has fallen into a bathtub and been knocked unconscious while playing with her doll, Nanny runs the child's evening bath and unknowingly drowns her. She is heartily loathed (and feared) her other charge, Joey, (William Dix), who knows her secret. His real mother, the depressive, emotionally weak and selfish Virgie Vane (Wendy Craig) is quite ill-suited to raising children, while her husband (James Villiers) is the archetypal distant father, too busy with his high-powered career as a Queen's Messenger to take much interest in his son. All responsibility for Joey's emotional and physical needs is therefore devolved onto Nanny, who, like the witch in "Hansel and Gretel," intends to kill him. The witch wants to eat Hansel, but Nanny merely wants to save her reputation. The film is a brilliant depiction of all the power-struggles and psychological mine fields of family life. Significantly, a key scene takes place around the dinner table, where parental authority has always been traditionally enforced, and where eating rituals have been indoctrinated. Joey, however, refuses to eat the meal Nanny has cooked.

"Joey, eat your dinner!" his father commands. Virgie tries a more conciliatory approach.

"How about a piece of cake? Nanny bought it just for you."

"I know," Joey replies, implying that that is precisely why he won't eat it, fearing she has poisoned it.

"Are you going to eat anything?" Mr. Vane asks.

"No," Joey replies.

"Very well then, go to your room."

"I'm glad you're going away tomorrow," Joey shouts back. "I hope you don't come back."

Virgie then bursts into tears and her husband throws down his knife and fork.

"Damn and blast it to hell," he shouts. "I'm going to the club."

The Will to Power, the horror of eating and the fear of death combine in this seemingly civilized setting, leaving Nanny quietly to clear away the dishes.

Joey, like all children, desperately wants his parents to love him, but he equally dreads infanticide and being consumed by them, or the witch/Nanny who personifies them. Joey escapes such a fate, but the girls of *Slender Man* are not so fortunate, being ingested by the trees of the forest where their fears have brought them. In a sense, their destiny is an extreme variation of what happens in Algernon Blackwood's story "The Man Whom the Trees Loved," but Blackwood's art is one of psychological threat and supernatural suggestion. In *Slender Man*, we watch as the girls are actually osmosed into the bark, their flesh covered with black tendrils before they are completely absorbed. From a narrative point of view this is the cause of some confusion: Is Slender Man a personification of the forest, or are the trees merely his servants? But the confusion is hardly relevant as the imagery here is all that really matters. Similarly, the mother in *Wakewood* is consumed by the earth, sucked down (presumably to the realm of the dead) at the end of that film, and the same anxieties are paraded in *The Blob* (dir. Irvin Yeaworth, Russell Doughten, 1958), which must be the ultimate "osmosis" horror film, in which a corrosive alien pink jelly rampages its way through two towns in Philadelphia.

In *The Mist*, Frank Darabont's 2018 adaptation of Stephen King's novel, the characters are trapped in a supermarket, which sells all manner of pre-packed foods; these consumers are then consumed by the extra-dimensional beings, who lurk in the mist that accompanies their arrival. (A similar situation had in fact featured many years before in the culminating scenes of Terence Fisher's *Island of Terror*, in which the islanders are trapped in a Village Hall and under attack from Sillicate monsters, which break in through the windows.) Like one of the girls in *Slender Man*, who is grabbed by an unseen force through her bedroom window, Norm, a bag boy (Chris Owen) is dragged from the prosaic certainties of his storeroom by the tentacles of one of these marauding entities. Violent demise visits many others, but again the most disconcerting fate seems to be another reference to absorption—in this case being cocooned in a spider's web. Of course, such imagery is all based on quite natural techniques used by insects in our own dimension. Darwin had already dwelt on such behavior in his *Voyage of the "Beagle"* (1839), describing "wasp-like creatures" that stuff their cells "with half-dead spiders and caterpillars, which they seem wonderfully to know how to sting to that degree as to leave them paralyzed but alive, until their eggs are hatched; and the larvae feed on the horrid mass of powerless, half-killed victims—a sight which has been described by an enthusiastic naturalist as curious and pleasing!"[22] He continues with imagery no doubt close to Darabont's heart:

> When any large insect, as a grasshopper or wasp, is caught, the spider, by a dexterous movement, makes it revolve very rapidly, and at the same time emitting a band of threads from its spinners, soon envelops its prey in a case like the cocoon of a silkworm. The spider now examines the powerless victim, and gives the final bite on the hinder part of the thorax; then retreating patiently waits till the poison has taken effect.[23]

Horror is, of course, largely a matter of scale. What can be brushed aside during a picnic becomes life threatening when magnified, and what Darwin describes in his account happens to the human victims of the fourth-dimensional, much larger insect creatures in *The Mist*. Other characters are mutilated in ways to which we will return in a later chapter, and Darabont also parallels alien feeding techniques with those of more familiar creatures by having the flying, locust-like beings that break into the store, rip off flesh from a human body—not that such an image will dissuade the majority of its viewers from eating meat themselves. It does, however, highlight the conflict between any residual Tennysonian horror of nature "red in tooth and claw" and the desire to eat flesh, but, again, it is usually the *manner* in which we eat rather than the actual manna itself that counts.

As we have seen, *Eraserhead* also has its dining scene in which Henry is asked by his father-in-law to carve a chicken that starts to bleed from between its legs and then moves, suggesting a very unappetizing form of menstruation. This disturbing dish causes Henry's mother-in-law to become increasingly agitated before she runs from the room, ruining the meal, which would hardly have been a success in the first place. Eating is therefore equated with copulation, and indeed both have the same purpose to sustain life, but both must pay the price of suffering and disgust. Harry's father-in-law, Bill, suggests that life in general may well not be worth all that suffering: He explains that he put in all the pipes in town, but the only pipe we see leads directly to a puddle. This suggests that all the effort of putting his own pipe into his wife, so to speak, has been equally futile: his own daughter is merely a waste product.

Eraserhead leads us to the subject of human waste in general—that inevitable consequence of eating. Excrement is even more of a social taboo than sex, as *Chemical Wedding* (dir. Patrick Doyle, 2008) demonstrates in comically graphic terms. The scene in question concerns the discovery of a giant turd that has been deposited on a university professor's desk. Before it is revealed to us, we are shown the horrified reaction of the professor's secretary, leading us to expect something much more demonic. The culprit, played by Simon Callow, is the academic Oliver Haddo, who is by now the host of the reincarnated spirit of Aleister Crowley. *Chemical Wedding* also features a spectacular display of urine when Crowley/Haddo micturates on his assembled students during a recitation of Crowley's infamous reworking of Hamlet's "To be or not to be" as "To pee or not to pee." Of course, there is no such option. We must all pee, and we must all open our bowels on a regular basis, as Gilbert and George made clear in their pseudo-ecclesiastical series of artworks, "The Naked Shit," from 1995. Echoing a Michelangelo mural, their fecal iconography echoes, but with deeper resonance, the Biblical truism, "Thou art dust and unto dust thou shalt return," for if dust is the by-product of death, excrement is surely the by-product of life. Gilbert and George here celebrate the fact, their message being that shit is nothing to be ashamed of. Their imagery is not presented as a matter for disgust, and as such it breaks an even stronger taboo than sex. Movies, however, have rarely taken such an enlightened approach to feces.

In *Playing for Time* (dir. Daniel Mann, 1980), Vanessa Redgrave, as Fanya Fénelon, a Jewish cabaret singer imprisoned in Auschwitz, gives one of the most compelling depictions of a disgust at eating, along with a simultaneous need to do so. Given a piece of sausage by a fellow inmate who has earned it by giving her body for the sexual gratification of one of the Nazi guards, Redgrave's character at first refuses to eat it on moral grounds, but as hunger takes over, she tastes the sausage (which looks disturbingly like a piece of excrement). She then consumes it, before almost regurgitating it, not so much because of its taste but more from the moral dilemma it represents: Having previously argued against her friend cheapening herself "like a piece of rotting meat" through such prostitution, eating the phallic sausage becomes a betrayal of all she stands for. The camera stays close on Redgrave's anguished profile during this harrowing scene.

However, the most starkly disturbing cinematic manifestation of excrement and eating is assuredly to be found in *Salo,* Pier Paolo Passolini's controversial 1976 adaptation of the Marquis de Sade's immense and obsessive rumination of sexual depravity, *120 Days of Sodom*. Among the many debaucheries and tortures on display in what is surely the cinema's most powerful critique not only of fascism but also of consumerism in general, is a wedding banquet in which the President of Salo force-feeds shit to his male bride at a wedding breakfast. "Eat, my exquisite bride," he insists, spooning in the repulsive morsels, "You must prepare for our night of love. Nothing's worse than a breath without odor." The political point here is that depravity feeds on itself, and that a society based on consumption (fascism is, after all, consumption *par excellence*) ends up as nothing much more than a waste product of the capitalism that creates it. In 1953, the French surrealist writer André Pieyre de Mandiargues had similarly equated coprophagia with fascism in his novel, *Portrait of an Englishman in His Chateau*. Here, Sadean sexual excess, torture, eating and murder combine in a powerful allegory of the Nazis' occupation of France. "I never eat shit without first proposing a toast to France," says the eponymous Englishman. "Vive la France!"

"The French are nothing but thieves who've gone around stealing everybody else's ideas," says another. "Eating shit is a German invention, before the war, you could get it in any good restaurant in Berlin."[24]

Tom Six's trilogy of *Human Centipede* films (2009, 2011 and 2015), while inspired more by the desire to be noticed than any firmly held political convictions, does nonetheless have things to say about the essential vileness of the human condition and the state of 21st-century politics in the wake of 9/11. A former producer of the *Big Brother* television franchise, Six is obviously driven by publicity and motivated by thinking up the most disgusting thing he can think of, which is in this instance enforced coprophagia. A German surgeon, who has specialized in separating Siamese twins, has decided to reverse the process, sewing the mouth of his second female victim to the anus of first, and the anus of the first to that of a Chinese male. Thus, the man's feces pass from anus to mouth, forming a single alimentary canal. The knee ligaments of each three are also disabled, forcing them to walk on all fours, hence the title. The first film is thus something of a one-joke movie, but it is also a response to *Salo*, tailored for an audience where politics has become so degraded there scarcely seems any point in making a film about it other than to show how corrupt it has become; not that 21st-century politics had at that point become quite so barbaric as it was in Nazi Germany, but by casting the German actor Dieter Laser as at the surgeon Dr. Josef Heiter, we are invited to make comparisons with the Auschwitz Doctor of Death, Dr. Josef Mengele.

The Human Centipede films also suggest that if we are so disgusted by what we generate and carry about within us before evacuating and flushing it away, we are also fundamentally disgusted by ourselves. Some of the *Centipede* films have achieved their goal of publicity at all costs by having been banned in several countries. This, of course, has always been the aim of publicity-conscious artists, but the offense these films has caused is precisely that of Caliban staring at his own image, for far worse is reported in the media on a daily basis: we regularly hear of beheadings, sexual mutilation, pedophilia, to say nothing of the effects of poverty and disease. In such a context of current affairs, it seems illogical at least to take offense at shit. One can deny neither Dr. Mengele's crimes against humanity nor the truths the Nazis as a whole revealed about the capabilities of human beings, and the sexual imagery of the human centipede is also not so far removed from many sexual practices, not to mention the coprophagic variety.

The way in which the trilogy is constructed is both clever and considered. In the second film, a perverted fan of the first film aims to apply its methods to his own reality. Filmed in art-house black and white, Six seems to be referencing the nightmare world of *Eraserhead*, while simultaneously sending up that film's artistic pretensions. The last film is a graphic satire on the draconian punishments of terrorist suspects in Guantanamo Bay, in which all the orange-clothed prisoners are surgically sewn together to create an immense human centipede. A more graphic exposé of the sadistic state of affairs that exists in a supposedly liberal Western democracy it would be hard to imagine. By continuing with employ Dieter Laser as Dr. Heiter, Six does indeed seem to be suggesting that America and its allies such as the United Kingdom have become a kind of Fourth Reich.

The conspiracy of the living has little time for these films, and Six seems to be having too much fun directing in and appearing in his own nightmare visions for many critics to be entirely confident that he has anti-fascist sentiments at heart, but the satire is definitely there. *The Human Centipede* films are profoundly cynical, but that does not affect their insight into what human beings are capable of doing to members of their own species.

The comic potential of vomit, that other form of excrement, was sensationally exploited towards the close of *Monty Python's The Meaning of Life*, when the sensational obese and greedy Mr. Creosote's over-indulgence leads to positively volcanic eruptions of bile amid the polite environment of a high-society cafe, where for a woman to announce the onset of her period is considered to be much less of a social *faux pas* than to break wind. John Cleese's headwaiter is keen to explain the richness of the food on offer to his monstrous customer: "the jugged hare is very high and the sauce is very rich, with truffles, anchovies, Grand Marnier," etc. Mr. Creosote immediately vomits on the menu, on the carpet, on the cleaning woman, on everything, before exploding and trashing the entire restaurant, thus exposing what the institution actually stands for, which is, of course, digestion, but digestion disguised by manners.

Cronenberg combined our horror of vomit with our perhaps greater revulsion against the eating habits of houseflies, which liquefy what they eat by regurgitation. In *The Fly*, the consistently mutating body of Jeff Goldblum's Seth Brundle does just this in a moment that is guaranteed to cause a reaction from any cinema audience, but, as in *The Meaning of Life*, it is poised between revulsion and comedy, thanks to Goldblum's carefully judged performance. Rather more disturbing vomit is disgorged by Logan Browning's cellist, Lizzie, in Richard Shepard's convoluted psychodrama *The Perfection* (2018). As with so many of the films I have mentioned, such carnivals of body horror contain some or all of the other categories into which this book is divided, so I will be returning to *The Perfection* in other contexts later. Here, however, my focus is on vomit containing maggots. In fact, the maggots are a hallucination, deliberately induced by Lizzie's friend Charlotte (Alison Wilson), who has deliberately given Lizzie a mind-altering drug, rightfully assuming that when Lizzie imagines that insects are also crawling under her skin, she will

"Absolutely stuffed." Terry Jones as Mr. Creosote with John Cleese's waiter in *Monty Python's Meaning of Life* (dir. Terry Jones & Terry Gilliam, 1983).

dismember her own hand. To achieve this, she uses the meat cleaver Charlotte has usefully brought along with her before both girls had set off for a holiday. Charlotte's intention, we later learn, is unexpectedly benevolent: she knows that Lizzie, like Charlotte, has been inducted into an elite sex cult at the music school where both have been star students. If musical perfection is not attained, the rules of the cult decree that the musician concerned will be subjected to gang rape. Charlotte therefore "merely" wants to save Lizzie from such a fate by destroying her musical career. There are further horrors, but the concept of vomiting creatures that have spawned inside one's own stomach—creatures, what is more, that are associated with death and decomposition—combines both the horrors of the digestive tract and the anxieties about reproduction, which we explored in part one. As the films encountered there demonstrated, the idea of a living being growing inside one's own body, natural though that may be in terms of human reproduction, is often presented as profoundly disturbing. To vomit an alien creature is perhaps to express that anxiety. To consume them, as Ray Milland does in Roger Corman's *The Premature Burial* (1962), is to *ingest* death, completely inverting the purpose of eating. The irony here is that humans prefer their food to have died before they consume it: Milland's death potion is still alive.

The complex and symbiotic relationship between life (eating) and death (food/prey) is so primitive, so primordial and so essential that it is to be expected that horror films will be fascinated by it. In purely biological terms we are indeed little more than a digestive tract that can locomote, and therefore not so very far removed from the vegetable horrors of John Wyndham's triffids. Our anxieties about these murderous creatures are, *ipso facto*, anxieties we have about ourselves. "'Triffids, huh! Nasty damn things, I reckon. Not natcheral as you might say,'"[25] as one of the characters in Wyndham's novel puts it, is as much a comment about our own bodily anxieties as the plants themselves.

Vegetable life is as grotesque and ruthlessly competitive as any other life-form in a world the Cathars believed to be the creation of the Devil rather than of God. There are many vegetable fictions that promote the Cathars' point of view, from the monstrous beanstalk of Jack the Giant Killer, which is a version of the Tree of Knowledge, and the invasive thicket that encloses the Sleeping Beauty's castle, to Edwardian tales of terror that to a greater or lesser extent explore the anxieties of Empire. One of them, "The Flowering of a Strange Orchid," was written by H.G. Wells in 1894. The dénouement is explicit in its vampirism:

> He was lying, face upward, at the foot of the strange orchid. The tentacle-like aerial rootlets no longer swayed freely in the air, but were crowded together, a tangle of grey ropes, and stretched tight, with their ends closely applied to his chin and neck and hands. She did not understand. Then she saw from under one of the exultant tentacles upon his cheek there trickled a little thread of blood. With an inarticulate cry she ran towards him, and tried to pull him away from the leech-like suckers. She snapped two of these tentacles, and their sap dripped red.[26]

"The Purple Terror," by Fred M. White, followed in 1899. In this, a purple orchid with a "queer, sickly fragrance ... the perfume of a corpse"[27] retaliates against a plant collector:

> The horrible green spines were round Tarrer's body like snakes. His face was white, his breath came painfully, for the pressure was terrible. It seemed to Scarlett to be one horrible dissolving view of green, slimy cords and great weltering, purple blossoms. The whole of the circle was strewn with them. They were wet and slimy underfoot.[28]

It is from these literary origins that malevolent cinematic vegetation took nourishment. Early among them are the monstrous plant forms examined by Dr. Van Helsing in F.W. Murnau's *Nosferatu* (1922), which, as the English title card puts it, offer "strange correspondences to human life." He begins with a carnivorous plant, the famous Venus Fly Trap. "Astonishing, isn't it, gentlemen?" he explains, as the plant devours a fly. "That plant is the vampire of the vegetable kingdom." He then moves on to another type of vampire: "a polyp with claws ... transparent, without substance, almost a phantom." These unnerving parallels between plants, cannibals and vampires may well have informed Thomas Mann's description of similar comparisons between ice crystals and vegetable forms in his great 1947 novel about German Romanticism, *Doctor Faustus*. (Mann had seen and much enjoyed *The Mummy* [dir. Karl Freund, 1933] in 1935,[29] and was therefore probably aware of Murnau's film as well.)

> Impudently, deceptively, they imitated the vegetable kingdom: most prettily of all, fern fronds, grasses, the calyxes and corolla of flowers. ... Creatively dreaming Nature dreamed here and there the same dream: if there could be a thought of imitation, then surely it was reciprocal.[30]

Another experiment observed by Mann's narrator involves a vessel of crystallization "three-quarters full of slightly muddy water—that is, dilute water-glass—and from the sandy bottom there strove upwards a grotesque little landscape of variously colored growths: a confused vegetation of blue, green, and brown shoots which reminded one of algae, mushrooms, attacked polyps, also moss, then mussels, fruit pods, little trees or twigs from trees, here and there of limbs.... It turned out that these growths were entirely inorganic in their origins; they existed by virtue of chemicals from the apothecary's shop."[31]

Mushrooms, because of their seemingly intermediary position between plant and animal life, along with their mysteriously sudden appearance and disappearance, have also acquired an unnerving reputation, and were well-chosen by Walt Disney for the most balletic moment in *Fantasia* (dir. Wilfred Jackson, Hamilton Luske, James Algar, et al., 1941). The Disney mushrooms are actually of the poisonous fly-agaric variety, and they dance to Tchaikovsky's Chinese Dance from *The Nutcracker*. Accordingly, they are given "inscrutable" oriental features à la Fu Manchu. Ostensibly "charming," their lurid green stems and vivid orange caps could so easily become malevolent in the manner of a Hanns Heinz Ewers horror tale, and the hallucinogenic effects of mushrooms has, of course, inspired many a cinematic "trip" from the psychedelia of *Yellow Submarine* (dir. George Dunning, 1968) to the nightmare vision "beyond Jupiter" in Kubrick's *2001—A Space Odyssey* (1968).

Naturally, the carnivorous plant is by far the most popular vegetable motif in horror films. We encounter a particularly grotesque one in *The Werewolf of London* (dir. Stuart Walker, 1935), which resembles an octopus, waving its tendrils around in pursuit of nutrition before an unfortunate frog is placed in its vulva-like mouth. "Evolution was in a strange mood when that creation came along," exclaims Werner Oland's Dr. Yogami. "It makes one wonder just where the plant world leaves off and the animal world begins."

It is also appropriate that Dr. Moriarty, the sophisticated nemesis of Sherlock Holmes, should also be a plant fancier. In *The Adventures of Sherlock*

Holmes (dir. Alfred Werker, 1939) George Zucco plays a bearded incarnation of the criminal mastermind, who admires his exotic blooms to the sinister flute accompaniment of an exotic servant, whom we at first see only as a shadow. Moriarty is almost more concerned about his plants than he is with his audacious plan to steal the Crown Jewels. "I'm away for a few weeks," he complains to his manservant, "and I return to find my Anthurium magenta— my incomparable Anthurium magenta—withered, ruined!" He accuses the unfortunate servant of neglecting them: "How does it happen that I find a spider's web spun across the spout of the watering can? ... Nothing is as important as the care of my flowers! Through your neglect this flower has died. You've murdered a flower! And to think that for merely murdering a man I was incarcerated for six whole weeks in a filthy prison cell." Plants thus form a comforting substitute for the humanity Moriarty despises, presumably because they are just as ruthless, amoral and voracious as he is himself.

In *Dragonwyk* (dir. Joseph L. Mankiewicz, 1946), Vincent Price, as the alcoholic and Roderick Usher–like Nicholas Van Ryn, poisons his invalid wife with a noxious oleander plant. "How alive it is," he purrs in admiration of it, "as if it were thinking, as if it had thoughts of its own and desires of its own." Glenn Langen's Dr. Turner later unmasks him: "I was never able to forget that plant," the doctor explains. "At first I thought that it was only very beautiful, but I've learnt since that it was also very deadly. It's a glucoside, similar in action to digitalis but much more toxic."

John Wyndham's infamous triffids therefore did not come from nowhere. *The Day of the Triffids* was first published in 1951, the first film adaptation following 11 years later in 1962. What makes the difference is the context in which the story appeared: a world still recovering from the Second World War, with the possibility of nuclear and chemical weapons bringing the threat of "crop diseases, cattle diseases, radioactive dusts, viruses, and infections not only of familiar kinds, but brand-new sorts recently thought up in laboratories."[32] The invasion of the triffids in post war London echoes those very real anxieties of a coming apocalypse:

> My father once told me that before Hitler's war he used to go round London with his eyes more widely open than ever before, seeing the beauties of buildings that he had never noticed before—and saying goodbye to them. And now I had a similar feeling. But this was something worse. Much more than anyone could have hoped for had survived that war—but this was an enemy they would not survive. It was not wanton smashing and willful burning that they waited for this time: it was simply the long, slow, inevitable course of decay and collapse.[33]

Triffids, capable of locomotion, armed with poison sacs, utterly malevolent and invasive are vegetable Nazis, just as the Daleks of *Dr. Who* are robotic ones. Wyndham is also keen to emphasize their sexual nature—an important aspect of their horror:

The dark green pod just below the cup was glistening and distended, about half as big again as a large apple. When it burst, it did it with a pop that was audible twenty yards away. The white seeds shot into the air like steam, and began drifting away on the lightest of breezes. Looking down on a field of triffids late in August you could well get the idea that some kind of desultory bombardment was in progress.[34]

Indeed, one can read the assault of the triffids as a monstrous rape or a voracious feast. The film adaptation, directed by Steve Sekely in 1962, is equally if not more concerned with the accompanying motif of blindness, which the meteor showers that open the novel have caused. Human blindness aids the Triffids, of course, making it easier for them to stalk their prey, for, as one of the characters in the film puts it, plants once found sufficient nutrient in the waste products of animals, but now they prefer the animals themselves.

Disaster films and dystopian apocalyptic fantasies are appealing precisely because they are a macrocosmic projection of our microcosmic anxieties. We can never be sure, after all, that we will survive the day, we have no idea what injuries may befall us before we return to our beds (if we do), and have no alternative but to take a great deal of life on trust. We depend on the conventions of common sense, which, as we have already seen, are largely illusory. Our relations with other people, with animals and, indeed, with plant-life, are fraught with potential dangers and conflicts. This is really the only explanation of why such films should be so appealing, exorcising as they do the anxieties and terrors we are forced to repress every day. Humanity survives at the end of *The Day of the Triffids*, with shots of grateful worshippers flocking into a church, as though God has had anything to do with their predicament. The original novel also offers hope, though acknowledges the supreme effort that is still required to "drive the triffids back and back with ceaseless destruction until we have wiped the last one of them from the face of the land that they have usurped."[35] That final sentence surely resonated with the survivors of a war that had only ended six years before the novel was published.

In *Dr. Terror's House of Horrors* (dir. Freddie Francis, 1965) made three years later, a vengeful vine eventually strangles Jeremy Kemp's government scientist Jerry Drake, who has earlier provided a brief overview, to the accompaniment of an illustrative black-and-white film, of the various kinds of plants in the world, from bacteria up to the carnivorous variety. (Such an illustrated "lecture" also opens the film version of *The Day of the Triffids*.) "Each stage, each adaption, each mutation," Drake explains, "is one step higher in the battle of the plant kingdom for survival. Now what if a plant were to take the next step, what if there were mutation that could develop intelligence, the ability to protect itself, perhaps even to know who its enemies were and destroy them."

"A plant like that could take over the world," adds Bernard Lee's pipe-smoking Hopkins, obviously referring to the audience's memory of Triffids, but also making a comment on humanity itself, which did, after all, beat plants to world domination. After killing a dog that tries to dig it up, the creeping vine strangles Drake, cuts the telephone wire and lays siege to the house. Only by accident do its hapless inhabitants realize that the plant fears fire (the leaves cower back when Hopkins lights his pipe), and this discovery enables their escape.

A kind of cut-price vegetable version of Hitchcock's *The Birds*, "The Creeping Vine" episode is perhaps more powerful than *The Day of the Triffids* film because it is so claustrophobically domestic. Budgetary constraints enforced this on Francis, but he turned these limitations to his narrative advantage. Taking his cue from Wyndham, who always juxtaposed terror with the mundanity of everyday life, Francis' creeping vine (which is also "merely" a vine, not a mutant monstrosity) is a classic example of our fear of life-forms that we otherwise take for granted and usually underestimate. (The same sort of imagery went on to inform the boa-constrictor-like behavior of the demonic plants in Kiersch's adaptation of *Children of the Corn*). Plant life is in fact just as ruthless, murderous and imbued with the will to power as any human, as Sir David Attenborough's natural history series for the BBC television, *The Private Life of Plants,* demonstrates with graphic stop-motion intensity.

All these influences are brought to bear on the opening shots of Jack Cardiff's *The Mutations* in 1974, in which Donald Pleasence, as a (significantly German) scientist, Professor Nolter, grafts, in distinctly Auschwitz/Mengele style, animal genes onto human beings. I will explore the mutation aspect later, but *The Mutations* opens with Nolter's lecture on carnivorous plants, which Cardiff illustrates with unnerving and somewhat erotically photographed stop-motion plant activity, principally of mushrooms:

> And we all know of carnivorous plants that behave like animals, such as this insect-eating specimen the sundew plant. The leaves of this remarkable plant are covered with numerous hairs and tipped air sticky glands. These bend and curl around the insect caught on the sticky tips completing its entanglement. Then the glands excuse a digestive substance enabling the plant actually to absorb the material from the insect's body. The Venus Fly Trap is an extraordinary example of a predatory plant. Its leaves fold rapidly when hairs on the inner surface are touched by an intruding insect. Many small digestive glans are scattered on the inner surface of each jaw. The jaws of the leaf are edged with interlocking teeth, which form a cage when closed to prevent the insect from escaping. Once triggered by the tension in the leaf tissue, the glands begin to work causing the insect to be ingested and absorbed.
>
> The Cobra plant is another unique example of natural mutation. Small insects are lured into the mouth of the plant by the secretions of nectar glands on the surface of the leaf. The captive continues through a glassy zone, finally to become enmeshed in an area of downward pointing hairs, which serve to complete the entrapment of the lured creature. Subsequent digestion occurs through the simultaneous action of bacteria living within the plant and juices serrated by the inner walls of the leaf.

These images and Pleasence's narration, along with Basil Kirchin's sonic accompaniment, are far more worrying than the eventual vegetable monster we see unveiled at the end of the film.

Schopenhauer, as so often and on so many different occasions, explains the underlying reason for the horror of the relentless appetites discussed in this chapter:

> every animal can maintain its own existence only by the incessant elimination of another's. Thus the will-to-live generally feasts on itself, and is in different forms its own nourishment, till finally the human race, because it subdues all the others, regards nature as manufactured for its own use. ... Many insects (especially the ichneumon flies) lay their eggs on the skin, and even in the body, of the larvae of other insects, whose slow destruction is the first task of the newly hatched brood. The young hydra, growing out of the old one as a branch and later separating itself therefrom, fights while it is still firmly attached to the old one for the prey. ... But the most glaring example of this kind is afforded by the bulldog-ant of Australia, for when it is cut in two, a battle begins between the head and the tail. The head attacks the tail with its teeth, and the tail defends itself bravely by stinging the head. The contest usually lasts for half and hour, until they die or are dragged away by other ants.[36]

As Schopenhauer goes on to explain, vegetable life and even the universe itself is similarly self-consuming: "the constant tension between centripetal and centrifugal forces which keeps the globe in motion ... is itself an expression of that universal conflict which is essential to the phenomenon of the will ... for, as every body must be regarded as the phenomenon of a will, which will necessarily manifests itself as a striving, the original condition or state of every heavenly body formed into a globe cannot be rest, but motion, a striving forward into endless space, without rest or aim."[37] The real horror of *The Mist* is its depiction of the aimless, self-consuming nature of the will to live. Life is thus inevitably horrific in itself.

FOUR

Mutilation

> "His legs and arms were then torn from their sockets by a team of four powerful horses. A crack, a shout and life flickered out, for the monster called Count Regula."
>
> —*Die Schlangengrube und das Pendel*, aka *The Torture Chamber of Dr. Sadism* (dir. Harald Reinl, 1969)

Horror films thrive on our perfectly natural horror of dismemberment: the musical hand in *The Beast with Five Fingers* (dir. Robert Florey, 1946), which performs a Bach chaconne on its own; the crawling hand chopped off from the mummy of Queen Tera in *Blood from the Mummy's Tomb* (dir. Seth Holt, 1972); severed heads galore, jars of eyeballs, and, as we shall see later, vats of female breasts.

Dismemberment is a worse horror than death itself because the physical horror of dismemberment is the gateway of an even more profound existential horror—that of identity. If we are no more than the sum of our parts, where does our center lie? Do we indeed have a center? If we can be dismembered or physically altered, we would appear to have no reliable reality other than that which a belief in the soul would bring. If we no longer believe in the soul, all we have is the body, which is transient, subject to injury or alteration by accident or malevolence. Our quest for a core is why we created the concept of the soul, which calms such a deep psychological anxiety. Everywhere we look, we find evidence of this need for wholeness and stability. Antony Easthope explains:

> Anthropology confirms that every known human society operates with a system of naming that designates a single person, however much that name links the bearer to others in their family, tribe or clan. And every human language has a means to signify the equivalent of "me" and "I."[1]

Easthope furnishes us with symbolic examples of this: the castle designs of Leonardo da Vinci are, for example, interpreted as models of the masculine ego.

> From its centre "one single guard watches the whole castle both inside and outside without moving." But this is not only for defence against the enemy without—it's also

a precaution against a possible enemy within. He claims that the commander "can always hear and see the conversations and movements of his garrison without being seen." Thus the commander "cannot be taken by treason of his own garrison." ...

> The castle is both stake and agent in a ceaseless struggle to keep itself together, to close all gaps, watch every move, meet aggression with aggression, ... to *master* every threat.[2]

Easthope also refers to the logo for the British television channel Channel Four, in which, when his book was first published in 1986, a figure 4 "comes to pieces and fits back together again."

> In one version of the station signal the 4 dissolves into dozens of tiny pieces and then is remade from the other side by as many fragments. ... In another version the 4 is broken into nine pieces, two each of yellow, blue, green and purple, and one red bit. These sail into the centre to make up a coherent 4, with the joins still showing as in a jigsaw or child's toy.[3]

This symbolism has much in common with the anxiety and desires of films that explore physical dismemberment. We seek, so to speak, a complete figure 4 in our approach to the body, even though we know it is made of many sections, each of which can easily be separated. We wish our bodies to be castles, which repel the invaders of disease and mutilation and which we may oversee from our omnipotent consciousness; but we know on a deeper unconscious level that there is no such safety, no such unity or completion, either physically or psychologically. Even if we can avoid accident or illness, we are all condemned through birth to inevitable dissolution and corruption.

Frankenstein is Western culture's primary expression of this dilemma, being a product of enlightenment principles, in which objective science began to prevail over religious orthodoxy and its belief in souls. *Frankenstein* reveals that we have no reality beyond our own bodies and that our bodies can be easily changed. Like the Channel Four logo, their component parts can be severed and reassembled, though the result is not necessarily always as attractive and satisfying. *Frankenstein,* the ultimate allegory of the horror of birth, is also an eloquent discussion about the horror we have of our own bodies. What we fear when confronted with Boris Karloff's monster in the James Whale Frankenstein films is our kinship with this artificial assemblage. The Creature is us. We are not only his psychological brothers, with all our shared need for love and compassion, but we are also the product of a process of creation. Rather than being assembled, we are instead the result of cell division. The former is inorganic, the latter organic, but in both instances the result is dependent on *manipulation*. The horror of birth, apart from its physical filthiness, lies in the fact that we are all constructed; and what can be constructed can easily be deconstructed, leaving us with no identity. Whereas Shelley's "indestructible" creature can only be dissected, we are all too subject to immolation while still intact.

Because our fear of dissolution is so profound an anxiety, a great many horror films dwell upon it, imaginatively reworking a basic theme. Though it was not the first adaptation of Mary Shelley's novel, James Whale's *Frankenstein* (1931) was the first film to explore Shelley's themes of psychological alienation and physical anxiety in the depth that perhaps only Whale at that time could have achieved. His *Frankenstein* is the ultimate "outsider" horror film. As we have seen, it is easy to see Frankenstein as a gay outsider, who rejects the women in his life so as to concentrate on creating life artificially. The Monster, whose appearance echoes the unemployed underclass of the depression era, is dispossessed, unwanted, victimized, and ultimately destroyed. Love is impossible for him, and only love can make life bearable. Whale is also careful to include scenes in which the comforts of religion are removed: the Monster rampages through a graveyard, overturning sacred imagery. There is no soul at work here, merely a brain, and a malformed one at that, as Frankenstein has unwittingly inserted a criminal's brain into the monster's skull rather than the "noble" organ he had in mind.

Much later, Gordon Hessler's *Scream and Scream Again* (1970) combined the basic ideas of Frankenstein and Dracula in a story about "composites," created by Vincent Price's mad scientist, Dr. Browning, who have a taste for vampirism. Browning keeps his laboratory stocked with assembled body parts, along with an acid vat to dispose of the experiments that go wrong. The film's most striking sequence appears right at the beginning when a jogger in a London park suddenly tumbles and subsequently wakes up in hospital to find that his limbs are gradually being removed from his body. These spare parts are destined for new composites, but the doctor's failure with what has turned out to be a psychopathic vampire called Keith means that the program is shut down by the powers that be (represented by Christopher Lee, who ultimately forces Dr. Browning into his own acid vat).

One line in the script plays with the film's other theme of identity. Keith, who is constructed from the body parts of other people, is played by the actor Michael Gothard. "What's your name," asks the girl he has picked up for a ride in his car. "Michael?" she volunteers. "Not today, lady," he replies, for Michael Gothard is playing someone else today, someone who, as Browning later says of another composite, "never really existed." It would be hard to find a better example of the fundamental lack of identity we all share with Keith than Keith himself, whoever he may be…

Imagery from this film was recapitulated in 1993 in Jennifer Chambers Lynch's *Boxing Helena*. Obsessed by Helena's unattainable beauty, the sexually frustrated surgeon, Dr. Nick Cavanaugh (played by Julian Sands), lures Helena (Sherilyn Fenn) to his luxurious home, only to be cruelly rejected by her, but a convenient car accident outside his house gives him the opportunity to amputate first her legs and then remove her arms, subsequently positioning the remaining torso amid his collection of classical statues. All is eventually revealed to have been a drug induced hallucination, but that is merely a plot device. Far more important is the way in which Lynch articulates the nature of sexual obsession. Cavanaugh is not interested in the real Helena, merely what she represents to him, which is a mixture of sexual allure and an antidote to his own sense of sexual inadequacy. In this sense, Helena is another kind of "composite"—as well as a construct of Cavanaugh's own imagination.

The film represents a reversal of the Pygmalion legend in which a statue comes to life. In *Boxing Helena,* Cavanaugh turns a living woman into a kind of statue—a portrait bust, so to speak, enthroned like an altar-piece and framed with a display of carefully arranged flowers. Lynch herself explained her own idea of the film as a response to the famous statue of the Venus de Milo, which, armless though it is, is always viewed as an image of beauty: "I thought I was broken and that maybe someday someone would find me beautiful. So this idea of a damaged boy who was in an obsessive situation who would try to recreate from his own view the one thing that didn't hit him or abandon him was this armless, beautiful woman."[4] It is through her amputation that Cavanaugh overcomes her rejection of him and, through her dependence on him, learns to love him. (It is appropriate that he enjoys listening to Puccini's *Turandot,* in which a similarly contemptuous princess rejects her various suitors, only to be conquered by the persistent Calaf.) It is, however, a curiously misogynistic film for a woman to have conceived and directed.

Like Gordon Hessler in *Scream and Scream Again,* Lynch keeps blood and gore to a minimum, and we certainly never see the amputations being executed, but the horror of the result is none the less for that, and not only reminds us of Hessler's film but also of the similarly afflicted character in Tod Browning's *Freaks* played by Prince Radian. Sands is the perfect choice for the sexually immature surgeon, his earlier performances as Percy Shelley in Ken Russell's *Gothic* (1987) lending an appropriate resonance of Frankenstein to his character here.

Seven years after *Scream and Scream Again*, Cronenberg's *Rabid* brought anatomical transposition into the equation by moving the normal scene of activity in a vampire story from the mouth to the arm. A skin graft leads to the arm of Marilyn Chambers' Rose developing its own "mouth," with which she attacks people and even a cow. On the one hand a satire on the vanity of plastic surgery, *Rabid,* as its title suggests, is also an expression of epidemic anxiety, indeed of the medical profession itself. (During one operation, an infected doctor dismembers a nurse's finger with a pair of scissors before feeding on her blood.) Once bitten by these rabid hosts, their victims become similarly voracious, with an uncontrollable thirst for blood. Filmed amid a bleak Canadian winter, there is no redemption in Cronenberg's Darwinian world-view: In the fight to survive, nothing else matters. Indeed, the disgust we might feel about having a mouth on one's arm was curiously prefigured by Darwin in account of *The Voyage of the "Beagle,"* in which he mentions a particular kind of invertebrate resembling a slug he discovered in Botofogo Bay, South America: "near the middle of the under crawling surface there are two transverse slits, from the anterior one of which a funnel-shaped and highly irritable mouth can be protruded. For some time after the rest of the animal was completely dead from the effects of salt water or any cause, this organ still retained its vitality."[5] Darwin's use of the adjective "irritable" along with the post-mortem persistence of this organ does rather resemble the mouth on Rose's arm. Everything in *Rabid* is similarly bleak and ruthless. The motorways are anonymous, the trees are lifeless, the landscapes flat.

Horror films have always responded to current anxieties as a kind of exorcism or psychotherapy in fantasy form. One of these is *The Hands of Orlac*, directed by Robert Wiene in 1924. Here, the consequences of a terrible accident are dwelt upon at great length. Two steam locomotives collide (though it was obviously too expensive to show the actual collision: Instead, two trains passing each other suggest a collision before the camera rapidly cuts away). Amid the carnage, steam and confusion, the concert pianist Paul Orlac (played with expressionist intensity by Conrad Veidt) is rescued, but his hands have been crushed and will never be able to perform concertos again. As Veidt lies in his hospital bed, his head bandaged and his hands virtually mummified, he could well be a casualty of the war that had ended only six years before the film was made. The surgeons, however, replace his crushed hands with those from an executed murderer, and Orlac is wheeled out to convalesce in the sunshine, as were so many the casualties of war; but like a genie released from Aladdin's lamp, the spirit of the murderer lives on in Orlac's adopted hands, Wiene emphasizing the fact by having the murderer's gigantic face appear from a cloud of smoke in Orlac's bedroom. Then, the gigantic image of a hand, clenched into a fist, descends over the sleeping pianist, like a nightmare vision from Max Klinger's celebrated "Glove" etchings. The epitome of an expressionist actor, Veidt is able to suggest that his own hands are somehow alien merely by the way he holds them and himself. The result is far more disturbing than the clever trick photography of the severed hand playing Bach in *The Beast with Five Fingers*.

Reunited with his piano (which he caresses, unlike the woman in his life), Orlac's murderous hands hover of the keys like spiders, two five-fingered beasts, indeed, but here attached to Veidt's equally spidery arms. The hands seem literally to pull Orlac's body along, his arms outstretched, to kill. And here, with only 10 fingers, Veidt and Wiene are able to symbolize both the Hitler and the Mozart within us all. Orlac returns to the surgeon, and on his knees, his arms outstretched, his fingers reaching for release, he pleads to have the murderous hands removed.

Four. Mutilation

Thrice remade, none of the later versions have anything of the expressionist power still less of the Gothic spirit of E.T.A. Hoffmann with which Wiene infused his vision. Lotte Eisner thought of Veidt performing "a kind of Expressionist ballet, bending and twisting extravagantly, simultaneously drawn and repelled by the murderous dagger held by hands which do not seem to belong to him,"[6] with "shadowy, ambiguous streets, a strange house with a long corridor people by weird figures, a devilish magician and his Hoffmannesque servant."[7] *The Hands of Orlac* is a nightmare of surgical trauma.

The following year, 1925, brought to the world Lon Chaney's tortured Erik, the famous Phantom of the Opera, in Rupert Julien's film of Gaston Leroux's novel, and Chaney's horrific "living skull" makeup also echoes the appalling facial disfigurements suffered by First World War veterans, as David J. Skal has pointed out.[8] Influenced by earlier Hollywood remakes, Hammer's Phantom (played by Herbert Lom) is disfigured by an accident with acid, after his own compositions have been stolen by an incompetent musical poseur (Michael Gough). Such a bourgeois revenge plot has, however, nothing to do with the original novel, which the first and still best adaptation followed with far more care. Chaney's Phantom, like Leroux's original Erik, is *born* hideous:

> But imagine, if you can, Red Death's mask suddenly coming to life in order to express, with the four black holes of its eyes, its nose, and its mouth, the extreme anger, the mighty hurt of a demon; *and not a ray of light from the sockets,* for, as I learned later, you cannot see his blazing eyes except in the dark.[9]

Erik's disfigurement is symbolic of the accident of birth itself. Whereas Lom's Phantom merely wants to reclaim the copyright of his music, so to speak, Erik uses his music as a surrogate for the sex his body denies him. He has composed *Don Juan Triumphant,* and wishes to consummate his marriage to music by having the young soprano Christine Daaé perform it. Erik is another esthete, and all esthetes, hideous or not, despise the world in which their ideals have become ensnared and thwarted. Erik hides behind his mask and looks into his soul, living solely for the beauty of music. He wishes music to cancel out his deformed body—indeed the ugliness of the whole world—which does not mean he is without vanity or fastidiousness. Ordinary life is too crude for him. "I began that work twenty years ago," he says of *Don Juan Triumphant.* "When I have finished, I shall take it away with me in that coffin and never wake up again. ... I sometimes work at it for fourteen days and nights together, during which I live on music only, and then I rest for years at a time."[10] Meanwhile, he sleeps in his coffin, to remind him of that other sleep where all life's troubles are cancelled out:

> The walls were all hung with black, but, instead of the white trimmings that usually set off that funereal upholstery, there was an enormous stave of music with the notes

"Feast your eyes!" Lon Chaney in *The Phantom of the Opera* (dir. Rupert Julien, 1925).

of the *Dies Irae*, many times repeated. In the middle of the room was a canopy, from which hung curtains of red brocaded stuff, and, under the canopy, an open coffin. "That is where I sleep," said Erik. "One has to get used to everything in life, even to eternity."[11]

(Erik would have found Cioran's response to the question "'What do you do from morning to night?': 'I endure myself,'"[12] much to his taste.) Erik's desire for Christine is really a symbol of his greater love for death, and his longed-for consummation is a kind of Liebestod. As he says at another point in Leroux's novel, "Talking of death, I must sing."[13] Music for Erik is a gateway to the release of death, where the imagination knows no bounds, and is uncontaminated by restrictions of living. Only in death can Erik attain the freedom, beauty and power he desires. His own life and those of other people exasperate him. It is also very much the attitude of that epitome of the decadent hero, Monsieur de Phocas, in Jean Lorrain's 1901 novel of that name. Discussing a highly effective poison, the friend of Monsieur de Phocas explains, "'It is instant death, certain but painless suicide, that I carry I this emerald. One bite'—and Ethal made as of to raise the ring to his lips—'and with a single bound one has quit the mundane world of base instincts and crude works, to enter eternity.'"[14]

In the climax of the film, Erik turns to face the crowd that is pursuing him. He raises his hand. The crowd cowers. He raises his other hand. The crowd cowers again, fearing it conceals a weapon, but in the end, Erik opens his fist to reveal nothing at all. Laughing the crowd to scorn, he welcomes the death they bring to him, for death is what he has wanted all along, and in death he gladly erases the error of his life. All this very much foreshadows what Cioran has to say in *The Trouble with Being Born*:

> Endlessly to refer to a world where nothing yet stooped to occurrence, where you anticipated consciousness without desiring it, where, wallowing in the virtual, you rejoiced in the null plenitude of a self anterior to selfhood.
> *Not to have been born*, merely musing on that—what happiness, what freedom, what space![15]

Leroux explains that as former construction engineer, Erik had been involved with laying the foundations of the Palais Garnier Ópera in Paris, and simultaneously created his own underground lair there. It is in this lair that Christine reveals his deformity. "Feast your eyes, glut your soul on my cursed ugliness!" he shouts (in both the novel and the Chaney film). "Look at me! I am *Don Juan triumphant!*"[16] In many ways he is the alter ego of the equally vain outsider (outsider because he was Jewish) Giacomo Meyerbeer, and Erik's music probably sounded rather like Meyerbeer's music.

Despite the several remakes of Chaney and Julien's classic, the most intriguing response to the film wasn't technically a remake at all, though it shares many of its themes with *The Phantom of the Opera*. *The Mystery of the Wax Museum* (dir. Michael Curtiz, 1933) concerns a disfigured creative artist (Ivan Igor, a sculptor in wax played by Lionel Atwill) who also terrorizes a beautiful woman (Fay Wray) before covering her in wax. Both films also have unmasking scenes in which the heroine recoils in horror at what is revealed. (*Wax Museum* was influential, inspiring several remakes and, not least, *Carry on Screaming* [dir. Gerald Thomas, 1966], in which Kenneth Williams' Dr. Watt manufactures fashion manikins using the same methods as Ivan Igor by stealing young women and in his case vitrifying them. The two Dr. Phibes films starring Vincent Price in the 1970s also drew heavily on Curtiz's film, not only with another disfigured genius, whose frightening features are for the most part disguised, but also in equipment used at the end: Phibes threatens his adversary with acid, Igor with wax, each liquids being passed through similar diffusers. Both films also blend comedy and art deco design with more traditional horrors.)

Perhaps the most interesting cinematic response to the subject of facial disfigurement can be found in *Les Yeux sans Visage,* Georges Franju's poetically surreal 1960 meditation on identity and plastic surgery. Dr. Génessier (Pierre Brasseur) attempts to graft a new face onto that of his disfigured daughter, Christiane (Édith Scob) but the operation fails, and Christiane is forced to resume wearing a facial mask. Génessier's obsession to restore his daughter's face leads to further murders and surgical failures until, sickened

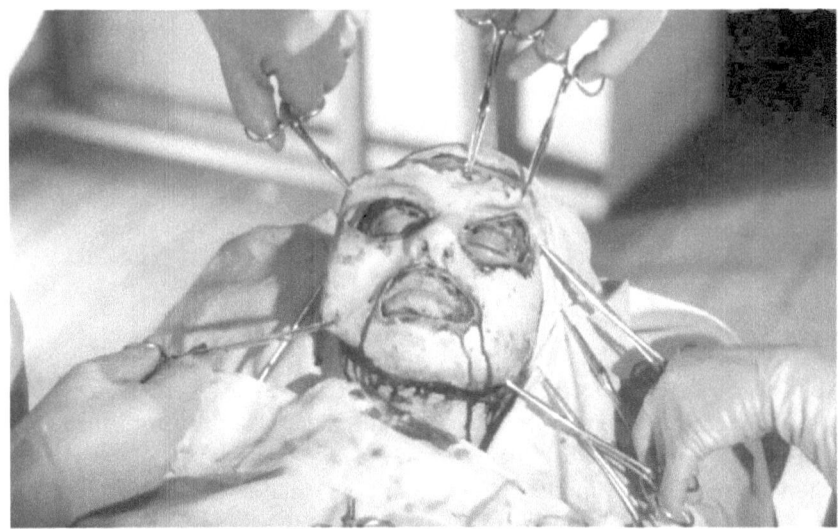

Face lift. The grisly operation in *Les Yeux sans visage* (dir. Georges Franju, 1960).

by the carnage committed in her name, Christiane lets loose her father's dogs, which maul him to death as she walks away to an uncertain future, accompanied by the doves she has also freed from the confines of the doctor's sinister laboratory.

Only 15 years earlier, the Nazi death camps had been liberated, revealing to the world the horrors that had been unleashed in the name of beauty, for what else is racism but the dark side of esthetics, the rejection of a physical type, a pigmentation of the skin? Hitler's program was motivated in the first instance by the pursuit of a particular kind of beauty, a particular kind of human, a particular kind of art, a particular kind of music and architecture. The result was the destruction of human beings, the destruction of art and the destruction of architecture. Similarly, Génessier's pursuit of the perfect face for his daughter is the cause of some of the most disturbing surgical scenes in any film, in direct line of descent from the shocking sliced eyeball in Luis Buñuel's surreal masterpiece, *Un chien Andalou* (1929).

Our faces can express but also mask our feelings, and they are never entirely to be trusted. If we lose our faces do we also lose our personalities, or do our personalities change? Édith Scob's face, when restored, is as expressionless and enigmatic as the mask she wears when it begins to degenerate, but in her masked condition she is the embodiment of isolation, another kind of Des Esseintes, indeed, who lives only in her own imagination. Disfigurement destroys her ability to interact with anyone, but Franju seems also to be suggesting that the accident has only heightened this tendency within her. Christiane has always been isolated.

The premise of *Les Yeux sans visage* was reprised in Robert Hartford Davis' *Corruption* (1968), but despite Peter Cushing's superb performance of the surgeon Sir John Rowan, the film lacks Franju's dreamlike quality, which, according to Cushing, was perhaps what *Corruption* was originally intended to exhibit. Cushing remarked, "Audiences did not get the idea that it was supposed to be based on a dream, which in fact did not justify some of the scenes that were presented. With any film you participate in, the company, if they so wish, can destroy your original interpretation of the role."[17] The final scenes in the film do explain this dream-like context, recapitulating as they do the opening party sequence, but not the accident that happens there. The implication is that the accident and all that follows it is the malicious fantasy of Rowan's very real sexual jealousy. We see Cushing's face in close-up and hear Anthony Booth's lecherous photographer, Mike Orme, saying to Rowan's fiancée (Sue Lloyd) "Undo your dress. Take it off." "That's enough," Rowan insists, as the film ends. In Franju's film, the disfigurement leads Christiane towards a self-renouncing apotheosis with doves; Hartford-Davis' film shows only the moral degeneration of Sue Lloyd's Lynn Nolan.

The cause of the disfigurement in *Corruption* is vanity (a lamp in Orme's studio falls on Lynn). Unknowingly foreshadowing the tragedy, Lynn complains, "You're spoiling my face!" as Sir John tries to kiss her before they go to the party. Sir John is also vain and very much aware of his reputation. "The more you succeed the more you fear the failures," he confesses during the main title sequence, as he emerges from an operating theater. Orme's interest in Lynn emphasizes Rowan's sense of alienation at the party amid the bright young things of the swinging sixties. The film demonstrates both a fascination with and a horror of sex and flesh. We hear the words "really kinky" and "don't be shy," the latter being repeated some time later when Rowan visits a prostitute with the intent of murdering her for her pituitary gland. After the scuffle between Rowan and Orme that leads to the lamp scorching Lynn's face, it is at first guilt that motivates the surgeon to restore it, but when the operation fails, it is Lynn's vanity that takes over. Like Lady Macbeth, she exploits her husband's guilt, driving him to commit a series of appalling murders to provide the raw materials required to restore her beauty. Whereas Christiane's accident exaggerates her natural sense of alienation, Lynn's accident magnifies her vanity.

There is, of course, another kind mutilation, which is deliberate self-harm. One of the most powerful depictions of this phenomenon can be found in Ingmar Bergman's *Cries and Whispers* (1972). This was made long before self-harm became the ubiquitous topic of media discussion that it is now, and Bergman's presentation of it is deeply shocking. He frames the self-harm within the 19th-century context of story in which Agnes (Harriet Andersson) is dying from cancer and cared for by her two sisters, Maria and Karin (Liv Ullmann and Ingrid Thulin), and their servant, Anna (Kari Sylwan). The death agonies of Agnes have none of the gore and splatter of so many body horror films, but are, in fact, far more grueling to watch than anything by Cronenberg or George A. Romero. Rarely has the reality of pain been conveyed as unflinchingly and honestly as in Andersson's performance here. Her cries of death agony are truly shocking, but neither have the whisperings of unhappiness, which lead to self-harm, been so un-sensationally evoked. As the two surviving sisters review their own lives and equally unhappy marriages, we learn more of their private anguish. Maria is unfaithful to her husband Joakin (Henning Moritzen), who, in despair stabs himself at his desk. Here there is blood, but no more than is needed to convey what he has done to himself. He recovers, but Bergman is keen to show us the psychological reality of self-harm far more than the gory details. The effect is consequently much more disturbing. Karin, meanwhile, is trapped in a loveless marriage with a diplomat. Having broken a glass of red wine during dinner, she collects one of the shards and later inserts it into her vagina, greeting her husband that night with blood on her legs, which she then smears on her mouth, smiling grotesquely, as few but Thulin can perform so unsettlingly. These two mutilations serve a profoundly psychological purpose, but Bergman's entire approach to this film is an intensely physical study of the human body. Much is shot in close-up—a series of faces when it is not a study in domestic claustrophobia. The predominant color is blood red. The carpets are red, so are the window draperies, the upholstery and eiderdowns. Scenes are divided by a "fade-to-red," often moving from one close-up to another. The color is not only suggestive of the blood of life itself, but also the family blood that unites this unhappy trio of sisters. The corruption of Agnes body is only the most extreme manifestation of this corporeality. Clocks are present throughout, ticking and chiming, reminding us of the inevitable disintegration of the flesh. At one stage, the doctor, David (Erland Josephson), with whom Maria is having an affair, asks Maria to look at herself in the mirror:

> Come here, Maria. Look in the mirror. You're beautiful. Perhaps even more than when we were together. But you've changed, and I want you to see how. Now your eyes cast quick, calculating side glances. You used to look ahead straightforwardly, openly… without disguise. Your mouth has a slightly angry, dissatisfied expression. It used to be so soft. Your complexion is pale now. You wear makeup. Your fine, wide brow has four lines above each eye now. You can't see them in this light, but you can in the bright light of day. You know what caused those lines? Indifference. And this fine contour from your ear to your chin is no longer so finely drawn.…the result of too much comfort and laziness. And there, by the bridge of your nose. Why do you sneer so often. You see that? You sneer too often. You see it? And look under the eyes. The sharp, scarcely noticeable wrinkles from your boredom and impatience.

These subtle mutilations of vanity and time, boredom and disillusionment are fully as profound as the stark disfigurement in *Corruption,* and qualify Bergman's harrowing but understated masterpiece as one of the cinema's most impressive examples of biological horror.

Brains and Severed Heads

The brain is often exposed in horror films. As Peter Cushing puts it in *The Gorgon* (dir. Terence Fisher, 1964), "It never ceases to amaze me why the most noble work of God—the human brain—is the most revolting to the human eye." It is revolting, of course, because if we can see it, it is fatally misplaced, but more significantly from a psychological point of view, the brain is what creates our impression of reality. Nothing exists for us without a brain to interpret the world around us, and here another aspect of Schopenhauer's philosophy comes into play. As we have already seen, Schopenhauer, via the philosophy of Kant, argues that we are unable to know the world for what it actually is, as our only means of interpretation are our highly unreliable senses.

> Are those representations, those objects, something more than and apart from representations, objects the subject? Then what would they be in this sense? What is that other side of them that is *toto genre* different from the representation? What is the thing-in-itself?...
> Whatever the thing-in-itself may be, Kant rightly concluded that time, space, and causality ... could not be its properties, but could come to it only after, and in so far as, it had become representation, in other words, belonged only to its phenomenon or appearance, not to it itself.[18]

We can never know exactly what it is that we are experiencing, having at our disposal only what the brains tells itself. Thus, we create our own reality, which is as fragile a construct as our physical existence, as Schopenhauer makes clear in his insistence that everything we experience is a *phenomenon of the brain*:

> a beautiful view for example, is also a *phenomenon of the brain*. Therefore its purity and perfection depend not merely on the *object*, but also on the quality and constitution of the brain. ... Accordingly, the picture of the same view appears in different heads, even when the eyes are equally keen.

He compares this to the way in which we perceive pain:

> Thus, just as we imagine we perceive things directly where they are, whereas in fact we do so in the brain, so do we also believe we feel the pain of a limb in the limb itself, whereas this pain also is felt in the brain to which it is guided by the nerve of the affected part. Therefore only the affections of those parts whose nerves go to the brain are felt, but not those whose nerves belong to the ganglionic system. ... Thus, in

the two phenomena here compared, what occurs in the brain is apprehended as outside the brain; in the case of perception, by means of the understanding extending its feelers into the external world; in the case of a sensation in the limbs, by means of the nerves.[19]

We are therefore doubly burdened. To the psychological and physical harm that birth bequeaths to us, is added the uncertainty of what exactly it is we are suffering from. This is why the brain is such a powerful symbol in horror films, for it is we who create the horror for ourselves. The neuroscientist V.S. Ramachandran would appear to be in agreement with this, for he argues that the brain creates not merely phantoms but also very real sensations of pain when there are no physical causes for it, as, for example, in the phenomenon known as a phantom limb. This sensation he describes as "an arm or leg that lingers indefinitely in the minds of patients long after it has been lost in an accident or removed by a surgeon."

> Some wake up from anesthesia and are incredulous when told that their arm had to be sacrificed, because they still vividly *feel* its presence. Only when they look under the sheets do they come to the shocking realization that the limb is really gone. Moreover, some of these patients experience excruciating pain in the phantom arm, hand or fingers, so much so that they contemplate suicide. The pain is not only unrelenting, it's also untreatable; no one has the foggiest idea how it arises or how to deal with it.[20]

Ramachandran then goes on to "overstate the argument deliberately," by suggesting that "we are hallucinating all the time and what we call perception is arrived at by simply determining which hallucination best conforms to the current sensory input. But if ... the brain does not receive confirming visual stimuli [due to brain damage], it is free simply to make up its own reality."[21] He adds, with regard to so-called "neglect" patients (who, due to a stroke ignore everything on either their right- or left-hand side, but are completely unaware that they do so):

> This raises profound philosophical questions about how sure we can be that our own grasp on reality is all that secure. An alien four-dimensional creature watching us from his four-dimensional world might regard our behavior to be just as perverse, inept and absurdly comical as we regard the bumblings of neglect patients trapped in their strange looking-glass world.[22]

Not all films featuring brains take this on board, some choosing merely to exploit the revulsion we feel for a brain displaced from its skull, but even a film such as *Donovan's Brain* (dir. Felix E. Feist, 1953) perpetuates our need to feel that there is an essential core to the personality that can survive dismemberment and death, which Ramachandran's investigations strongly suggest is not the case. In *Donovan's Brain*, the brain originally belonged to the callous millionaire, Mr. Donovan, who is killed in an air crash before the action of the film gets going. His brain, however, is kept alive in a tank of nourishing chemicals by Dr. Cory (Lew Ayres), who is assisted by his wife (played the future first lady of the United States, Nancy Davis, later to be known as Nancy Reagan, and Nancy's husband, Ronald, who was also an actor before becoming U.S. president, had a famous line in *King's Row* [dir. Sam Wood, 1942] with its own identity issues. Having had his legs severed, Reagan's character, Drake McHugh, shouts, "Where's the rest of me?"—foreshadowing the jogger in *Scream and Scream Again*).

Donovan's brain forms a telepathic means of communication with Dr. Cory, which grows increasingly powerful, affecting his personality and inspiring him to indulge in criminal activity. The story is hence another variant of *Dr. Jekyll and Mr. Hyde,* but the main idea had fact been previously explored in Arthur Lubin's *Black Friday* (1940), in which Stanley Ridges upstages Boris Karloff in a remarkable performance as both a mild-mannered professor of English literature and the ruthless gangster whose brain is transplanted into the professor's body, with predictable results.

The idea that the personality can survive in the brain alone is not so far from the belief that it can survive death in spiritual form. Donovan's brain is eventually destroyed by the intervention of a thunderbolt (thus reversing the process of Frankenstein's method), and this is deemed a positive resolution, as the brain is obviously malevolent, but what if the brain had been benevolent? Well, there would have been no story, and that, in itself, demonstrates Schopenhauer's contention that life fluctuates between boredom and striving. Heaven must be a desperately boring place, while hell is surely so full of torment.

The basic theme of *Donovan's Brain* was bloodily reworked by David Cronenberg in *Scanners* (1981) in which telepaths are able to destroy other humans merely by willing them to die—either increasing their heart-rates to bursting point or, as in the film's most famous opening scene, exploding their heads, which are surely among the most spectacular examples of body horror. (Cronenberg reworked this effect towards the end of *Videodrome* when Max shoots Les Carlson's Barry Convex and his entire body erupts, the mask of his face cracking into bloody shards.) The two main characters of *Scanners* (Michael Ironside's Darryl Revok and Steven Lack's Cameron Vale) are eventually revealed to be brothers, each imbued with powerfully destructive psychic potential, and the film ends with a psychic duel between them. "I'm going to suck your brain dry," Revok insists. "Everything you are is going to become me."

Anton Leader's *Children of the Damned* from 1964 dealt with telepathic powers in a more abstract manner, but Cronenberg, for whom the body is all there is, expresses this mental duel in the most physical of terms, the effort of concentration and hostility being represented by blood and veins bursting through the skin of the two men. Vale's eyes are sucked from their sockets, while Revok's turn white, like the undead in Hammer's *Plague of the Zombies* (dir. John Gilling, 1966) and Boris Sagal's *The Omega Man* (dir. 1971). We are finally shown Revok with Vale's eyes in place of his own, the personality transfer complete.

Fiend Without a Face (dir. Arthur Crabtree, 1958) is really a B-movie horror version of *Forbidden Planet* (dir. Fred M. Wilcox, 1956). Both are concerned with our anxiety over technology coupled with the destructive potential of our own brains. We are continually reminded of the cold war context of *Fiend Without a Face*, with its deliberately threatening shots of radar dishes, jet planes and, even more disturbing, the lingering sounds of machinery either throbbing or shrieking, which even interrupts a funeral at one stage. The air-force personnel take all this noise for granted and express irritation at the local residents who don't. "They'll probably blame the death on our atomic reactors," says one of them. "It's this fear of radioactive fallout," says another. Marshall Thompson's straightforward Major Cummings complains, "We're not exploding atom bombs, we're just using atomic power for our radar experiments," as if that isn't anything to worry about. "What a bunch of backward people," adds his assistant.

There is further considerable irony when Cummings insists, "We're all human here! We're not monsters from outer space," but surely any intelligent alien would regard a species preparing for its own nuclear annihilation as being exactly that. Technology in the film is constantly seen as a threat. When asked to provide more atomic power for the radar experiments, a technician reluctantly agrees. "It's your funeral. Mine too probably."

Atomic power is indeed involved in the murders that surround the base, but it is not exactly due to the military. Rather, an eccentric profes-

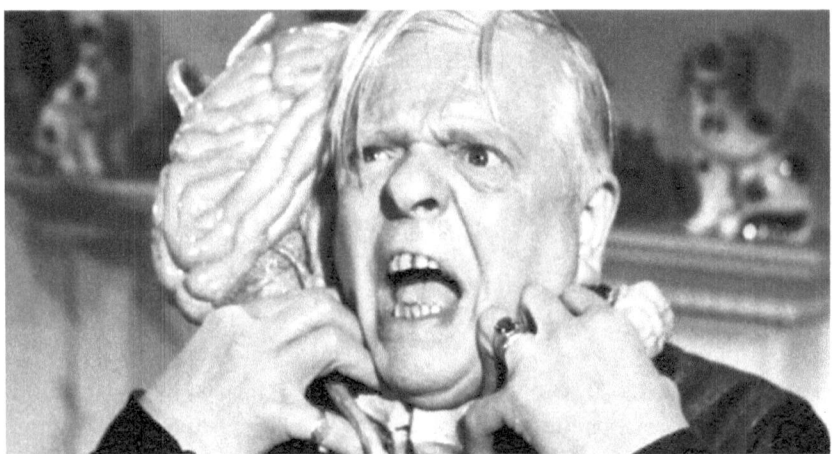

Brain power. Lauce Maraschal as Deputy Mayor Melville under attack by the eponymous monster in *Fiend Without a Face* (dir. Arthur Crabtree, 1958).

sor played by Kynaston Reeves who, like Walter Pidgeon's Dr. Morbius in *Forbidden Planet,* has unleashed his own brain power and created a psychic monster, a "kind of mental vampire." The professor has achieved this materialization of thought by exploiting the atomic power at the airbase. As in *Frankenstein,* a thunderbolt gives the professor's instruments a charge of power, and this releases the thoughts from his brain. He then devises a being "into which the thought, once released, could enter and preserve itself for all humanity. I envisaged something akin to the human brain, with life and mobility but without the limitations of man's body." When, at the end of the film, the military personnel start shooting these flying brains, the film provides us with a graphic, if unintentionally comic representation of our will to self-destruction. The film's most impressive still shows Kim Parker being attacked by one of these brains, along with its attached spinal cord. It appears, however, as if it is her own brain that is being drawn from her skull. Our essential sense of self-revulsion could not find a more powerful expression than this: what is essential for life within the body becomes horrific when removed from it. We are repelled by our own internal reality.

Herbert J. Leder, who had written the screenplay for *Fiend Without a Face,* created one of the most arresting images of a severed head in *The Frozen Dead,* which he also wrote and directed in 1966. Here, Dana Andrews plays the ex–Nazi scientist, Dr. Norbert, who, 20 years after the end of the Second World War, is continuing his cryogenic program. Dr. Norbert has a cellar filled with Nazis on ice awaiting resurrection, but he needs to study a living brain to perfect his technique. (*The Boys from Brazil* [dir. Franklin J. Schaffner, 1978], updated this conceit to genetics with Hitler clones, nurtured for future world domination.) An opportunity for Norbert to acquire the brain he needs arises when his niece and her friend, Elsa (Kathleen Breck) arrive home from boarding school a little earlier than expected. Elsa soon finds herself decapitated, and with the aid of eerie blue light and pallid make-up, Breck gives one of the cinema's most moving performances of a severed head. Like a female Baphomet, she glowers and mutters and eventually uses her own brainpower to activate a row of amputated arms to strangle Norbert and his Nazi employer. Breck's evocation of suffering, whispering "bury me!" at the end of the film, could well be seen as popular culture's response to Dido's lament ("Remember me!") at the end of Purcell's opera, *Dido and Aeneas.* As a secular symbol of human suffering it might even bear comparison not only with the Lutheran hymn "O Haupt voll Blut und Wunden" but also with images of Christ crucified. Our own heads, however, do not need to be severed to suffer from the horrors of the body. Fixed to a moveable platform, their horrors are hardly any the less for that.

A different kind of frozen dead, or frozen head at least, occurs in *Corruption,* in which Peter Cushing's surgeon stores a severed head in the freezer

"Bury me!" The severed head of Elsa Tenney (Kathleen Breck) observed by Philip Gilbert and Anna Palk in *The Frozen Dead* (dir. Herbert J. Leder, 1967).

box of his refrigerator. It had once belonged to a woman he murdered on a train for her pituitary gland, and it is discovered by another girl, who is rather prosaically making sandwiches. This head cannot speak, however, and is therefore rather less horrific.

Decapitation can sometimes be grisly but historical, rather than overtly horrific, as is the case at the end of adaptations of Dickens' *A Tale of Two Cities*, but as the ultimate mutilation, horror films are obviously attracted to it most of all, hence the guillotine imagery that brings *The Curse of Frankenstein* to a close and opens its sequel, *The Revenge of Frankenstein*. The same imagery opens *Frankenstein Created Women* (dir. Terence Fisher, 1967), which involves two executions later on. In this film, Frankenstein exploits the situation in which he finds himself to aid the transplantation of a male soul into a female body. The resulting psychopath, played with suitably doll-like demeanor by Susan Denberg, unfortunately worships the severed head of her old body, which strongly suggests the Freudian equation between decapitation and castration.[23] *The Omen's* most infamous moment of body horror is the decapitation of David Warner's head by a sheet of plate glass, but decapitation can also be amusing given the right treatment. *Horror Hospital* (dir.

Anthony Balch, 1973) cheerfully chops off a variety of heads throughout its 95 minutes, as Michael Gough's mad surgeon attempts to create a bodyguard of lobotomized hippies. A customized limousine, equipped with Boudican blades, sets heads rolling, while sheets stained with blood hardly provide a sense of security to the guests in his Gothic mansion (in fact Lord Lytton's Knebworth House).

Hospitals are the temples of body horror, which is one of the reasons why Cronenberg set a great deal of *Rabid* in one (Cohen based the first half of *It's Alive* in hospital too), but the hospital in *Rabid* is a much more brutalist "soulless" building than Knebworth House, suitably reflecting the highly materialistic world-view Cronenberg wishes to present, in which the body, as he relentlessly insists, is all there is. There is no room for sly humor or Gothic (i.e., "spiritual") attenuations in Cronenberg's vision of an increasingly materialistic culture in the 1970s. Body horror is about the agonies and accidental uncertainties of life (hence Cronenberg's relentless contemporaneity), whereas Gothic horror is mostly about death and the past. *Horror Hospital* somehow manages to straddle and satirize both sides of this equation. Ex-porn star, Robin Asquith's irrepressible desire to undress women emphasizes that this is a life-enhancing film, despite the casual murder that takes place all around him, and it is possible, indeed appropriate, to interpret the action along Nietzschean lines—as an indomitable "Yes" in the face of existential horrors. Cioran, also suggests that it is possible to make of death "an affirmation of life."[24]

> It is true that negation is the mind's first freedom, yet a negative habit is fruitful only so long as we exert ourselves to overcome it, adapt it to our needs; once *acquired* it can imprison us—a chain like any other.[25]... Having exhausted my reserves of negation, and perhaps negation itself, why should I not run out into the street shouting at the top of my lungs that I am on the serge of discovering a truth, the only one that is worth anything? But I do not know yet what that truth is; I know only the joy which precedes it, they and the madness and the fear.[26] ... Yet we must learn to think against our doubts and against our certitudes, against our omniscient humors, we must above all, by creating for ourselves *another* death, one that will be incompatible with our carrion carcasses, consent to the undemonstrable, to the idea that something exists...
>
> Nothingness may well have been more convenient. How difficult it is to *dissolve* oneself in Being![27]

This, it seems to me, is exactly what comedy horror films like *Horror Hospital* attempt to do: To laugh in the face of death ("lachender Tod"—"laughing Death," as Wagner has Siegfried and Brünnhilde sing at the end of his third *Ring* opera, *Siegfried*). And it works. Lou Costello's response to Lon Chaney's line in *Abbot and Costello Meet Frankenstein* (dir. Charles Barton, 1948) is the perfect example: "You don't understand," Chaney's Wolf Man explains, "every night when the moon is full, I turn into a wolf," to which Lou replies, "You and fifty million other guys!"

By the post-modern times in which *Barton Fink* (dir. Ethan and Joel Coen, 1991) was released, the black comedy of a severed head had become harder to interpret. Fink (John Turturro) is a left-wing playwright, but probably not a particularly good one, despite his modish success on Broadway. He is certainly a man of intellectual pretensions, claiming to understand "ordinary" people but in fact having nothing in common with them. His play on an everyman theme is an apparent critical success and attracts the attention of Hollywood. By selling out to tinsel town, even though his artistic collateral was probably not all that high in the first place, he truly sells his soul to the Devil.

Barton Fink is thus really a re-working of Marlowe's *Faust* and Dante's *Inferno*. Fink checks into a decaying art deco hotel, where wallpaper peels off the walls of his suffocating apartment, everyone perspires and ultimately everything bursts into flames. This is Hell and no mistake. His introduction to this establishment is an indication of what is to follow. After a long wait, the receptionist, summoned by an endlessly vibrating desk-bell, eventually appears from below the reception counter, as through a trapdoor in the floor. Though he is subservient to the grander demons, who run the studios, he is a demon nonetheless.

The Hollywood that Fink now encounters is pretty much the kind of hell described by Bernard Shaw in *Man and Superman*—a place of bland materialism, concerned only with subduing its audiences and extracting cash in return. Shaw's Devil explains that hell "is the home of the unreal and of the seekers for happiness."

> It is the only refuge from heaven, which is, as I tell you, the home of the masters of reality, and from earth, which is the home of the slaves of reality. ... But here ... you are a ghost, an appearance, an illusion, a convention, deathless, ageless: in a word, bodiless. There are no social questions here, no political questions, no religious questions, best of all, perhaps, no sanitary questions. Here you call your appearance, beauty, your emotions love, your sentiments heroism, your aspirations virtue, just as you did on earth; but here there are no hard facts to contradict you, no ironic contrast of your needs with your pretensions, no human comedy, nothing but a perpetual romance, a universal melodrama.[28]

Placed on a "wrestling picture" (the last kind of project with which Fink would have wished to be associated), he is shown film rushes to give him a flavor of what is expected from him, and his state of mind is brilliantly evoked by the astonishing sound design of Skip Lievsay.

Fink, like Dante before him, aims for higher things, and these higher things are represented by the photograph of a woman, which hangs in his hotel apartment. She sits on a beach, one hand raised against the sun, and though we never see her face, she actually manifests herself to Fink later in the film as an equivalent of Dante's Beatrice—a symbol of hope and salvation, which unfortunately elude him in the end. It is hell to which Fink belongs, like the rest of us, and he begins to realize the true nature of his predicament when the "ordinary man" in the adjacent apartment (played by John Goodman) is revealed to be a serial killer who decapitates his victims. The Coens make sure to remind us that man is not the only other lost soul in this hot(h)el(l), for we continually hear the sounds of sobbing and suffering in the corridors. These noises fill the corridors, which resemble the terrifying negative spaces of Kubrick's Overlook Hotel in *The Shining* (1980). Eventually, the flames of hell engulf those corridors, but Fink survives to walk along the Californian beach where he finally meets his Beatrice. However, there seems little of redemption in the encounter, and rather more bewilderment along with a sense that the only enlightenment all his suffering has brought is an understanding of life's essential futility.

Prisons of the Flesh

Horror films also explore our sense of being trapped within our bodies, rather than merely *being* our bodies. This idea is entertainingly expressed in Robert Irwin's novel *The Arabian Nightmare*:

> It was the Dawadar's opinion that opium gave no positive pleasure. It merely eased the pain of being in a body, the congestion of blood in the veins, the scraping of sinew against bone, the shaking of the brain's porridge within the skullcase, all part of our everyday level of pain which was to be noticed only when opium alleviated it. For the Dawadar, pleasure was the absence of pain, while good could be defined only as the absence of evil.[29]

The body is a prison, a restriction, a parody, even a parasite. We are desperate to believe that something exists apart from or at least in parallel with our bodies. In both *The Revenge of Frankenstein* and *Frankenstein Must Be Destroyed*, Peter Cushing's Baron transplants the brain of one man into the body of another. (In the former, Michael Gwynne sympathetically plays the result before his tastes turn cannibalistic. In the latter, the thoroughly disorientated victim is played with even more tragic melancholy by Freddie Jones. Frankenstein must indeed be destroyed for committing such an outrageous imposition upon another man's brain.) Such interchangeability of not merely body parts but also of personalities creates a kind of physical schizophrenia.

Cast in the form of a science fiction thriller rather than a horror film, *The Man Who Changed His Mind* (dir. Robert Stevenson, 1936) confronts this dilemma directly. While no physical brains are exchanged, the *contents* of one brain are channeled into another, with the same effect. Boris Karloff plays Dr. Laurience, a scientist who develops this technique. At first he exchanges the minds of a violent chimp and a docile chimp, before moving onto humans. (Dr. Stein would, of course, follow the same trajectory in *The Revenge of Frankenstein* 22 years later.) Laurience swops the personality of his disabled assistant (Donald Calthrop) with that of an arrogant newspaper magnate, Lord Haselwood (Frank Cellier), before transferring his own personality into the body of Haselwood's son, Dick (John Loder). He also murders Haselwood, but this not before he murders Haselwood, thus ensuring (he hopes) that he will not only inherit his "father's" money when in his new body, but that Dick, in Laurience's body, will pay the ultimate price for the murder.

Hammer added a gender element to this kind of story in *Frankenstein Created Woman*, which is a rather more metaphysical film, dealing, as it does, with the concept of the soul as opposed merely to the personality, but Hammer returned to more straightforward personality exchange by means of brain transplant in *Frankenstein Must Be Destroyed*. The complexity of *The Man Who Changed His Mind* emphasizes the existential element of the story: that we really have no fundamental identity at all, consisting, as we do, of little more than a complex of cultural constructs and sensory impressions with their inevitable contradictions. Can one really claim to having an inherent personality if it is dependent upon not having been shut in a cupboard since birth? Environment and experience are what "form" the personality, and it might thus be possible to argue that personalities are as interchangeable as they are in the Karloff film, but without the need for expensive laboratory equipment. Other people see us differently too, so in a sense there are as many different "I"s as there are different people who construct our own idea of ourselves. Such fluidity of identity is disconcerting, but perhaps not so surprising as it was when *The Man Who Changed His Mind* was first released in 1936. Certainly, Hammer's gender exchange in *Frankenstein Created Woman*, in which a male soul is transplanted into a female body, anticipated the trans-gender issues of our own time, which is much less disconcerted by gender fluidity than we were in 1969.

In *Before I Hang* (dir. Nick Grinde, 1940), Karloff continued this theme with one of his most beautifully judged performances of understated unease as a scientist who has developed an anti-aging serum. Unfortunately, he uses the blood of a convicted murderer in the mix, thus turning himself into a murderer when he experiments on himself. All these personality-altering films are, as I pointed out earlier, variants on the Jekyll and Hyde story, in which the unconscious destroys the super-ego. This results in a form of psychological suicide, which society finishes off by executing the physical host in one way or another. The rebellious nature of the Id, as Dr. Morbius discovers in *Forbidden Planet*, suggests once more that we are somehow pre-programmed to self-destruct. Freud contemplated this idea in "Beyond the Pleasure Principle" and his later essay "The Ego and the Id," in which he put forward "the hypothesis of a *death instinct*, the task of which is to lead organic life back into the inanimate state ... to re-establish a state of things that was disturbed by the emergence of life. The emergence of life would thus be the cause of the continuance of life and also at the same time of the striving towards death; and that life itself would be a conflict and compromise between these two trends."[30]

Arthur Koestler, however, had another explanation. To be born as a human being means also to inherit the cerebral cortex, which Koestler believed had evolved disproportionately to the ape brain. (Koestler eventually committed suicide himself as a result not only of his terminal illness but also of his own horror of and disillusionment with the human predicament.) Koestler claimed that the cerebral cortex was "a tumorous overgrowth" which we should not congratulate ourselves about: "we ought to pause and examine the possibility that man ... might carry a constructional fault inside his skull."[31] The technological abilities the neo-cortex permits humanity to develop are extremely dangerous when linked with the emotional primitivism of the old brain we also carry about with us.

> The cause which contemporary research seems to indicate is not increase in size, but *insufficient co-ordination* between archicortex and neocortex—between the phylogenetically old areas of our brain, and the new, specifically human areas which were superimposed on it with such unseemly haste.[32]

Koestler's conclusion in that "the rise of the human neo-cortex is the only example of evolution proving a species with an organ which it does not know how to use."[33]

Gender Games

Gender fluidity has traditionally been regarded with unease by horror films, because horror films are largely created for and designed to appeal to the male gaze. The victims are traditionally women, who are rescued by men, the villains are also usually male, and their excesses are curbed in the end by men who operate within more civilized boundaries, but we are also encouraged to admire such villains. Female vampires also perish, but not before we have been given ample opportunities to gaze upon their increasingly revealed cleavage, and it is because of this predominantly male gaze that horror films find gender fluidity as perhaps the most horrifying thing of all. Easthope clarifies the situation by arguing "male sexuality, like all human sexuality, is unevenly divided and has a bisexual potential." He goes on:

> [T]he dominant version of masculinity treats masculinity as undivided, and so must find means to deny, exclude and contain male femininity and homosexual desire. ...
> The aim is to put forward masculinity as a pure essence defined against what is wholly

other than it, femininity as a pure essence. Men and women, male and female, masculine and feminine are to be compartmentalized, sorted into opposed categories and assigned to separate place.[34]

Hammer Films was keen to exploit both the loosening of censorship and the emerging gender politics of the 1970s. Hence, lesbian vampires appeared in *The Vampire Lovers,* who were staked with phallic ruthlessness by male vampire hunters. More intriguing, however, was *Dr. Jekyll and Sister Hyde* (dir. Roy Ward Baker, 1971), which went beyond the cleverness of its title tentatively to explore homosexuality, which had only previously been included in a mainstream horror film by Roman Polanski's *The Fearless Vampire Killers* (1967). Instead of turning into a Neanderthal monster, Ralph Bates' Dr. Jekyll, in his pursuit of an elixir to extend life, transforms, by means of female hormones, into the curvaceous form of Martine Beswick. "Man or woman? Or both?" as the trailer teasingly asked. Mrs. Hyde in turn attracts the attention of Lewis Fiander's Howard Spencer, who lives in the flat above with his prudish mother and annoyingly virtuous sister; but there is one scene in which Howard encounters Jekyll in a London street. Jekyll whispers Howard's name and touches his chin tenderly before departing, causing Howard to draw his own conclusions as he realizes what kind of shop the good doctor has been visiting: a French corset maker.

But all these approaches were, like Terence Fisher's white of egg, quite tasteful, which *Frankenhooker* (dir. Frank Henenlotter, 1990), a horror satire on male chauvinism, was certainly and deliberately not. The tastelessness, indeed, made its premise all the more interesting. A dropout medical student called Jeffrey (James Laurinz) attempts to resurrect his girlfriend, Elizabeth (Patty Mullen), who has been dismembered by a lawn mower. He is only able to save her head, however, and decides to assemble the rest of her body from the limbs of assorted prostitutes. Henenlotter's depiction of bosoms, legs, and bottoms says much about the commodification of sex in modern America (or anywhere else for that matter), in which body parts are merely objects of male desire, easily separable from the women they belong to in the name of sexual gratification. One scene shows Jeffrey sorting through a pile of bosoms as one might select mushrooms in a supermarket. "These are no good. Mutt and Jeff!" he shouts. Body parts in pornography are indeed interchangeable, the person to whom they belong being much less important than the stimulation they can generate.

"Want a date? Going out? Looking for some action? Need some company?" the resurrected Elisabeth asks on being reactivated, her prostitute body parts having more control over her than her previously respectable head. *Frankenhooker* is even more a satire on prostitution than it is of *Frankenstein*. Nowhere is this made more explicit than in the scene when all the hookers' limbs and heads erupt from Jeffrey's storage tank and spill out over the feet of the prostitutes' pimp, Zorro (Joseph Gonzalez). Severed hands grab him, bosoms press against him and a severed head kisses him, before they drag him back into the tank.

Feminism, however, has its revenge at the end of *Frankenhooker*. Zorro decapitates Jeffrey, and Elisabeth brings him back to life. She can only do this using Jeffrey's method, which, being estrogen-based, is dependent upon female body parts, and so it is that the film ends with Jeffrey screaming in horror on finding his head attached to a composite prostitute, with a bosom, painted fingernails and no penis. "Where's my Johnson?" he shrieks, before Henenlotter brings the proceedings to an abrupt conclusion, like Thackeray at the end of *Vanity Fair*, which is surely the world's first literary equivalent of a cut-to-black:

> Ah! *Vanitas Vanitatum!* Which of us is happy in this world? Which of us has his desire? or, having it, is satisfied?—Come, children, let us shut up the box and the puppets, for our play is played out.

Five

Infection

> "Swifter, more awesome than the black death: The plague. In the first moments, every muscle, every fibre will be afire with torment and agony."
>
> —Christopher Lee as Dracula in *The Satanic Rites of Dracula* (dir. Alan Gibson, 1973)

An essential aspect of the horror of our own bodies is their susceptibility to infection. This perennial anxiety has increased in cinematic terms of recent years, at a time when superbugs, antibacterial resistance and the Covid-19 pandemic have reminded us of a period when science was less able to defend us against such enemies. In her 2017 book of essays, *Body Horror: Capitalism, Fear, Misogyny, Jokes*, the feminist writer Anne Elizabeth Moore blames capitalism's quest for profit as the Frankenstein behind these particular body horrors:

> An autoimmune response is when the body's own immune system starts attacking its host instead of foreign invaders like viruses. This results in illness or disability or pain or weird body functions that are the result of a hyperactive immune system seeking to wipe itself out. Autoimmune responses seem to be triggered by a couple of different things, only one of which is genetics. Another is when additives are placed in food.
> ...I'm very very very allergic to soy, as are a lot of people, yet it is considered a normal food ingredient because of food policy, because the government wants it that way, because it's a way of promoting commerce.
> So what I describe in the book is that we've created a system largely intended to curb global hunger—which additives have helped to do, for sure—that also injects what turn out to be poisons into the bodies of certain people around the world, mostly women and poor folks.[1]

Long before these contemporary concerns, vampires in old-fashioned horror films had lent themselves to medical allegory, sometimes made explicit, as, for example, in *House of Dracula* (dir. Erle C. Kenton, 1945), in which John Carradine's Count seeks a medical cure for his condition. Later in Hammer's *Kiss of the Vampire*, vampirism is specifically described as a disease. Clifford Evans' Prof. Zimmer describes the fate of his daughter in terms that initially suggest syphilis, but which he makes sure we realize is even more worrying:

> I had a daughter. She was all I had in the world. I idolized her. When she was very young she ran away from home, ran away to the city. She drifted in with a so-called smart set and finally she was living with a certain man. She came home eventually— what was left of her came home. She was riddled with disease ... and she was a vampire.

Hammer's equation of vampires with disease reached its peak in *The Satanic Rites of Dracula,* in which Freddie Jones gives a bravura performance as Professor Julian Keeley, a bio-chemist, who has been given the job, by Dracula himself, of developing a plague virus to destroy humanity—and Dracula himself—for good. Professor Keeley explains:

> I found the new strain: bacillus pestis, but more virulent than any known specie. I grew the bacilli in agar and then exposed them to radioactive neutrons. An infected creature suffers the most indescribable symptoms: The flesh literally rots on the bones and the contagion spreads by touch like wild-fire. Everything accelerates beyond any imagination. Within seconds the disease takes over the whole system.

In the final scenes of the film we witness these effects as Dracula compels one of his middle-aged disciples to crush a phial containing the virus, but, in the event, he is the only one to be infected, as he is ultimately burned to death in the culminating conflagration, the bacillus with him.

In Werner Herzog's *Nosferatu* (1979), the plague caused by Count Dracula (Klaus Kinski) and his army of rats is ultimately defeated when the vampire is destroyed through the self-sacrifice of Lucy (Isabelle Adjani). Roger Corman's *The Masque of the Red Death* (1964) also confronts our fear of plague. Prince Prospero's attempt to outwit the microbes of this suppurating invader fails in the final frames, as the Red Death invades his fortress. The guests he has assembled there all fall too, their faces streaked with blood, and when Prospero encounters the face of the Red Death, he discovers that it is his own.

Disease had previously been used by Hammer as a political metaphor, channeling cold war anxieties along the lines of Don Siegal's *The Invasion of the Body Snatchers.* In *Quatermass 2* (dir. Val Guest, 1957), government officials are "infected" by what are termed "overshots." These sinister objects originate in what is presumed to be a secret government research establishment. It is, in fact, an alien base. A wound on the hand indicates extraterrestrial infection, which transforms whoever carries it into an alien host. A similar eventuality had previously occurred in Hammer's earlier *The Quatermass Experiment* (dir. Val Guest, 1955), in which an astronaut, played with great compassion by Richard Wordsworth, gradually turns into a giant cactus-like creature, his own personality and body entirely taken over by the invading alien bacteria.

As the optimistic 1960s gave way to the much chillier 1970s, infection became more topical. *Doomwatch*, an apocalyptic/environmental British television science fiction series created by Gerry Davis and Kit Pedler, who had previously worked for *Doctor Who*, inspired a spin-off movie of that name directed by Peter Sasdy in 1972. Starring Judy Geeson and Ian Bannen alongside members of the original cast, *Doomwatch* the film continued the TV series' preoccupation with ecological issues, and combined infection with the issue of mutation. Growth-stimulating hormones have leaked from cans dumped in the sea around a remote British island, causing acromegaly, the disfiguring disease that had afflicted the actor, Rondo Hatton, who was able to exploit what he couldn't cure by appearing in horror films and Sherlock Holmes mysteries. *Doomwatch*, however, relied on make-up, and required from the actors who wore it, increasing degrees of aggression, leading to insanity. The islanders are convinced that the affliction is divine punishment upon them rather than the result of commercial greed. Suspicious and ashamed, the afflicted are hidden away from the inquisitive troubleshooters who come to investigate. *Doomwatch* is perhaps more interesting for its parallels with other films rather than its own paper-thin plot. In several ways it anticipates the following year's *The Wicker Man* (dir. Robin Hardy). Both films have remote island settings, both suggest a conspiracy amongst the islanders, who gather in the local pub, and both societies are dominated by their religious beliefs. Also similar is the isolation of the marooned Dr. Shaw (Ian Bannen) who visits the island to investigate its problems, much as Edward Woodwood's Sgt. Howie flies to Summerisle. *Doomwatch* also looks forward to *The Ghoul* (dir. Freddie Francis, 1975), for the monstrous acromegalics are kept locked away, much as Peter Cushing's Dr. Lawrence keeps his depraved cannibalistic son locked in a room at the top of the house. The various shots of villagers moving their unfortunate relatives around the island under cover of darkness is also reminiscent of the midnight gatherings of the villagers in *The Witches* (dir. Cyril Frankel, 1966). Redeemed by the cast's stalwart performances and Sasdy's location work, the infection-driven action of *Doomwatch* suggested the shape of things to come, as well as providing one of horror cinema's most notable stills of a deformed villager lurking in the shadows and raising a club aloft.

The following year, George Romero developed the premise of *Doomwatch* for the much more disturbing action of *The Crazies* (1973), in which ordinary people are infected by a contaminated water supply. The result was another zombie film, but one which was also an allegory of the Vietnam War, still in progress at the time. Two years later, the BBC TV series *Survivors* began its 38-episode contemplation of the consequences of a pandemic caused by a Chinese scientist, who featured in the soon-to-be very familiar title sequence.

Five. Infection 105

Acromegaly screaming. Judy Geeson responds to a close encounter with the heavily made-up Michael Brennan in *Doomwatch* (dir. Peter Sasdy, 1972).

The ghost of Fu Manchu of course haunts this somewhat racist presentation of a "yellow peril," though whether the pandemic of *Survivors* was an accident or a deliberate act of terrorism was never explained. However, this short opening sequence, perhaps because of its ambiguity, caught the spirit of the age, reflecting the geopolitical anxieties of the time and the increased awareness that air-travel had removed natural quarantine boundaries, for no one is safe in a global economy. (Eleven years earlier, the epilogue of Terence Fisher's sci-fi adventure *Island of Terror* had suggested a similar oriental threat. Having just been informed that the threat of the bone-dissolving "silicate" creatures might never have been contained if the outbreak had not taken place on an island, we are shown a Chinese laboratory, with doors usefully marked in both Chinese characters and English translations, where a similar experiment with identical consequences has just taken place. The scientist opens the door, disappears ... and screams.)

A mushroom cloud had blasted off the title sequence of the original *Doomwatch* TV series, and nuclear war scenarios tended to pre-occupy the fantasy market rather more throughout the 1980s, but disease movies gradually became more popular from the 1990s onwards, one film spawning another in increasingly rapid succession. There are various reasons for this: ecological anxiety fueled by the threat of global warming, the electronic "viruses" of the internet age, on-line "trolling", which we have already explored with regard to the *Slenderman* phenomenon, and, of course medical epidemics, such as the Ebola outbreak in Zaire in 1995, which exposed the possibility of pandemics affecting the affluent West, but there are also political and social anxieties, which more socially aware directors have discussed via the infection sub-genre.

One of the first of these was Wolfgang Petersen's 1995 *Outbreak*, a mainstream event from Warner Brothers with A-list stars such as Donald Sutherland, Morgan Freeman and Dustin Hoffman. Although the subject is very much one of biological horror (an infection caused by a monkey, which leads to what the film calls "the greatest medical crisis of all time"), there is very little graphic body horror in what is essentially a cross between a disaster film and a war film. Made in the wake of the Zaire Ebola crisis, Laurence Dworet and Robert Roy Pool's screenplay imagines what might have happened if the entire United States of America had only 48 hours left before a virulent virus destroys the entire population. Danny Boyle's *28 Days Later* (2002) was a British variation on this theme, with a virus spread by another contaminated chimpanzee, unwisely released from captivity by an animal-rights protestor, which leads to a "rage" virus destroying the U.K. *Doomwatch* had been prescient in this respect, and Boyle merely updated the *Doomwatch* scenario, taking into account the country's much larger population by that time, the phenomenon of "road rage" and the internet's baleful assault on privacy and behavior.

Developing this approach, Chris Gorak's 2006 apocalypse thriller, *Right at Your Door*, mixed in the added anxiety caused by 9/11 by having the pandemic caused by terrorist "dirty" bombs. With Àlex and David Pastor's *Carriers* (2009) viral infection was also used to symbolize a society that has become both politically and morally toxic, a situation summed up in the line: "Never touch anything that's not disinfected." This suggests that not only are the infected dangerous but are also socially undesirable. There is a nihilism here, which though on the surface seems to be being resisted, is, on a deeper level, seems to be in accord with the anti-natalist agenda of David Benatar. "Everyone dies," says Chris Pine's Brian, who, when infected himself, ultimately sees the struggle for survival as less desirable than film heroes did in the past. He pleads to be killed, just as a doctor had earlier practiced euthanasia on a group of infected children. The film's conclusion is consequently very bleak indeed, suggesting that extinction is probable and, under the circumstances, for the best. While Benatar advocates a more peaceful path to extinction (a subject to which I will return later), *Carriers* nonetheless has much in common with that view.

Infection films thereafter rapidly began to pick up speed, indeed to tumble over each other in pessimistic somersaults. Steven Soderbergh's 2011 *Contagion* adds political allegory to the physical fear, previously explored in *The Satanic Rites of Dracula*, of touching contagious individuals. The command "Don't talk to anyone. Don't touch anyone. Stay away from other people" suggests that we also fear being contaminated by foreigners, the poor, the internet—everything beyond which we are in control, indeed. A bio-weapon is at first thought to have been responsible for this pandemic, which kills 26 million people, but we later discover that it was caused by a bat dropping a banana into a pig pen, which begins a chain of events leading to the first human infection.

Contagion is a really a medical thriller, whereas Barry Levinson's *The Bay* from 2013 moved the subject fully into the aesthetic of body horror. As with Romero's *The Crazies*, an infected water supply is the cause of the problem. This breeds an isopod parasite that eats human organs "from the inside." By this time, horror films in general were familiar with what was already the cliché of invasive organisms moving under human skin, but what Levinson adds is an allegory of the failure of the American Dream in general. Like Roland Emmerich's distinctly post-modern science fiction *Independence Day* from 1996, he places the action, which purports to be reportage, on 4 July celebrations.

Eric England's *Contracted* appeared in the same year, featuring a sexually transmitted disease caused by a man having sex with a corpse in a morgue. Whereas traditional vampire films have always had an undertone of syphilis about them, Eric England expresses AIDS anxiety (the two girls at the center of the story are lesbians) much more explicitly here, with bleeding vaginas from which maggots emerge. Samantha, played by Najarra Townsend, then finds her eyes become bloodshot, her hair falls out, her fingernails fall out, and her teeth tumble, as she turns into as a zombie before finally being shot.

Hank Braxton's *Chemical Peel* kept up the momentum in 2014, in which a group of women are trapped in an isolated farmhouse that is suddenly surrounded by toxic air in the aftermath of a railway accident. This infection film is thus a response to anxieties about pollution, as well as an ironic comment on the feminine cosmetics industry. In an inevitable homage to *Psycho*, Kimberly (played by Leigh Davis) deliberately showers herself to death, to protect her friends (water increases the chemical reaction). The film also features Beethoven's Moonlight Sonata as an ironic counterpoint to the mayhem, suggesting that post-modern sensibilities can no longer take on face value the Romantic certainties of the past.

The following year brought along the much more interesting *Condemned*, directed by Eli Morgan Gesner. Body horror here effectively meets political satire set in a condemned tenement block in New York to which a runaway rich girl, escaping from her bickering parents, finds herself cohabiting with a group of drug junkies and social degenerates. The virus, which turns them all into homicidal maniacs, is bred from the noxious waste that seeps into the water supply. "There is something seriously wrong with this building," says the disillusioned graduate/model Tess (Lydia Hearst), perhaps the most interesting character here, who reflects on her academic disillusionment while taking a shower: "'What are you planning to do with this this degree in post-modern literature,' her father asked her in a soul-crushing but ultimately accurate fashion," she reminisces. And it is Tess who has the film's most significant lines as she raves about the gentrification caused by the likes of rich girl Maya (Dylan Penn). Before we arrive at that visceral, but also parodic moment (so appropriate for a student of post-modern literature), Maya is confronted by the leader of this unorthodox flat-share as she takes out the garbage. To take out garbage in this film has a sociological connotation, for her cohabitants are regarded by the police and by society in general as just that. Indeed, one of the characters (Cookie) is accidentally knocked down by a reversing police car, which then simply drives away as such a casualty is not deemed worth bothering about. The community leader who confronts Maya asks: "Do you mean that you're sorry, like when they [the police] find out that people are living here, illegally, are you sorry like that? Is that the kind of 'sorry' you're feeling? Or are you sorry that when the NYPD come here with their riot gear and tear gas and throw everybody in this building out into the cold, into the streets—I mean, are you sorry like *that*?"

Condemned rehearses all the old fears about what worried middle-class Victorians termed "the residuum" of society: the poor the dispossessed, the malcontents. How to contain them? How to deal with the fear that they might rise up and revolt, while simultaneously not wishing to invest in them? After one of the grisly attacks has taken place in the apartment block, Maya wants to phone for the police, but it is explained to her, "these people have shit. This building is all they have. It's their home. If you call the cops they'll have nowhere to live. We'll have nowhere to live!"

Tess' culminating rant, delivered with a carving knife that's been thrust into her bloody eye, says it all:

> Now who's going to hire me? You've ruined New York City. You know that, right? You rich girls, who grew up watching *Sex in the City* thinking it's all Cosmos and Jimmy Choos. So you get knocked up by some investment banker and make him buy you a loft in the fucking West Village. Well, you know who used to live in the West Village? People like me! Artistes, immigrants, Mark Twain, Jackson Pollock, Isadora fucking Duncan. Now, Manhattan's a fucking gated community and look where the little people end up: here! In a fucking abandoned building with a knife in my face.

Obviously, the film's body horror and infection are servants to Gesner's political agenda here, which aims to show just how much America has degenerated since the 1970s, when the apartment block was closed down.

Travis Zariwny's *Cabin Fever* in 2016 responded to the mass shootings that were by then characterizing a particularly self-destructive aspect of the American zeitgeist. A group of teenagers take a vacation in a woodland cabin but find themselves infected by a virus when a hermit drowns in a reservoir and, again like *The Crazies,* infects the water supply. One of the group, Karen (Gage Golightly), finds herself with an infected groin while having sex with her boyfriend, which somewhat dampens the mood, and during a fireside tale, we are treated to the sight of nails being driven into the backs of a group of tenpin bowlers (this has nothing to do with the film's plot, being merely a grisly aside). The unenlightened views of the far right are represented by local inhabitants, who know full well what has been going on: Infected people become cannibals, and dogs attack humans. (We briefly see the dog's POV, through a blood red filter, not unlike the camera work of Freddie Francis' *Legend of the Werewolf,* back in 1976, though there the similarities end.) Along with the inevitable shootings, infected children bite distraught teenagers, and a screwdriver is thrust though the ear and brains of a dim-witted local. Such violence is not exactly new (a comb had achieved the same result in Hammer's *To the Devil a Daughter,* when Honor Blackman's Anna Fountain is dispatched, and, of course, a similar thing happened to Milton Reid's Manservant in *Dr. Phibes Rises Again*), but *Cabin Fever* is a lot more bloodily cynical.

So too is *Viral* (dir. Ariel Schulman), also from 2016, by which time the infection trope was becoming somewhat repetitive. The suburban setting here provides a false sense of security, which the infection disrupts: A town is put into quarantine after an outbreak of "worm flu" which usefully combines the horror of maggots and corruption with that of an invisible virus. (Worms emerge from the orifices of the infected hosts.) The somewhat lame official advice is "Lock every window and every door," and so the military is eventually summoned, but the town is not obliterated, as was the case with the town in the previous year's *Hidden* (dir. Matt and Ross Duffer). The drastic action in that film was taken in an attempt to contain another deadly virus.

Things reached a pinnacle in John Suits' *Pandemic* in 2016, which combined dystopia, war and apocalypse with, as the title suggests, a viral infection. "You are humanity's last stand," screams the trailer, and it does indeed seem as if all those ecological protest groups such as Extinction Rebellion were wasting their time. Extinction does appear to be a kind of subconscious death wish in films like this—again suggesting that Benatar actually has more followers than he dares to hope for, even though they may be in denial. There are five types of survivor in *Pandemic*: those with flu-like symptoms, which were initially mistaken for Ebola; those who have begun to hemorrhage; those with brain damage from blood loss who are extremely aggressive; those who are in a hibernation stage, comatose and unresponsive before becoming murderous when they wake up (like the children in *Carriers* these unfortunates were about to be euthanized but the authors ran out of potassium chloride), and finally those with severe brain damage who are rabid and extremely vicious. Again, *Pandemic* is really a re-run of *The Crazies* in that the infected are slaughtered in military raids, but whereas *The Crazies* was a response to the Vietnam War, *Pandemic* takes on board the refined atrocities of the Iraq War, hence the emphasis on massacres in urban settings, which reflect that particular aspect of American foreign policy at the time. Needless to say, blood is smeared on every available surface and we are not denied a zombie ghoul with pale, emaciated face and blood red eyes.

This plethora of cinematic pandemics suggests a Zeitgeist at work, which seems to have been curiously predictive of the outbreak of the Covid-19 virus in 2020, the global response to which cannot wholly be separated from the panic and mass hysteria such films aim to stimulate.

Six

Mutation

> Animals are not brethren, they are not underlings; they are other nations, caught with ourselves in the net of life and time, fellow prisoners of the splendor and travail of the earth.
>
> —Henry Beston[1]

Animals suffer, of course, but they are never guilty. Necessity is their only law, for morality lies beyond their much simpler reality. Cioran puts it like this:

> A film about wild animals: endless cruelty in every latitude. "Nature" a torturer of genius, steeped in herself and her work, exults with good reason: there is not a moment when what is alive fails to tremble, to make others tremble.[2]

Horror films reference animals not to express their reality but, rather, our own. What we fear about them, apart from their ability to inflict physical harm, is what they reveal about ourselves. Some of the animals in horror films are merely zoological equivalents of human monsters, such as *Zoltan, Hound of Dracula* (dir. Albert Band, 1978), sometimes known more prosaically as *Dracula's Dog*. In this instance, alas, Zoltan lacks the Count's engaging personality. Horror films have always been fascinated by shapeshifting: the mutation of human into animal. In Hammer's *The Reptile* (dir. John Gilling, 1966) a young woman (Jacqueline Pearce) is cursed by a Malayan cult and becomes half human/half sndake, shedding her skin between bouts of terrorizing a Cornish village. *Dr. Renault's Secret* (dir. Harry Lachman, 1942) is revealed to be George Zucco's cross between a man and an ape in the form of J. Carrol Naish. *The Blood Beast Terror* (dir. Vernon Sewell, 1967) has Peter Cushing investigating a series of murders perpetrated by a woman (Wanda Ventham) who turns into a giant moth, while in *The Fly* (dir. Kurt Neumann, 1958 and later remade by David Cronenberg in 1987, who raised the level of graphic body horror), an insect's head is accidentally enlarged and transplanted onto a man's body. In *Return of the Fly* (dir. Edward Bernds, 1959), the fly does indeed return, along with another failed experiment at transmutation—the "rat man" with a rodent's hands and feet, but there is only one true mutant in the less obvious, much superior and British-made *The Curse of the Fly*, directed by Don Sharp in 1965. This mutant is the result of two deformed human experiments, teleported together and reintegrated as a mixture of body parts, soon dispatched with an axe by the Albert Delambre of Michael Graham. Cronenberg's version differs in the gradual transformation of the scientist Seth Brundle (Jeff Goldblum) from human to fly, along with the body horror cameos along the way (a baboon is turned inside out after a failed experiment; during an arm-wrestling match between Brundle and an overconfident opponent, the opponent suffers a double fracture, with bones exposed in classically Cronenberg style. Cronenberg also cannot resist the imagery of Seth pulling off one of his moribund fingernails, a grotesquerie that was, of course, recapitulated in England's *Contracted*). Cronenberg's version is consequently more of a metaphor for the process of aging and disintegration, but George Langelaan's original 1957 story on which all these fly films were based is really a popular version of Franz Kafka's short story "Metamorphosis," which appeared in 1915 during the real-life horrors of the First World War. The famous opening line, quoted by and rejected as "too good!" by Zero Mostell in Mel Brook's comedy *The Producers*, sums up the dilemma of "The Fly."

> As Gregor Samsa awoke one morning from uneasy dreams he found himself transformed in his bed into a gigantic insect. ...
> What has happened to me? he thought. It was no dream.[3]

Kafka's tale is often interpreted as an allegory of disability, the inability to operate one's own body in the way one used to, along with the way other people react to those changes—their reassessments, their strained tolerances and their often down-right rejections. Much the same can be said of "The Fly" and its film adaptations, and, as such, the story has a great deal to say not only about the terrors of the flesh and our sense of being imprisoned within it when the body malfunctions, but also of our attitude towards illness. Illness can corrode love and affection, affect our sense of identity, and cause us to question the nature of reality. What, after all, is real if what we thought of as certainty can change so drastically? "You're changing, Seth," says Geena Davis' Veronica in Cronenberg's *The Fly*. "Everything about you is changing. You look bad. You smell bad." These various versions of *The Fly* reflect the tragedies that take place in sickrooms all over the world.

Werewolf films are also tragic. The greatest of them all, *The Wolf Man* (dir. George Waggner, 1941), is also perhaps the most melancholy horror film ever made. Lon Chaney's Wolf Man, Larry Talbot, eloquently demonstrates the fundamentals of Schopenhauer's belief that a life lived without love is unendurable, while also making clear that a life requiring love to make it en-

Six. Mutation

Come into my parlor... Jeff Goldblum takes a meal in *The Fly* (dir. David Cronenberg, 1986).

durable is clearly futile in the first place, for it can have no satisfying meaning purely in its own terms. In his family life, Larry has suffered from repression and reservation. The Talbots, on the admission of his own father (played with great sympathy by Claude Rains) are of the "stiff-necked and undemonstrative" type, tendencies that have been carried to "very unhappy extremes."

"Don't I know that," Larry replies ruefully. Hence, we have a man who has not been encouraged to engage with his own emotions, let alone those of anyone else, which already marks him out as a suitable case for monstrous transformation—that classic mythical pressure value for repression. Of course, the werewolf legend allegorizes the need to sublimate our animal instincts before any civilized human relationship is possible (as we also observe in Jean Cocteau's 1946 *La belle et la bête,* which is at heart another werewolf film). Appropriately, Larry's potential girlfriend, Gwen Conliffe (Evelyn Ankers) works in a shop that advertises "Saneman Products" on the wall outside. Whatever these are in the retail sense, the name "Saneman" is psychologically revealing, for what makes men sane is the civilizing effect of love, but, fatally, Larry selects a wolf-headed cane decorated with a pentagram from her store, thus marking himself as one of the damned. The girl is already spoken for anyway, being engaged to be married to Frank Andrews (Patric Knowles), the manager of Larry's ancestral home, Talbot Castle, which is surrounded by fairytale forests, wreathed in swirling mist.

Having been bitten by the gypsy werewolf Bela (Bela Lugosi), Larry becomes a werewolf himself. In the struggle, Bela is killed by Larry's silver-headed cane, and Bela's mother, Maleva (Maria Ouspenskya), gives him her own version of the last rights. This amounts to a paraphrase of Adam's appeal to God in Milton's *Paradise Lost*, with which Mary Shelley introduced *Frankenstein*, combined with a certain Schopenhaurian insight into life's essential suffering.

> The way you walked was thorny
> Through no fault of your own.
> Your suffering is over, Bela, my son.

"There's something very tragic about that man," Frank had astutely observed of Larry, earlier in the film, but Frank lacks Larry's insight into the human condition and doesn't realize that he too is just as much a victim of that condition as anyone else. Larry's induction into werewolfdom, along with his various transformations, can usefully be read as metaphors of being born and becoming human in all its monstrousness and yearning: A werewolf after all has much more to do with human beings than with wolves. "Go now, and heaven help you," says Maleva, which is really all any mother can say to their children. Larry's release from the werewolf curse is similarly the release we all seek from the curse of life itself. Maleva sums up the whole process with the line, "Tears run to a predestined end."

Terence Fisher's approach to werewolves for Hammer Films takes a similarly tragic approach. Young Léon (Oliver Reed) is the product of a loveless coupling between a half-crazed beggar, unjustly imprisoned for many years, and a mute serving girl. This unfortunate origin (the equivalent of Talbot's emotionally repressed parents), is made worse by the fact that Léon is born on Christmas Day: an unwanted child born on the day of the Savior's birth is inevitably predestined for werewolf status, and thus does Léon's destiny prove to be. He, like Larry, finds relationships with women problematic, the werewolf within predominating over the human without, much as Mr. Hyde overwhelms Dr. Jekyll.

In 1981, by which time the traditional Gothic horrors of Hammer were seemingly beyond resurrection, John Landis unveiled his *An American Werewolf in London*, locating his creature in the traditional home of horror, but updating it with cynical dialogue and dwelling at great length on the gruesome physical mutation of his hero into a werewolf. Landis exploited the werewolf myth, much as Cronenberg did with *The Fly*, for its body horror potential. The physical pain of the transformation is emphasized, along with an almost clinical consideration of both its biological consequences and the physical scars of the werewolf's victim, Jack Goodman (Griffin Dunne). DC Superheroes such as The Incredible Hulk and Spiderman are relations of these more traditional transformations. The Hulk, like the werewolf, externalizes his inner psychosexual rage; while Spiderman, the victim of a radioactive arachnid, acquires the powers of the creature that has attacked him.

If wolves are the animals of choice when discussing the human condi-

Six. Mutation 115

A friend in need. Griffin Dunne as the mauled ghost of Jack in *An American Werewolf in London* (dir. John Landis, 1981).

tion from the male point of view, cats are more in tune with the feminine. Loosely based on Algernon Blackwood's tale "Ancient Sorceries," Val Lewton's *Cat People* (dir. Jacques Tourneur, 1942) is the most famous example of this, with kitten-faced Simone Simon terrified by the more sinister feline features of Elizabeth Russell into believing that she is the victim of an ancient Serbian curse, which turns her into a killer cat. Here, the imagery concerns the destructive aspects of the anima, rather than the animus of the wolf, and though the film is far more ambivalent about the physical transformation of Simon's Irena (taking a much more overtly psychological approach to the story), the implication is the same. Irena finds life intolerable due to her "curse" and eventually commits suicide, having been unable to consummate her marriage due to her fear of intimate physical contact and of passing on the cat curse to her children. Irena's fears are explained as the consequences of similar childhood traumas to those suffered by Larry and Léon, and her apparent transformation is the result of unwanted but uncontrollable sexual feelings, as is the case with the werewolves. That Irena finds the burden of living too great again suggests a parallel with the anti-natalist agenda. Despite a man who loves her and gives her every encouragement, her life is simply not worth the suffering it brings with it.

With *The Uncanny* (dir. Denis Héroux, 1977), Peter Cushing plays Wilbur, a neurotic writer who is convinced that cats are trying to organize a *coup d'etat* against humanity. This is hardly news to any one who has ever owned one, and the film doesn't take itself too seriously, but Wilbur's observation, "We think we're the masters and they're merely pets, but we're wrong. They're the masters," was more seriously handled in both Alfred Hitchcock's *The Birds* and *Planet of the Apes* (dir. Franklin J. Schaffner, 1968). In both cases, animals are shown to usurp humanity's traditional place at the top of the food chain, but for reasons that have much more psychological insight than *The Uncanny*. *The Birds*, unlike other Hitchcock movies, presents no obvious narrative resolution at the end. As Donald Spoto remarks, "Federico Fellini called it an apocalyptic poem,"[4] and the multi-layered symbolism of the birds themselves does indeed function poetically and allusively, facilitating multiple interpretations. The birds can in particular be viewed as metaphors of feminine anima—the callous cruelties of the various female characters in their struggle for the sexual favors of Mitch Brenner (Rod Taylor). The avian attacks begin in the previously peaceful Bogeda Bay setting only when the brittle and distinctly selfish Melanie Daniels (Tippi Hedren) arrives, and it is not long before the birds kill one of her rivals, Annie Hayworth (Suzanne Pleshette). (Spoto compares this aspect of the story to a comment made by the bird-obsessed Norman Bates in Hitchcock's previous *Psycho*, in which he observes that we all "scratch and claw, but only at the air, only at each other."[5]) This is only the first killing, however, and perhaps most obvious layer of Hitchcock's complex onion. The apocalyptic elements suggested by Fellini also reflect the period in which the film was made, only months after the Cuban missile crisis, which brought the world to the brink of nuclear war. The attack of the birds is a powerful expression of this anxiety, especially given the traditional association of birds as harbingers of death. There is also a prescient ecological aspect at work, in which the bird attacks represent the revenge of nature on humanity and its destructive exploitation of natural resources. All these interpretations are valid and together inform the poetic power of the film, but even more powerful is Hitchcock's concern with the vulnerability of the body and our complacency with regard to it. Schopenhauer, whose writings were of course well-known to Hitchcock, would have found much to admire in *The Birds*, as it is a graphic depiction of his theory that life moves from striving to survive, thence to boredom and subsequently back to striving. For Schopenhauer, the process is essentially painful and cruel:

> The life of the great majority is only a constant struggle for this same existence, which the certainly of ultimately losing it. What enables them to endure this wearisome battle is not so much the love of life as the fear of death, which nevertheless stands in the background as inevitable, and which may come on the scene at any moment....
>
> [It] is worth that, as soon as want and suffering give man a relaxation, boredom is at once so near that he necessarily requires diversion and amusement. The striving after existence is what occupies all living things, and keeps them in motion. When existence

is assured to them, they do not know what to do with it. Therefore the second thing that sets them in motion is the effort to get rid of the burden of existence, to make it no longer felt, "to kill time," in other words to escape from boredom.[6]

One of the most celebrated scenes in *The Birds* clearly illustrates this passage: Melanie sits outside a school, waiting to talk to Annie. Behind her, ominous black birds gather on a children's climbing frame. Melanie is bored at first, smoking a cigarette as there is nothing else to do, but when the birds begin to attack, she must fight for survival. The fact that the birds then attack the school children who have previously been chanting a highly repetitive song inside the school, amplifies the Schopenhauerian allusion. We carry the horror of the body around with us throughout life, but only realize our predicament when external forces press it upon us.

The nightmare imagery of this scene is also indebted to the ominous mood of Edward Hopper's alienated landscapes and lonely houses. (The schoolhouse itself distinctly echoes the Bates house in *Psycho,* which was also based on Hopper's example.) The mood of nightmares is usually rooted in the mundanity of reality, which has been weirdly transformed into a context of anxiety and terror. Hitchcock himself said that he did not make costume dramas, because the people in those kind of films never went to the toilet. "You see, it's the juxtaposition of the norm, of the accurate average, against the fantasy. ... That's what makes the thing interesting."[7] Nightmares are never irrelevant adjuncts to reality; they are psychological *comments* on reality, and that reality is unquestionably a nightmare for those who approach reality in realistic terms, stripped of its moral and what Benatar calls its Pollyanna principles: "We tend to have an exaggerated view of how good things will be," he explains. "The Pollyannaism [a tendency towards optimism] typical of recall and projection is also characteristic of subjective judgments about current and overall well-being. Many studies have consistently shown that self-assessments of well-being are markedly skewed towards the positive end of the spectrum."[8]

Hitchcock makes quite clear the basic horror of the body by showing in such graphic detail how easy and yet how horrible it is to die. Out of normality and seemingly benign environments, death, as Schopenhauer observes, can strike at any moment and for no reason at all. The shock of the pecked-out eyes of the dead farmer who is discovered by Jessica Tandy's Lydia is an extreme example of this visceral horror (and may also refer the audience to the myth of Oedipus, who similarly plucked out his own eyes in despair at having unwittingly married his own mother. If so, it furnishes another possible interpretation of the relationship between Lydia and Mitch), but Hitchcock's critical depiction of the latent horror that surrounds us even in the most mundane of situations is the moment of the avian attack at a gas station: Melanie finds herself caged, like the "bird" she is, in a telephone box while burning petroleum consumes everything around her and the birds attack everyone in sight. Ultimately, Hitchcock transforms our point of view to an aerial shot from high above the mayhem, where birds assemble before swooping down like divebombers to increase the carnage down below. There is no real dramatic meaning here. Hitchcock's aim is a purely poetic one, creating a powerful visual symbol of existential horror. To be born is automatically to made vulnerable to pain and subject to death.

Because of our desire to maintain what we regard as our own corporeal normality, freak shows featuring abnormal or damaged bodies have always held a grim fascination for cinema audiences. Early in the history of the horror film, Tod Browning's *Freaks* caused such offense that it remained banned in the United Kingdom for 30 years after its original release in 1932. MGM was accused of inducing a woman to suffer a miscarriage while watching screen tests; faced with critical condemnation and public outrage, several scenes were cut, which so far have not been rediscovered. After that debacle, Browning's career never really recovered. Greater understanding now acknowledges *Freaks* as the counter-cultural masterpiece it is; far from being an exploitation of deformity we can now see it clearly as an indictment of the vile way in which a "normal" woman treats those less fortunate than herself in the pursuit of material wealth.

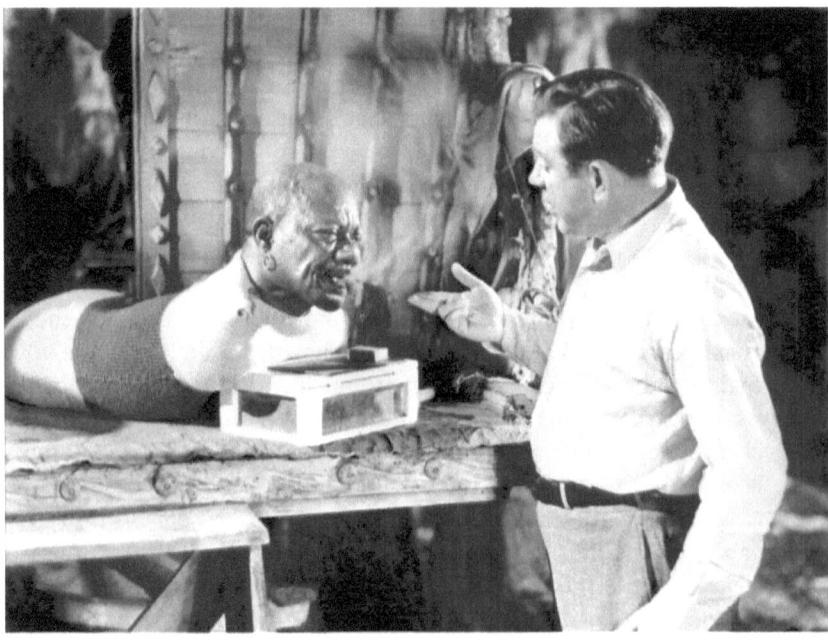

Alternative living. Prince Randian as "The Living Torso" with Johnny Eck as "Half Boy" in *Freaks* (dir. Tod Browning, 1932).

The film apparently explains its approach in the rolling script of the opening frames. This informs us, "in ancient times anything that deviated from the normal was considered an omen of ill luck or representative of evil."

> Gods of misfortune and adversity were invariably cast in the form of monstrosities, and deeds of injustice and hardship had been attributed to the many crippled and deformed tyrants of Europe and Asia. ... The accident of abnormal birth was considered a disgrace and malformed children were placed out in the elements to die. If, perchance, one of these freaks nature survived he was always regarded with suspicion. Society shunned him because of his deformity and a family so hampered was always ashamed of the curse put upon it. Occasionally one of these unfortunates was taken to court to be jeered at or ridiculed for the amusement of the nobles. Others were left to eek out a living by begging, stealing or starving, for the love of beauty is a deep seated urge which dates back to the beginning of civilization. The revulsion with which we view the abnormal, the malformed and the mutilated is the result of long conditioning by our forefathers. The majority of freaks themselves are endowed with normal thoughts and emotions. Their lot is truly a heart-breaking one.

Doubts remain, however, as to Browning's real motivation. After all, *Freaks* was marketed as a horror film. We are invited to be horrified and even to be repelled, just as much as we are encouraged to be sympathetic. "But for the accident of birth you might be as they are," says the freak show exhibitor at the beginning of the film. "They didn't ask to be brought into the world but into the world they came," he continues, suggesting, perhaps that we should be just as horrified by ourselves as by the freaks, but in the final chase scene in which the freaks crawl like animals in pursuit of Olga, the trapeze artist, who has offended the freaks code by theft and unfaithfulness, Browning loses no opportunity to exploit his assembly of grotesques for horror effect.

The sequence takes place during a Gothic thunderstorm, and summons comparison with *The Island of Lost Souls* (dir. Erle C. Kenton). Made in same year and continuing Hollywood's portrait of the West's state of mind in the 1930s, with the Depression haunting capitalism in America and fascism looming over European civilization, *The Island of Lost Souls* has Charles Laughton as Dr. Moreau, a white-suited sadist, intent on turning animals into human beings, with only limited success. The closer the animals are manipulated towards humanity the more they suffer. The premise of the film (and the novel by H.G. Wells on which it is based) has much in common with that of Heinrich von Kleist's 1810 essay on "The Puppet Theater," which later so inspired Philip Pullman's *His Dark Materials* trilogy. Kleist argues here that the only way to regain the "grace" of paradise, from which consciousness has excluded us, is either to have "no consciousness or an infinite amount of it."[9] Unfortunately, the "humanimals" in *The Island of Lost Souls* are denied this and must remain, like the rest of us, in the unfortunate state of paradise lost to which consciousness has condemned us.

Hindsight allows us to view the scene in which Moreau is discovered at his unholy surgical work as an uncanny premonition of the medical horrors of Auschwitz, but in those countries where the film was banned at the time of its release, condemnation was usually along the lines that it was an affront to nature. ("Of course it's against nature," Laughton's wife, Elsa Lanchester, quipped. "So's Mickey Mouse."[10]) Again, the critical rage was really the rage of Caliban at his own reflection, and what was soon to overtake world events would prove this only this too well. The horror we have of ourselves knows no bounds, and must therefore be strictly contained or laughed to scorn. It is for this reason that horror films have always suffered adverse criticism along with other materialistic philosophies.

Both *Freaks* and *The Island of Lost Souls* informed two vegetable variations on this theme. The first was Hammer's *The Quatermass Experiment*, which paved the way for the company's *The Curse of Frankenstein* in 1957. Richard Wordsworth portrays a "monstrous" human being, who gradually mutates into a predatory plant-like organism after his return from a space mission. One of the film's most compelling shock scenes shows Wordsworth's Caroon (whose first name is Victor, like Frankenstein's), thrusting his hand into a cactus under the influence the alien entity within him. The scientist who is studying Caroon realizes that he is now "only the shell of a man being transformed. If one of these cacti is subject to the same mutation there could be an affinity—a union—between plant and animal," with the ability to multiply at will. By the end of the film, amid the Gothic arches of Westminster abbey, Caroon has completely transformed into a gigantic, octopus-like Lovecraftian monster ("It must be twenty feet across!"), in which the human element has been completely absorbed by the cactus. Such a transformation is more unnerving than "mere" animal metamorphosis. Most of those transformations take the shape of mammals, with which we have so much in common. Reptilian transformations are, of course, rather more alien in effect, but mutation into a plant is a much wider genetic leap to take. Again, the horror of sex and the language of infection are added to the mix to increase our anxiety. Earlier on we have been introduced to this thing's reproductive prowess, but now it is "twenty times the power of reproduction. Those nodules: if they get to spore this time nothing will stop them. They'll break out. They'll spread by the million wherever there's air and wind."

In Jack Cardiff's *The Mutations*, Professor Nolter similarly creates a hybrid of plant and animal. The images that illustrate Nolter's opening lecture, which we have already encountered, are accompanied by indeterminate roaring sounds on the soundtrack, lending them an alien, animal-like nature. "This is not a flower," he explains, "however much it may resemble one." We see next a sea anemony: "It is an animal with certain characteristics that normally one would expect to see only in plants."

After his disquisition on carnivorous vegetables, Nolter informs his stu-

Six. Mutation 121

Meat and veg. One of the experiments in *The Mutations* (dir. Jack Cardiff, 1974).

dents: "You may think you are normal, but you are all the product of mutation. Your ancestors—*our* ancestors—were *freaks*, who only survived because they were stronger than the other forms of life around them." Unfortunately, Nolter's own experiments result in monstrous vegetable mutations.

This idea had been explored earlier by Gustav Meyrinck in his 1905 story "Dr. Cinderella's Plants," in which the eponymous Doctor cultivates similar plant-animal hybrids:

> Everywhere the same wooden trellis-work and, as I could now clearly see, overgrown with veins, evidently all patched together in which blood was coursing. In amongst them countless eyeballs glistened horribly, sprouting alternately with hideous warty nodules like blackberries. Eyes of all sizes and colours, from brightly shining irises to the light blue tone of the eye of a dead horse, fixed immovably upwards. Some, shrunken and black, looked like over-ripe nightshade berries. The main stems twisted their way out of jars filled with blood, drawing up their juice by means of some unfathomable process....
>
> And all seemed to be parts of living bodies, fitted together with indescribable art, robbed of any human soul, and reduced merely to vegetative organisms.[11]

Following on from Thomas Mann's observations about Nature, Nolter believes that "all living things are closely related—and all matter is related." His aim to create a new species "composed of the characteristics of both plants and animals ... plants able to move ... animals able to harness the rays of the sun directly through photosynthesis, absorbing nourishment through exposure to light." He justifies this program by his fear that humanity is facing extinction. Like some kind of Nazi botanist, Nolter wants to create "a new race of men with all the miraculous properties of a plant." The purple light in which he is bathed as he pronounces this ambition (one of Jack Cardiff's more painterly touches) emphasizes the decadence of his program. Like the frog earlier fed to the plant in *The Werewolf of London,* Nolter now feeds his huge and greedy Venus Fly Trap with a live rabbit. "Regretfully, this is necessary," he explains with sanguine indifference, Pleasence obviously relishing the ghoulish absurdity of the moment, which cleared the path, so to speak, for the man-eating, Muppet-like plant in Frank Oz's *Little Shop of Horrors* in 1986: "Feed me, Seymore!"

Nolter's activities have distinct echoes of Dr. Moreau's Nazi inspired experiments, but there is also a subplot concerning a group of circus freaks, 10 in all (including their diminutive ring master): a Bearded Lady, a Monkey Woman, a Human Pincushion, the Frog Boy, the Alligator Skin Girl, the Human Skeleton, the Pretzel Man, Popeye (literally) and the Lizard Woman of Tibet. At one stage, during a birthday party, they even chant, "We accept you. He's one of us," echoing the famous chant of "We accept her: one of us," in Browning's *Freaks.*

By far the most troubling mutations, however, are those that reorganize human anatomy and contaminate it with those of other species. This happens a great deal in John Carpenter's 1982 remake of Christian Nyby's 1951 *The Thing,* and, even more so, in Matthijs van Heijningen, Jr.'s 2011 prequel to that film with the same title. In both films, an alien entity, of no permanent shape itself, infects a group of scientists in a remote Antarctic research base, and replicates their human forms until its real genetic nature breaks out and combines with other humans, mostly by consuming them. The restructuring of human anatomy is disturbing enough, but what seems to unnerve audiences most is van Heijningen's combination of human forms with insects (particularly spiders) and elements of sea life. Such "alien" forms had previously been exploited by H.P. Lovecraft for his Cthulu mythology, as in this passage from "The Call of Cthulhu."

> The awful squid-head with writhing feelers came nearly up to the bow-sprit of the sturdy yacht, but Johansen drove on relentlessly. There was a bursting as of an exploding bladder, a slushy nastiness as of a cloven starfish, a stench as of a thousand opened graves.[12]

The natural world may be beautiful but it is also horrifying. As Oscar Wilde knew so well, "all art is at once symbol and surface. Those who go beneath the surface do so at their peril."[13] The surface beauties of the world disguise a myriad of horrors in their struggle to survive. Living, as we do, at the top of the food chain, we face no pressing fears of being eaten, but we can imagine it nonetheless. The eating habits of spiders and insects in general are usually considered to be revolting, but we are hardly without our own disgusting feeding habits. We too must kill food and consume it. In van Heijningen's *The Thing*, we observe an autopsy of one of these shape-shifting aliens, which reveals the half-digested body of its human prey. The thought of being the meal of a hideous alien monstrosity is obviously disturbing, but the reality underlying such anxiety is the unease we have with our own digestive processes. We would rather not think that the bacon sandwich we have just eaten is actually a pig, and thus abstract our chosen food products from their biological origins. Even vegetables can be worrying. Significantly, in Nyby's *The Thing*, the alien, though possessing only one form (which is reminiscent of Boris Karloff's Monster in *Frankenstein*), it is referred to as a giant carrot by the men on the research base, and they accordingly "cook" it with an electrical charge.

But we do not need to travel to other planets to discover disturbing alternative realities. The hidden landscape of the body is itself an alien world that haunts the surface reality of our lives. We cannot touch this hidden reality by any means other than accident, surgery or violence, and it is for this reason that we dread it and find it loathsome, while remaining utterly dependent upon it. We do not wish to visit this strange world within us, which we carry around every day of our lives but which is largely unknown and mysterious to us. Nonetheless, it is our only reality. Our organs are essential but simultaneously horrifying, their fleshy, bloody, slimy qualities, their pulsating animation, their appetites, their secretions seem somehow independent of our conscious sense of self and they accordingly revolt us. In fact, we do with our internal anatomy what we do when consuming food, preferring to ignore, or at least abstract it. This revulsion against our inner selves ensures a reaction when human anatomy is exposed, especially when it is rearranged or contaminated by the anatomy of creatures whose eating habits repel us even more.

We are all waiting to become cadavers, and there is perhaps nothing more terrifying than our own flesh and blood. When we see our organs exposed, it is like diving into the depths of the ocean and discovering terrifying, viscous sea creatures with goggle eyes and devouring mouths. We carry a monster within, which illness occasionally reveals to us, like the hinted horrors we read about in Lovecraft's subterranean tales. Indeed, the fleshly horrors that lie beneath the seemingly untroubled surfaces of our skins are what Lovecraft's characteristic art is really all about. The primordial vocabulary of "Yog-Sothoth," so often heard in Lovecraftian incantations is nothing more than the sound of our own corporeal functions: the gurgling of our bodily fluids, the pulsation of our blood, the creaking of our bowels and their concomitant stench. When Lovecraft describes his eldritch horrors, he is really presiding over an autopsy:

> The odour arising from the newly opened depths was intolerable, and at length the quick-eared Hawkins thought he heard a nasty, slapping sound down there. Everyone listened and everyone was listening still when It lumbered slobberingly into sight and gropingly squeezed Its gelatinous green immensity through the black doorway into the tainted outside air of that poison city of madness.[14]

Cthulhu lies deep within each one of us.

Any human encounter—from shaking hands, to penetrating a lover—is really a confrontation with a towering abomination of quivering meat, a sack of surging blood and sticky secretions, foul-smelling fleshy tubes and twitching muscles. The American fantasy writer, Fitz-James O'Brien, was very much aware of this when writing his astonishing 1857 story "Seeing the World," which very much foreshadowed Roger Corman's highly metaphysical science fiction film, *X—The Man with X-Ray Eyes* (1963). The hero of O'Brien's story is a poet called Cipriano, who has been given the power to see *everything* in the world—an X-ray vision indeed:

> Through the garments and the flesh he saw the triangular artery called the heart beating in the young girl's bosom. He saw the blood coursing up to the roots of her hair, and forming the delicate blush upon the cheeks that he had loved so much. Wretched man! In those eyes so beautiful and full of love he found nothing more than a species of *camera obscura*, made of a reticulated membrane and a drop of liquid. In that graceful walk, he saw only the play of ingenious mechanism. Alas! Charlotte was no longer an angel upon earth for him, and the object of his purest hopes. She was nothing more in his eyes than an anatomical preparation.[15]

There is indeed little to distinguish the hidden reality of our own bodies from the monsters in *The Thing*, where what seem to be human comrades turn out actually to be hideously voracious life forms, which have merely imitated human shapes, lurking within them until they mutate into hybrids of human, spider and jellyfish, with devouring mouths and monstrous appetites. The monsters in van Heijningen's *The Thing* are really only ourselves turned inside out, combined with our anxieties about the natural world in which we are forced to live. Such films exorcise our biology, externalizing them as "other" and not what, deep-down, we know to be our own reality. All our worst antisocial prejudices, all our hatred of the "other" ultimately derives from the loathing we have of ourselves. Jonathan Walker's character, Colin, in van Heijningen's *The Thing*, says, at one point, "This is wrong." He is talking about the paranoia that has led to unjust persecution among his colleagues, who can no longer trust each other, knowing that one of them is in fact an alien imitation, but in a larger sense, his comment applies to the rearranging of human anatomies. It is "wrong" to see our own bodily organs, and even more wrong to regard parts of our own anatomy combined with spider's legs and the tentacles, sucking mouths and scales of unknown sea life. We long for biological purity and order. The dangers of racism and misogyny are consequently never far away, and Lovecraft was indeed one of their number. Racists project the horror they have of the "alien" elements within their own bodies onto others. The ancient Greeks celebrated our Apollonian appearance in their statues, but body horror movies are monuments to our inner Dionysian reality.

Cronenberg's *Dead Ringers* features a "sexual mutant"—an actress called Claire Niveau (Geneviève Bujold). She has a "trifurcated cervix," which means that she is very unlikely to have children, but this is really incidental to the film's main story concerning two identical twins, both played by Jeremy Irons, who have sexual relations with Niveau. The elder twin, Elliot, begins the affair and then encourages his more introverted brother, Beverly, to take over, suggesting that he pretends to be Elliot. When Claire discovers the deception she is outraged, but continues to see Beverly, who now finds himself falling in love with her. This causes a rift between the two brothers who are so close that there is really no room for a loving relationship with anyone else to come between them without profound psychological consequences. The two brothers therefore use Niveau and other women to sublimate their own almost hermaphrodite love for each other. In this drama about identity, Cronenberg seems to be suggesting that where sex is involved, we are all no more than objects—obscure objects of desire, to use the title of Luis Buñuel's 1977 film. It is no coincidence that they are both also gynecologists, who are distinctly cavalier and chauvinistic in the way they examine the genital areas of their patients. There is a great deal of red: red clinical robes, red clothing, and incidental red objects such as a truck, a traffic cone, furnishings, etc. The implication of menstrual blood is obvious.

Beverly and Elliot are so dependent upon one another they resemble the situation of Siamese twins. Indeed, Cronenberg's visualization of a dream experienced by one of them demonstrates this graphically, by showing both men actually joined at the waist by a gruesomely fleshy growth, which the woman whom Beverley is having sex with at the time attempts to sever with her teeth. To ramp up his sex life, Beverly starts to take drugs and becomes an addict. (He collapses in one scene and it is significant that Elliot pushes Niveau away to give him the kiss of life. "Don't touch him," he shouts. "He's my brother.") The addiction distorts Beverly's grip on reality and he comes to resemble one of the characters in Jean Lorrain's decadent novel, *Monsieur de Phocas,* who "was always in a kind of waking sleep, stupefied by opium. His vitreous eyes and his bloodless complexion seemed to have preserved all the oppressive lethargy of Oriental poisons."[16] Obsessed by Claire's "mutant" cervix, Beverly increasingly believes that all patients look fine on the outside, but inside they are deformed, and this contrasts with Elliot's earlier statement that we should learn to see the beauty of our insides not merely the shell of external appearance.

Beverly eventually looses contact with reality altogether, commissioning a series of eccentric medical instruments with which he surgically murders his brother in a grotesquely symbolic "operation" to separate himself from his sibling. All of which brings me to the bodily horror of insanity.

Seven

Disintegration

"We forgive only madmen and children for being frank with us: others if they have the audacity to imitate them, will regret it sooner of later."

—E.M. Cioran[1]

A great many horror films end in physical disintegration: the vampire is staked and the cheated centuries catch up with him; flesh falls away from Dracula's skeleton, which then turns to dust; deprived of its mystical life force the mummy collapses in a tangle of bandages and desiccated bones; Frankenstein's unfortunate monster has been subjected to dissection, incineration and immersion in acid, while those who attempt to cheat death by means of various elixirs usually come to a similarly catastrophic collapse. Dorian Gray's portrait is corrupted by the sins of its model; the years catch up with Anton Diffring at the end of *The Man Who Could Cheat Death* (dir. Terence Fisher, 1959). "I'm going to die!" he shouts, which, of course, applies to all of us. Even Ursula Andress' immortal Ayesha disintegrates at the end of *She* (dir. Robert Day, 1965), which H. Rider Haggard had described in his original novel with a rather cruel misogyny:

> Smaller she grew, and smaller yet, till she was no larger than a monkey. Now the skin was puckered into a million wrinkles, and on the shapeless face was the stamp of unutterable age. I never saw anything like it; nobody ever saw anything like the frightful age that was graven on that fearful countenance, no bigger now than that of a two-months' child, though the skull remained the same size, or nearly so, and let all men pray they never may, if they wish to keep their reason.
> At last she lay still, or only feebly moving. She, who but two minutes before had gazed upon us the loveliest, noblest, most splendid woman the world has ever seen, she lay still before us, near the masses of her own dark hair, no larger than a big monkey, and hideous—ah, too hideous for words![2]

In Terence Fisher's sci-fi package, *Island of Terror*, the distinctly low-budget Silicate monsters dissolve human bone, leaving "just a horrible mush with the eyes sitting in it," according to Sam Kydd's policeman, who eventually suffers the same fate, and how many horror films feature those most poetic lines from the Book of Common Prayer, which form the hallowed service for the dead?

> ...Man that is born of a woman hath but a short time to live, and is full of misery. He cometh up, and is cut down, like a flower; he fleeth as it were a shadow, and never continueth in one stay.... In the midst of life we are in death ... earth to earth, ashes to ashes, dust to dust.

We must all eventually disintegrate, and it is due to this shared fate, which we spend most of our lives trying to ignore and avoid, that we have horror films in the first place. 2007 even saw a film entitled *Disintegration* (dir. Roger McLeod). "He's coming undone. He's coming unglued, ... coming apart at the seams. His life in unraveling," the trailer explains, but the disintegration here is more mental than physical in a film that finds holding itself together even more of a challenge.

Convention argues that we should also fear the collapse of reason, for reason is the artificial plot each human "novelist" imposes upon the essentially irrational, plot-less nature of existence. When reason collapses, we enter raw reality, rather like walking into a radioactive zone without protective clothing. Lunatics, who until relatively recently had always been seen as a danger to society, were consequently isolated in asylums.

Madness appears to have been of particular interest to director Ken Russell. All his composer biopics (which all contain a strong doses of fantasy) feature mad scenes. In *Mahler* (1974) Robert Powell's Mahler visits David Collings' Hugo Wolf in his asylum. Hugo thinks he is the Emperor of Austria. Later, naked in his cell, he wipes his bottom with one of his own songs: "The critics say that's all they're fit for!" he complains. His madness is attributed to having had to conduct the music of other men while failing to have his own even acknowledged, let alone performed. In Russell's Tchaikovsky film, *The Music Lovers*, Tchaikovsky's ill-fated bride, Antonina Miliukova, similarly ends her days in an asylum. "He's never loved another woman, has he, mother?" she asks, preferring to forget the fact that the man who was once her husband is a homosexual. "But I have so many lovers!" she proclaims, as grimy hands reach up between her legs from the dungeon grille on which she stands. In *Lisztomania* (1975), Richard Wagner, as portrayed by Paul Nicholas, is presented a combination of Count Dracula and Baron Frankenstein, who steals Liszt's music to make his Aryan superman, Siegfried, live. Later, he becomes a version of Karloff's Frankenstein monster, shooting Jews with a glam-rock gun-guitar. For Russell, Wagner was definitely mad, but he reserved his greatest mad scenes for *The Devils* (1971) where Christianity drives an entire convent of nuns insane with lust. The body horror depicted here very much involves the disintegration of reason.

Seven. Disintegration

Insanity also informs much of Bram Stoker's *Dracula,* the arch vampire's slave, Renfield, being an inmate at Dr. Seward's sanatorium. Renfield fluctuates between lucidity and seeming incoherence, though what Seward regards as zoophagous degeneracy (the eating of flies) Renfield regards as a quite rational aspect of his devotion to the vampire. Renfield believes that the blood is the life, that the more blood he consumes the longer his life will last. He graduates from flies to kittens and ultimately receives the Count in a kind of vampire communion, but Renfield breaks faith with his master and Dracula responds by murdering him. A John the Baptist figure, Renfield heralds the arrival of a vampire Messiah in Victorian England. He thus finds himself suffering a similar fate to his Biblical model: Dracula may not decapitate him but he does breaks Renfield's neck. In Gerald Savory's television adaptation of the novel for the BBC in 1977 (still the most faithful), Renfield (Jack Shepherd) is much concerned with the transience of life and his own corresponding desire for immortality. He quotes William Blake's poem "The Fly," which, in a curious way, suggests the horror film of that name and its remake by David Cronenberg in 1987:

> Little Fly
> Thy summer's play,
> My thoughtless hand
> Has brush'd away.
>
> Am not I
> A fly like thee?
> Or art not thou
> A man like me?
>
> For I dance
> And drink & sing;
> Till some blind hand
> Shall brush my wing.[3]

Renfield's fear of death has led him into the dark corridors of immortality, but at the eleventh hour he realizes his mistake: it is not death but life itself that is the real enemy. Death, on the contrary, is a liberator. The Christian context of the tale gives this new understanding a metaphysical significance: Renfield's only way into paradise is to recant his devotion to earthly life. Having discussed the subject of souls with Mina Harker (Judi Bowker), a subject for which he formally had no interest, he pleads with Dr. Seward (Mark Burns) to let him leave the sanatorium to escape the wrath of Dracula and retain his own soul: "Dr. Seward, you must let me go at once from here. Now: This very hour. Let them take me in a straight waistcoat. Manacled! Leg-ironed! Even to prison, but let me go!" He gets down on his knees: "I'm not a lunatic in a mad fit. I'm a sane man fighting for his freedom!" But Dr. Seward does not permit this, and, as Renfield predicted, Dracula's next visit to him certainly brings death but not paradise. Sade, Schopenhauer and Nietzsche would all, of course, have felt that Renfield's real madness was his ultimate acceptance of the soul at the expense of continuing to invest his energies in the body.

In John Badham's film remake of the story in 1977, much is made of Dr. Seward's lunatic asylum, which is here much bigger and far more populated than the one in the BBC version. The asylum scenes here are a clear metaphor of the fact that irrational urges underlie the orderly world of apparently rational civilization: the sanatorium is physically attached to Seward's elegantly furnished Victorian living quarters. Here, Seward (Donald Pleasence) and his daughter Lucy (Kate Nelligan) greet their new neighbor, the urbane, handsome, witty, sophisticated, exquisitely mannered psychopath that is Frank Langella's Count Dracula.

Badham's film constantly exploits our anxiety that the lunatics will break free, and, like Dracula, contaminate civilization. The prime text in this regard is Edgar Allan Poe's 1845 story "The System of Doctor Tarr and Professor Fether," in which a visitor to a lunatic asylum discovers that the inmates are actually running the institution themselves. The superintendent of the asylum "grew crazy himself, and so became a patient." But he escapes and with the help of other inmates overpowers the keepers who were "first well tarred, then carefully feathered, and then shut up in underground cells."[4] Poe's idea formed the basis of the father of all horror films, Robert Wiene's *The Cabinet of Dr. Caligari* in 1919. Inspired by the aftermath of the First World War, Wiene demonstrated, with catastrophic clarity, that civilization is merely a cage for the homicidal tendencies we all have in common. In *Caligari*, the director of the lunatic asylum in which the story is framed, is ultimately exposed as a madman himself. Obsessed by the story of an 18th-century mystic called Caligari, this director (Werner Krauss) has experimented on one of his own somnambulist patients (Conrad Veidt), using him to commit a series of murders along the lines of the original 18th-century Caligari and his somnambulistic accomplice, Cesare. The film thus works admirably as an allegory of the murderous German State and its over-obedient population, but it also has wider implications about human civilization in general: Does insanity lie at the heart of all human behavior?

A less powerful, though still enjoyable variation on this theme occurs in Roy Ward Baker's 1972 film for Amicus, *Asylum*, which is also derived from Poe's tale in which the Maison de Santé is described "a fantastic château." The spectacular building in *Asylum* (New Lodge in Winkfield, Berkshire) is in rather better repair than Poe's "much dilapidated, and indeed scarcely tenantable"[5] one, but director of the asylum, one Dr. Starr (a disguised allusion to Poe's title), is just as murderously insane.

Such stories exploit our more general distrust and/or resentment of all authority figures in life, who often seem to be presiding over a nightmare in which reality is revealed to be really only a matter of opinion. Schopenhauer certainly felt this to be the case:

> A clear and complete insight into the nature of madness, a correct and distinct conceptions what really distinguishes the sane from the insane, has, so far as I know, never yet been found. Neither the faculty of reason nor understanding can be denied to the mad, for they talk and understand, and often draw very accurate conclusions. They also, as a rule, perceive quite correctly what is present, and see the connexion between cause and effect. Visions, like the fancies of an overwrought brain, are no ordinary symptom of madness; delirium falsifies perception, madness the thoughts. For the most part, mad people do not generally err in the knowledge of what is immediately present; but their mad talk relates always to what is absent and past, and only through these to its connexion with what is present. Therefore, it seems to me that their malady specially concerns the memory. It is not, indeed, a case of memory failing them entirely, for many of them know a great deal by heart, and sometimes recognize persons whom they have not seen for a long time. Rather it is a case of the thread of memory being broken, its continuous connexion being abolished, and of the impossibility of a uniformly coherent recollection of the past. ... In his memory the true is for ever mixed up with the false. Although the immediate present is correctly known, it is falsified through a fictitious connexion with an imaginary past. Mad people therefore consider themselves and others as identical with persons who live merely in their fictitious past.[6]

It is certainly the case that the same event may easily be remembered in quite differing ways by those who experience it. Reality is really only what we make of it, and it is reason's unsettling kinship with insanity that both attracts us to and repels us from the subject. Madness is so fascinating because it is so close to us, and this fascination was eloquently explored in *Bedlam* (dir. Mark Robson, 1946), one of Val Lewton's elegant fantasy films made for RKO. *Bedlam* was marketed as a lurid horror feature, promising vicarious chills from the "loonies," as Boris Karloff's character, Master Sims calls them. In fact, *Bedlam* is far more of an historical drama concerned with both the inhumanity of man to his less fortunate fellows, and encouraging a compassionate approach to those who differ from the perceived norm. Anna Lee as Nell Bowen begins by sharing the unsympathetic views of her class, laughing at the "loonies" and claiming to have no pity for these "animals without souls," but at an entertainment organized by Sims, at which he exhibits his "loonies" for the entertainment of assembled aristocrats and politicians, she changes her mind, finding it uncomfortable to laugh at such unfortunates, especially when one of them (Glenn Vernon), dressed ironically as an allegorical figure of "The Golden Age of Reason" expires. "What say you to this Wilkes?" laughs Lord Mortimer (Billy House), "a mad boy playing 'Reason!' That's a Tory joke for you!" To which the Whig politician, Wilkes (Leyland Hodgson), replies, "And only the Tories will laugh at it. The opposition wonders what the effect will be on the poor sick boy. The Tories care only for the jest."

As the boy attempts to recite his poem ("To this pretty world, there came, heaven sent, divinely inspired, the blessing of our age, this man set like a jewel, this prince of men, this paragon Lord Mortimer...") he struggles for breath. Wilkes thinks he knows the reason for his trouble: "Somewhere I heard that the human body must breathe through its pores. If you shut those pores..." The boy, covered in gold paint (as Shirley Eaton would be in *Goldfinger* [dir. Guy Hamilton, 1964]), expires from suffocation.

In the end, Master Sims, who runs the Bedlam Hospital in London, is stabbed in the back by a Madonna-like inmate and then walled up by the others in revenge for his cruelties, which in itself suggests two other Poe tales, "The Cask of Amontillado" and "The Black Cat." Lewton and Robson suggest here that the insane are far more worthy of our respect than anyone in authority. In the end, the madness of society is presented as being far more repellent than that of Bedlam. In a sense we are all inmates in the asylum of society where there is no real asylum at all. Nell is incarcerated in Sims' Bedlam, as many a Victorian heroine found herself thus abused (both Wilkie Collins in *The Woman in White*, and Sheridan Le Fanu in *The Rose and the Key*, exploited this narrative device), but *Bedlam* suggests that it is hardly any worse than being free in the pernicious and sadistic world at large.

Although Miloš Forman's *One Flew Over the Cuckoo's Nest* (1975) is not a horror film, it inhabits a place so often exploited by the genre and presents a negative presentation of the authority. An indictment of lobotomy, Forman's film is in agreement with the outraged Doctor Martin played by Robert Powell in *Asylum*, who asks Patrick Magee's Dr. Rutherford:

"Do you believe that surgery is a substitute for psychiatry?"
"It's effective."
"Yes, its effect in turning human beings into vegetables."

Some eight years before *Asylum*, Patrick Magee had made a particularly powerful impression on the stage in Peter Brook's production of the Peter Weiss play often abbreviated as the *Marat/Sade*, in which the Marquis de Sade puts on a play about the French revolution in the lunatic asylum of Charenton, where Sade was actually incarcerated. Brook filmed his production with its original cast in 1967. In one scene, Sade himself describes how Robert-François Damiens was executed in public for attempting to assassinate King Louis XV in 1757. It is one of the greatest pieces of writing about the savage insanity of humanity and our inherent horror of the body. "Man is a destroyer," Sade insists, "but if he does not destroy with passion, he is a mere machine. He should destroy with passion, unlike the mechanical murder advocated by Marat, who is in charge of the French Revolution. Sade then describes how Damien was pulled to pieces while Casanova looked through a window and "felt under the skirts of women watching." Damien's calves, thigh and legs were split open, and molten lead was poured into them; ropes were tied to his arms and legs and four horses were attached to the ropes to pull them apart, but not before they had sawed into them, as the horse couldn't manage it unaided.[7] (Christopher Lee's Count Regula was similarly pulled to pieces in the opening scenes of Harald Reinl's *Die Schlangengrube und das Pendel* aka *The Torture Chamber of Dr. Sadism,* even though the film rather has more in common with Poe than Sade.)

Weiss' Sade has no faith in mankind but even less in those who repress passion in the name of morality. He is horrified by mankind but accepts the horror of it all:

> I do not know if I am hangman or victim
> for I imagine the most horrible tortures
> and as I describe them I suffer them myself
> There is nothing that I could not do and
> everything fills me with horror.

He explains how he once watched a tailor, a gentle, philosophical, cultured man, foam at the mouth "and raging and screaming attack with a cudgel a man in Switzerland," tear open the breast of the defeated man, pull out his heart and swallow it. As soon as his soliloquy ends, one of the patients says:

> A mad animal
> Man's a mad animal
> I'm a thousand years old and in my time

"Man's a mad animal!" Poster for *Marat/Sade* (dir. Peter Brook, 1967).

> I've helped commit a million murders
> The earth is spread
> The earth is spread thick
> with squashed human guts.⁸

Ken Russell's *The Devils* inhabits a similar universe, for it is a similarly political film concerned with the nature of social and religious freedom. Cardinal Richelieu aims to eradicate the protestant Huguenots from France. When the priest, Grandier (Oliver Reed), refuses to allow the walls of his city, Loudon, to be demolished in order to facilitate Richelieu's plans, he finds himself accused of sorcery, via the sexual hysteria of Vanessa Redgrave's Mother Superior. The film's contention that repressed sexual desire leads to madness, reminds one of Cioran's remark, "'O Satan, my Master, I give myself unto thee forever!' How I regret not remembering the name of the nun who, having written these words with a nail dipped in her own blood, deserves to figure in an anthology of prayer and concision!"⁹

The Mother Superior and her Ursuline nuns are described by Grandier as "secluded women. They give themselves to God, but something remains, which cries out to be given to men." The Mother Superior scourges herself in an attempt to exorcise her lustful thoughts, but, as Grandier knows, "pain is sensuality; and in its vortex brings images of horror and lust." (A similar idea is depicted in Michael Reeves' *The Sorcerers* [1967], in which Catherine Lacey plays a repressed, elderly woman, who becomes corrupted by her lust when given the opportunity to experience vicarious excitement via her telepathic communion with the youth, sexual activity and physical violence of Ian Ogilvy's Mike.)

All the nuns find Grandier attractive and none of them can endure the news of his marriage. The Mother Superior is even jealous of her own nuns' fantasies about Grandier. As Grandier puts it, "Anything found in the desert of a frustrated life can bring hope, and with hope comes love, and with love comes hate. So I possess this woman" (i.e., The Mother Superior). Richelieu and his envoys exploit this situation to rid themselves of Grandier's intransigence. Threatened with execution, the nuns are persuaded to accuse Grandier, and this leads to the famous orgy scene in which Russell graphically depicts the insanity of the Catholic Church's obsession with sexual repression. Sex is part of what Grandier calls "this hideous state of existence."

Russell juxtaposes sexual depravity with the depravity of torture, even of medical procedures. "What fresh lunacy is this?" Grandier exclaims when interrupting the absurd practices of two doctors in attempting to cure a woman of the plague. Piles of dead plague victims remind one of the bulldozed corpses of Auschwitz, and the corpses piled on railway sleepers after the British fire-bombing of Dresden, which does rather make us question Grandier's dictum that "if God wants you to suffer, you should accept that suffering." Russell was a Catholic convert and God is definitely an off-stage character in *The Devils*. God is contrasted with the "perversion of Christ's teaching," which we observe Richelieu's agents gleefully committing. Even so, Russell does not shy away from the idea that nothing generates violence like belief, but much of the violence depicted in *The Devils*, which generated such controversy and censure at the time of its release, is in fact highly stylized. As Russell pointed out himself, the film was made with a considerably ironic attitude, and the violence, while grotesque, is often so exaggerated that it verges on the comedic (along the same lines as the cartoon violence of Tom and Jerry).

Grandier accuses Richelieu's agents of having "seduced the people in order to destroy them," which further suggests Nazi politics. Grandier is subjected to torture (his tongue is pricked, his kneecaps smashed), and this tests even Grandier's faith ("Oh God, I thought I had found You and now You have forsaken me"). A show trial, again like those resurrected during the Third Reich, follows, in which Grandier is inevitably condemned to death. "Learn the meaning of Love," he shouts at the nuns as he endures his auto da fé. The ecstasy of the mob, which has always relished an execution, is comparable to the Marat/Sade. Russell shows people enjoying themselves on a balcony as Grandier is put to death, just as Casanova felt under the skirts of women watching Damien's dismemberment during the French Terror. Consumed by their own madness in the name of power, Russell's vision even foreshadows the nuclear catastrophes of Nagasaki and Hiroshima. The walls of Loudon are blown up and the city is destroyed; God has abandoned the city and its defenders, presumably (from a Catholic point of view) because humanity has abandoned God.

Werner Herzog concurs with Russell's vision of the self-destructive impulse of humanity:

> The Germans were a dignified people, the greatest philosophers, composers, writers and mathematicians. And, in the space of only ten years, they created a barbarism more terrible than had ever been seen before.[10]

Herzog's film *The Enigma of Kaspar Hauser* (1974) is not really interested in the actual enigma of this individual, who appeared from nowhere, having spent the first 17 years of his life tied to the floor in a cellar with only a toy horse to play with. The original German title, *Jeder für sich und Gott gegen alle* ("Every Man for Himself and God Against All"), is more to the point. Herzog is not concerned with Hauser's ancestry or how he was placed in such a strange situation. Deposited in a town square, after his long, unexplained isolation, his innocent, "uncontaminated human dignity"[11] is shown to be in stark contrast to the interests and behavior of the townspeople. Many of them are well intentioned, other less so, but in the end he is murdered for no reason other than his difference from the norm, and this is exactly Herzog's point.

> Kaspar's story is about what civilization does to us all, how it deforms and destroys us by bringing us into societal line; in Kaspar's case this stultifying and staid bourgeois existence. …
>
> There is a scene in the film when a young child holds a mirror up to Kaspar's face, the first time he has ever seen his reflection, something which confuses and shocks him. This is actually what Kaspar is doing to everyone around him: forcing them to confront their day-to-day existence with new eyes.[12]

Herzog demonstrates that Kaspar is "certainly the most intact person in this unnamed town. … It is clear that Kaspar is strictly forbidden to imagine anything, and that his creativity is suffocated and suppressed. We sense that everything spontaneous in Kaspar is being systematically deadened by philistine society, though people like the professor think they are behaving decently with their attempts to 'educate' Kaspar."[13] It would be easy at first sight to regard Kaspar as being in some way deficient, simple-minded, even "mad," but Herzog shows that he was none of those things. He simply had no experience. (He has, for example no sense of fear and does not know what danger is.) Herzog writes, "Kaspar was, in the purest sense, a being without culture, language and civilization, an almost primitive human being. … Not an idiot, rather a saint like Joan of Arc."[14] He learns to write, even to play the piano. He

Variations on an enigma. Bruno Schleinstein in the title role of *The Enigma of Kaspar Hauser* (dir. Werner Herzog, 1974).

has "genius" even if only in his way of looking at reality, in which he delights (as when feeding a bird, as he does in one scene, for example). Like Schopenhauer's definition of madness quoted above, Kaspar lives only in the present, and, because of this, he is able to regain Kleist's lost paradise. Indeed, Kaspar's real life guardian, Mr. Von Tucher, described Kaspar as "being such as we may imagine in Paradise before the fall; a precious, unique, ever to be remembered embodiment, which shone like a ray of heaven's own light upon this impure, degraded world of sinners."[15] Memory does not corrupt or congest Kaspar's response to the world, a quality understood fully by Schopenhauer:

> The mad person's knowledge has in common with the animal's the fact that both are restricted to the present; but what distinguishes them is that the animal has really no notion at all of the past as such, although the past acts on it through the medium of custom. Thus, for instance, the dog recognizes his former master even after years. ... On the other hand, the madman always carries about in his faculty of reason a past in the abstract, but it is a false past that exists for him alone.[16]

Schopenhauer also believed there was a connection between the genius and the madman because of these factors:

> Now from what we have stated, we see that the madman correctly knows the individual present as well as many particulars of the past, but that he fails to recognize the connexion, the relations, and therefore goes astray and talks nonsense. Just this is his point of contact with the genius; for he too leaves out of sight knowledge of the connexion of things, as he neglects that knowledge of relations which is knowledge according to the principle of sufficient reason in order to see in things only their Ideas, and to try to grasp their real inner nature which expresses itself to perception, in regard to which one thing represents its whole species, and hence, as Goethe says, one case is valid for a thousand. The individual object of his contemplation, or the present which he apprehends with excessive vividness, appears in so strong a light that the remaining links of the chain, so to speak, to which they belong, withdraw into obscurity, and this gives us phenomena that have long been recognized as akin to those of madness. That which exists in the actual individual things, only imperfectly and weakened by modifications, in enhanced to perfection, to the Idea of it, by the method of contemplation used by the genius.[17]

Kaspar is exactly this kind of genius, and this is why Herzog includes so many scenes of natural phenomena in the film to represent Kaspar's way of seeing things:

> Some of the shots in Kaspar Hauser seem to be held for an unusually long time, like the one near the beginning of the rye field blowing in the wind. I felt it was important to hold this image because in some small way I wanted the audience to empathize with Kaspar by looking anew at the things on this planet, seeing them almost with Kaspar's youthful eyes. For some of these kinds of shots I mounted a telephoto lens on a fish-eye lends which gave the image a very strange quality.[18]

Our redemption from the terrors of the flesh would therefore seem to lie in how we perceive the relation of our own bodies with the world around it. The terror does not go away but the deadening influence of civilization, with its dull perception, is replaced by what in Germany is regarded as the opposite of civilization: Kultur. Genius and its brother, madness, lie in direct opposition to civilization. While we find ourselves in the world, the best way of dealing with it is to be either a genius or a madman; ideally, both.

Herzog's film has been compared with François Truffaut's earlier study of instinctive culture versus sophisticated civilization, *L'enfant sauvage* (1970), in which Dr. Jean Marc Gaspard Itard (another historical figure, this time played by Truffaut himself) rescues another kind wild boy with no known history. Herzog, however, resists the comparison:

> In Truffaut's film—which I saw after I made Kaspar Hauser—there is a child who has the nature of a wolf and is taught how to act as a member of so-called civilized society. Yet Kaspar has no nature whatsoever, not that of bourgeois society, nor of wolves. Simply, he is human. On the surface the subjects of the two films appear similar, but on close inspection it becomes clear that there are real tangible differences between them.[19]

Indeed, the two directors take opposing philosophical views. Herzog seems to follow the ideas of Jean-Jacques Rousseau, who regarded civilization as a corrupting force. Michael Newton, who has written about both films and their historical inspirations, observes that "there is something nightmarish in Rousseau's lost ideal: his children of nature inhabit a world without beauty, art, love or friendship, where mutual need instantly becomes ownership and oppression."[20]

> Itard was as anxious to disprove Rousseau as he was to validate his new educational methods. Itard knew that Rousseau had lied. He had woven a beautiful and enchanted spell around our vision of the natural human. He had, as a kind of injustice, painted a pernicious illusion. The state of nature was not magical, attractive or beautiful: it was a state of vacuity and barbarism, an empty, ugly, and unmeaning condition of entrapment.
>
> Itard sought to prove that Rousseau was wrong. He knew that a human life can only be realized within society. Yet something in the young doctor pined for that same vision of savage freedom that his reason consciously rejected. Itard despised Rousseau, but could not, even in antagonism, escape his influence. He learnt from Rousseau that there is an innate human instinct for sympathy. Our nature leads us inevitably into relation with others.[21]

Truffaut's film might more properly belong to the category of the werewolf fantasy, for the wild boy does indeed learn to become human before reverting to his wolf nature. One of the doctors, who examines him, regards him as an inferior being, lower than an animal—an idiot, in fact, but the boy is not an idiot. He grows to understand the meaning of words like "Lait" (milk), and also learns sorrow, which he never knew in his savage state. Itard calls the boy Victor, immediately suggesting comparison with Mary Shelley's Victor Frankenstein, whose attempts to create a perfect human being fail, just as the boy Victor fails to become a perfect human being. (In contrast to this, we at no point regard Herzog's Kaspar to be anything less than a perfect, if uncivilized, human being.) When Victor weeps, the doctor says, "I regretted having known him. I condemned the curiosity of the man who had wrenched him away from his innocent and happy life," the implication, following Rousseau's belief, being that civilization is always ultimately worse than the natural state. Though Herzog distances his film from Truffaut's, both films attack civilization in favor of a condition that is uncontaminated by it, and both the wild boy and Kaspar Hauser represent the purer more perceptive outsider status shared by madmen and geniuses.

Eight

Extinction

> "A Monster however horrible, secretly attracts us, pursues us, haunts us. He represents, enlarged, our advantages and our miseries, her proclaims us, he is our standard bearer."
>
> —E. M. Cioran[1]

Freud's controversial theory of a death-instinct underlying human motivation first appeared in his essay, "Beyond the Pleasure Principle," written in 1920, after the cataclysm of the First World War. Somewhat to his own surprise, Freud acknowledged that he had "unwittingly steered our course into the harbor of Schopenhauer's philosophy." He acknowledged that for Schopenhauer, "death is the 'true result and to that extent the purpose of life,' while the sexual instinct is the embodiment of the will to live."[2] In "The Ego and the Id" published three years later, he elaborated, "the hypothesis of a death instinct, the task of which is to lead organic life back into the inanimate state.... The emergence of life would thus be the cause of the continuance of life and also at the same time of the striving towards death; and life itself would be a conflict and compromise between these two trends."[3]

Attempting to explain to himself and others the psychological impulses that had led to the catastrophe of the then-recent war, Freud suggested that this death instinct "would thus seem to express itself—though probably only in part—as an instinct of destruction directed against the external world and other organisms."[4] Adding his habitual sexual interpretation of this observation, he suggests that "for the purposes of discharge the instinct of destruction is habitually brought into the service of Eros,"[5] thus psychologizing the well-known connection between sex and violence, which, as we shall see later, is a driving force behind a great many war films, of which Francis Ford Coppola's *Apocalypse Now!* (1979) is perhaps one of the most honest.

If Freud was right, we have a deep subconscious drive towards what a Buddhist would call Nirvana—a restoration of the tranquil nothingness that existed before the breath of "the One" disturbed it:

> Then there was neither death nor immortality,
>   nor was there then the torch of night and day.
> The One breathed mindlessly and self-sustaining.
>   There was that One then, and there was no other.[6]

Richard Wagner, who arrived at Buddhism via Schopenhauer's philosophy, to some extent anticipated Freud's formulation of a death instinct. In a letter to Liszt in 1855 discussing Schopenhauer's advocacy of the denial of the will to live and its similarity to Buddhist thought, he wrote:

> Admittedly, it puts forward a myth in which the world is created by God; but it does not praise this act as a boon, but presents it as a sin committed by Brahma for which the latter atones by transforming himself into the world and by taking upon himself the immense sufferings of the world; he is redeemed in those saints who, by totally denying the will to live, pass over into "nirvana," i.e., the land of non-being, as a result of their consuming sympathy for all that suffers.[7]

According to Schopenhauer:

> *Brahma* is supposed to have created the world by a kind of fall into sin, or by an error, and has to atone for this sin or error by remaining in it himself until he has redeemed himself out of it. Very good! In *Buddhism* the world arises as a consequence of an inexplicable clouding of the heavenly clarity of the blessed state of Nirvana after a long period of quietude. Its origin is thus a kind of fatality.[8]

As we shall see, some fantasy films contemplate and indeed depict the final release of extinction, but 19th-century entertainment had already begun to explore this idea in novels such as Mary Shelley's 1826 *The Last Man*, in which a pandemic destroys the entire human race, leaving but one man standing at the end. Lord Byron, with whom Shelley had spent the celebrated haunted summer of 1816 on the shores of Lake Geneva, which gave rise to *Frankenstein*, had also addressed the death of humanity his poem "Darkness." Written in the same year as *Frankenstein*, "Darkness" had been immediately inspired by the unusually gloomy weather caused by the eruption of Mount Tambora in the Dutch East Indies, which had created in its wake the effects of what we would now call a nuclear winter.

> The world was void,
> The populous and the powerful was a lump,
> Seasonless, herbless, treeless, manless, lifeless—
> A lump of death—a chaos of hard clay.
> The rivers, lakes and ocean all stood still,
> And nothing stirr'd within their silent depths;
> Ships sailorless lay rotting on the sea,
> And their masts fell down piecemeal: as they dropp'd
> They slept on the abyss without a surge—
> The waves were dead; the tides were in their grave,
> The moon, their mistress, had expir'd before;

> The winds were wither'd in the stagnant air,
> And the clouds perish'd; Darkness had no need
> Of aid from them—She was the Universe.[9]

Frankenstein was also a response to the mood of that summer, but it approached the human condition from the other way around. Rather than extinction, it is life that Shelley presents as the fundamental problem. The generation of new life is regarded here as the great evil, Frankenstein's Creature symbolizing all humanity—its need for affection, its suffering, its resentment, its desire for death; but Frankenstein's creation cannot die. That is its tragedy, an even greater tragedy than being born.

Written much later in Shelley's life, *The Last Man* charts the decline and destruction of all humanity.

> I was alone in the Forum; alone in Rome; alone in the world. Would not one living man—one companion in my weary solitude be worth all the glory and remembered power of this time-honoured city. Double sorrow—sadness, bred in Cimmerian caves, robed my soul in a mourning garb. The generations I had conjured up to my fancy, contrasted more strongly with the end of all—the single point in which, as a pyramid, the mighty fabric of society had ended, while I, on the giddy height, saw vacant space around me.[10]

Here, Shelley foreshadows Neville Shute's post-apocalyptic romance, *On the Beach*, later filmed by Stanley Kramer in 1959. Unlike *The Last Man on Earth* (dir. Ubaldo Ragona, 1964) and *The Omega Man*, *On the Beach* does not flinch from depicting the absolute destruction of humanity. The deserted city streets we are shown at the end of Kramer's film really are empty, and will remain empty for all eternity. There are no vampires, no mutations and no survivors. A banner with the words, "There is Still Time, Brothers" is, of course, deeply ironic, for time has definitely run out. The Marquis de Sade of Peter Weiss' play would have observed that nature couldn't care less about all this:

> Every death even the cruelest death
> drowns in the total indifference of Nature
> Nature herself would watch unmoved
> if we destroyed the entire human race[11]

Sade claimed to hate Nature, "this passionless spectator this unbreakable iceberg-face,"[12] but to anti-natalist philosophers like David Benatar, extinction is not a negative. He does not advocate its achievement through nuclear war or any other kind of man-made suffering, promoting instead voluntary birth control, which would lead to the gradual, peaceful extinction of the species:

> I shall not assess arguments and evidence for competing views about when human extinction will occur. We know it will occur, and this fact has a curious effect on my argument. In a strange way it makes my argument an optimistic one. Although

things are now not the way they should be—there are people when there should be none—things will someday be the way they should be—there will be no more people. In other words, although things are now bad, they will be better, even if they first get worse with the creation of new people.[13]

In the light of anti-natalist philosophy, the conclusion of *On the Beach* might even be interpreted as optimistic, providing, as it does, an end to human conflict, and the anxiety, pain and terrors of the flesh. Conversely, despite its title, in Terence Fisher's science fiction masterpiece, *The Earth Dies Screaming* (1964), a small group of people survive an alien attack, in which everyone else in the small town in which the action is set, are killed. This apparently optimistic ending might therefore be regarded as pessimistic, for it suggests that the terrors of the flesh will continue.

Hammer's *The Plague of the Zombies* can easily, if perhaps unadvisedly, be read as a Marxist allegory (it was hardly intended as such). In it, Squire Hamilton (John Carson) runs his Cornish tin mines on classically capitalist lines, his workforce recruited, however, from the decaying but exploitable zombies, summoned from the grave by means of voodoo to become an obedient (and cheap) proletariat. To equate the labor force with the undead might be said to be accurate in that the conditions capitalism prefers its workers to endure is indeed often a kind of living death. (Marx certainly thought so.) Hamilton's workers fail to organize a rebellion against him; instead they merely catch fire, but one of them does strangle the Squire at the end. Victor Halperin's *White Zombie* (1932) had also used the undead to symbolize slavery in general and those slaves in particular who "are made to work in the sugar mills or the fields at night."

"They work faithfully," says zombie-master, "Murder" Legendre (Bela Lugosi). "They do not mind long hours." If these zombies were ever to regain their souls, Legendre agrees they would tear him to pieces, just as Marx hoped the exploited proletariat would destroy its capitalistic overlords if their consciousness was awakened, and the true cause of their plight exposed. "But that, my friend," Legendre adds, "shall never be," and, indeed, it is not the zombies who kill him in the end but the man who wants to use his voodoo knowledge to zombify the woman he loves (the white zombie of the title). Legendre is a Gothic capitalist, and thus rather more of a political horror than the role that had made Lugosi famous the year before in Browning's *Dracula*. Dracula does of course suck blood, as capitalists do in a symbolic sense, but Browning's film has no real political comment to make out of it in the way that Marx had done in *Capital* and the Halperin brothers demonstrated in *White Zombie*

According to Marx, capital "is dead labor, which, vampire-like, lives only by sucking living labor, and lives the more, the more labor it sucks."[14] Richard Matheson elaborated this metaphor in his 1954 novel *I Am Legend*, which has been filmed three times, first with Vincent Price in the aforementioned *The Last Man on Earth* (dir. Ubaldo Ragona, Sidney Salkow, 1964), the second with Charlton Heston in *The Omega Man*, and the last, so far, with Will Smith, which revered to the original title of Matheson's novel (dir. Francis Lawrence, 2007). This dystopian fantasy is really an allegory of capitalism in terms of body horror. Matheson in fact turns the whole human race into vampires rather than killing them off for good, and only one man, Robert Neville, survives this pandemic. (The problem is caused by mosquitos, consequently foreshadowing our own anxieties of global warming.)

George A. Romero later elaborated on this idea in his *Dawn of the Dead* (1978), in which zombies wander through a vast shopping mall, Romero obviously intending us to question whether they were really that different when they were alive. The extreme violence (mainly consisting of bullet wounds fired by M16 rifles) also reminds us that *Dawn of the Dead* is also an allegory of the Vietnam War. So too are Romero's other zombie film, *The Crazies* along with *The Night of the Living Dead* (1968), and all these films are as much about American gun culture and the eroticization of violence, which grimly foreshadowed the mass shootings in our own time.

Meanwhile, Neville, barricaded into his flat, is sustained by the products of a dead civilization. Outside, the vampires keep calling him. "Come out, Neville!" they shout, just as society forever keeps insisting that we play our part in the grotesque game of capitalism. The vampires are Neville's enemies, of course, but they are not really any worse than human beings had been before the epidemic:

Guns 'n ghouls. David Emge and Scott H. Reiniger with an M16 in *Dawn of the Dead* (dir. George A. Romero, 1978).

> The vampire may foster quickened heartbeats and levitated hair. But is he worse than the parent who gave to society a neurotic child who became a politician? Is he worse than the manufacturer who set up belated foundations with the money he made by handling bombs and guns to suicidal nationalists? Is he worse than the distiller who gave bastardized grain juice to stultify further the brains of those who, sober, were incapable of a progressive thought? (Nay, I apologize for this calumny; I nip the brew that feeds me.) Is he worse, then, than the publisher who filled ubiquitous racks with lust and death wishes? Really, now, search your soul, love—is the vampire so bad?[15]

The vampires want Neville's blood, just as the government wants his tax, and the water and electricity companies their fees. All of society is a kind of vampire, sucking us dry, making us conform to its rules, seducing us with its advertisements, resisting our attempts to overcome the restrictions of the body and retreat into our own imaginative universe. Indeed, Matheson revealingly observes that so many of our desires, including sex, are in fact mere commodities, which are only made desirable through peer pressure and advertising: "Sex was fast losing its meaning without the endless prodding of mass hypnosis."[16]

Ragona and Salkow's 1964 adaptation of Matheson's novel (*The Last Man on Earth*) follows Matheson's text reasonably closely, but the most interesting thing about it was that it was partly filmed in the suburb of Rome known as EUR (Esposizione Universale Roma), particularly the Palazzo della Civiltà Italiana and the steps outside the Palazzo dei Ricevimenti e Congressi, which had been created by Mussolini as the centerpiece of a World Fair to be held in 1939. The Second World War put an end to plans for the exhibition, but the buildings remain as striking examples of streamlined neo-classical Fascist architecture. Setting the film at EUR gives the post-plague location scenes a stylishly alienating quality, which is reminiscent of Michelangelo Antonioni's use of EUR in *L'eclisse*, filmed two years previously. Indeed, Antonioni had suggested imminent world catastrophe in his film by featuring the curious water tower at EUR (also seen in *The Last Man on Earth*), which resembles a mushroom cloud. He also complements other shots of people staring up at the vapor trails of jet fighters high above them in the stratosphere. All in all, the visual effect is similar to the urban anxiety captured in the paintings of Giorgio de Chirico. The final seven minutes of *L'eclisse*, which present a poetically charged visual poem based around the often-deserted locations where Antonioni's lovers planned to meet but never do, also seem to be echoed in *The Last Man on Earth*. (In those shots where we do see people, they are usually alone, waiting or seemingly anxious. The ultimate horror of the body is, of course, its isolation: we essentially both live and die alone.) Antonioni's vision has been called a self-indulgent, defeatist vision of despair,[17] which may well be true, though not necessarily in a pejorative sense. The same might also be said of *The Last Man on Earth*.

Fascist fantasy. EUR architecture and Vincent Price in *The Last Man on Earth* (dir. Ubaldo Ragona and Sidney Salkow, 1964).

The EUR setting also heightens the political subtext of the story by equating the fascist state with the infected survivors of the plague, who have managed to keep the disease at bay thanks to a serum. These survivors all wear black uniforms reminiscent of Mussolini's black-shirts who created EUR in the first place. Indeed, in the final pages of his novel, Matheson has Neville report how this new community of "dark men" enjoys killing just as much as any fascist:

> "But ... but did you see their faces when they ... they killed?" His throat moved convulsively. "Joy," he mumbled. "Pure joy."
> "Did you ever see your face," she [Ruth] asked, "when you killed?" She patted his brow with the cloth. "I saw it—remember? It was frightening. Are you weren't even killing then, you were just chasing me."
> He closed his eyes. Why am I listening to her? he thought. She's become a brainless convert to this new violence.
> "Maybe you did see joy on their faces," she said. "It's not surprising. They're young. And they *are* killers—assigned killers, legal killers. They're respected for their killing, admired for it."[18]

The title of Matheson's novel is now explained: Neville has become something of a celebrity, due to his indiscriminate killing of a great many members of this group, unaware that they were still alive, though infected. He is to them as much of a legend as Dracula and vampires had been to him. *The Omega Man* subsequently removed the vampire element of Matheson's original concept, turning the plague survivors into pale-faced, white-eyed mutants, dressed in inquisitor-style robes to signify their technophobic religion, which aims to be free of "forbidden tools...medicine, weapons, machinery, electricity." Their new "undead" community is another kind of fascist dictatorship: anti-urban, folkloric, cultish, obedient to its own Führer (played by Anthony Zerbe), at odds with reality, and fanatically loyal to its misconceived ideals.

The constellation of body horror, fascism and apocalypse created by these Matheson adaptations link them to other horror films that have allegorized the way in which political power has so often been enforced through the threat of physical violence and the infliction of bodily horror. Universal horror films of the 1930s had often evoked what was really going on in the torture chambers of the Third Reich. We have already seen one example of that in *The Island of Lost Souls,* but other echoes reverberated in Edgar G. Ulmer's *The Black Cat* (1934), not only in its fascination with the occult, which the Nazis shared, of course, but also in the final scene in which Bela Lugosi's Dr. Vitus Werdergast flays alive the Hjalmar Poelzig of Boris Karloff. The actual torture is left to our imagination, in contrast to how David Cronenberg might have filmed it, but the horror is there nonetheless, and it is perhaps even more horrific in that we can imagine something so much worse than any special effects might create. As David J. Skal has observed, "By indulging sadism in the guise of dispassionate science, the pointless and atrocious medical 'research' carried out by the Nazi doctors remarkably paralleled the typical activities of the mad movie doctors of the thirties and forties. ... These madmen were usually obsessed with some dream of world domination."[19]

Taking fascism as a kind of super-capitalism, Hans W. Geissendörfer later brilliantly applied Marx's vampire imagery to his allegory of Adolf Hitler's reign of terror in *Jonathan* (1970). Paul Albert Krumm's vampire here sports the Führer's hairstyle while sensibly avoiding the mustache, but the parallel is clear in this Gothic parable set in the Biedermeir period (as was Murnau's *Nosferatu*). Geissendörfer eschews body horror, in keeping with the Gothic parameters of his vision, but the final scene in which the vampires are driven to the seashore and are drowned does seem uncannily similar to Waltraud Reski's account of how her mother was serially raped by the invading Russians at the end of the Second World War, and how she was herself very nearly drowned in the mass suicide of her fellow inhabitants in the East German town of Demmin. "You can't imagine what it was like for her—to be raped ten or twenty times a day," she explained in an interview in the final episode the BBC's documentary *The Nazis—A Warning from History* (dir. Laurence Rees, 1997). "You're hardly human any more. My mother became an entirely different person for the rest of her life." Rather than endure the Russian occupation of their town, hundreds of people took the decision to commit suicide in the rivers that flow quietly around the town. "Women holding children by the hand were running towards the water. There were also whole families including elderly people. Many had tied themselves together. I didn't understand what they were doing. There were also individuals running up and down the riverbank, and children who had lost their families. There was the terrible sight of those who had gone into the water the previous night—those bloated bodies, reddish-blue. Mother grabbed us and wanted to run into the river with us. We were both screaming. We'd almost reached the river, but grandmother managed to stop us and we didn't jump in."

If it is indeed true that humanity has the seeds of its own self-destruction embedded deep within its own genetically inherited psychology, Koestler's arguments concerning "the gulf between our intellectual and emotional development," thanks to the exponential development of the neo-cortex, would seem to offer an explanation. He continues:

> Language, the outstanding achievement of the neocortex, became a more dividing than unifying factor, increasing intra-specific tensions; progress in communications followed a similar trend of turning a blessing into a curse. Even from the aesthetic point of view we have managed to contaminate the luminiferous ether as we have contaminated our air, rivers and seashores; you fiddle with the dials of our radio and from all over the world, instead of celestial harmonies, the ether disgorges its musical latrine slush.
>
> Of all exponential curves, that referring in destructive power is the most spectacular and the best known. ... The first atomic bomb on Hiroshima equalled twenty thousand tons of T.N.T. Ten years later, the first hydrogen bomb equalled twenty million tons. At the time of writing, we are stockpiling bombs the equivalent of one hundred million tons of T.N.T. ... [Before] the thermonuclear bomb, man had to live with the idea of his death as an individual; from now onward, mankind has to live with the idea of its death as a species.[20]

Our will to what Koestler calls genosuicide is, of course, much older than the development of our technological ability to achieve it. Milton's Satan in *Paradise Lost* is the prototype of the eponymous Dr. Strangelove in Stanley Kubrick's film. Unable to overthrow God Himself, Satan decides to destroy what is closest to God's affections. Humanity has always blamed its own sins on the temptations of a supernatural force beyond its control, but, of course, Satan is an allegory for what lives in the neo-cortex. Satan (and God) are the Biblical equivalents of Hans-Jürgen Syberberg's phrase, "The Hitler within us." Milton's Satan is so admirable because he is so easy to identify with—a recognition of which Percy Bysshe Shelley was fully aware:

> Nothing can exceed the energy and magnificence of the character of Satan as expressed in "Paradise Lost."... Milton has so far violated the popular creed (if this

shall be judged a violation) as to have alleged no superiority of moral virtue to his God over his Devil. …He mingled as it were the elements of human nature as colours upon a single pallet, and arranged them in the composition of his great picture according to the laws of epic truth.[21]

Thus, when Milton's Satan plans the destruction of humanity, it is really humanity contemplating its own destruction if not also the destruction of the Earth on which humanity is placed. Beelzebub—the Lord of the Flies, indeed, elaborates:

> Here, perhaps,
> Some advantageous act may be achieved
> By sudden onset, either with hell-fire
> To waste His whole creation, or possess
> All as our own, and drive, as we were driven,
> The puny habitants. Or, if not to drive,
> Seduce them to our party, that their God
> May prove their foe, and with repenting hand
> Abolish his own works.[22]

Though intended as warnings, films such as *The Day the Earth Stood Still* (dir. Robert Wise, 1951) and Val Guest's *The Day the Earth Caught Fire* (1961) nonetheless juggle humanity's will to self-destruction with its simultaneous fear at so doing. In the former, the visiting alien, Klatu (Michael Rennie), causes a massive power failure to demonstrate the authority of those he serves, using it as a warning of what may follow if humanity does not mend its ways and abandon the nuclear weapons that so endanger the peace of the universe. The fact that the universe, as Sade knew all too well, couldn't care less, is beside the point. The allegory here is certainly inspired by cold-war anxiety, but *The Day the Earth Stood Still* is above partisan patriotism and speaks of the Satan within us all. Its ultimate message, however, is a long way from Benatar's advocacy of peaceful extinction.

Wise's film wishes to preserve humanity by advocating what is surely impossible; for war, violence and distrust are as much a part of the human psyche as love, sexual desire and esthetics. What such films seem to be advocating is the creation of quite another species.*The Day the Earth Caught Fire* offers the distinct and far more imminent possibility of the destruction not only of humanity but of the planet itself. A newspaper journalist, Peter Stenning, played by Edward Judd, is ready at his typewriter to report the truly momentous event. His typewriter, however, has ceased up in the heat, because the nuclear weapons tests have not only tilted the axis of the Earth, but also changed its orbit, and the Earth is now on a collision course with the sun.

As Leo McKern's character, Bill McGuire, puts it, "It amounts to the biggest jolt the earth's taken since the ice age started." Uncannily presaging the global warming crisis of our own time, the way in which the film depicts the initial jubilation of the public at such unusually warm weather also captures exactly the inane attitude of global warming deniers in the 21st century. The Campaign for Nuclear Disarmament also features in the action, as does a fatuous broadcast by the Prime Minister designed to prevent panic. "Some of the seasons as we know them may be disturbed and change their intensity," he pontificates, at which Guest immediately cuts to shots of freak snowstorms, floods and, of course, heatwaves with their concomitant forest fires. Such denial and damage limitation is even more relevant now, nearly 60 years after the film was made. McGuire bluntly predicts that humanity will have about four months before "there's a delightful smell in the universe of charcoaled mankind."

As the film opens, an attempt by the joint governments of the world to correct the Earth's orbit by detonating more bombs has just taken place. London is evacuated. Big Ben tolls solemnly. "This is London," says the official announcement on the radio. "I feel that at this time it is senseless to minimize the gravity of our situation, or to deny the danger of the course decided upon," the Prime Minister intones. "Drastic conditions demand drastic action. ... And so, four thermonuclear bombs, the largest ever devised, will be detonated simultaneously one hundred miles apart in the West of Siberia."

We then return to the moment at which the film began, with Stenning dictating his peroration:

> It is exactly thirty minutes since the corrective bombs were detonated. Within the next few hours, the world will know whether this is the end or another beginning; the rebirth of man or his final obituary. For the last time, man pursued his brother with a sword and so the final fire was kindled. The Earth that was to live forever was blasted by a great wind towards oblivion.

Guest concludes with the film's most memorable image of Stenning walking down a deserted city street, the image tinted a sickly golden hue:

> So man has sown the wind and reaped the whirlwind. Perhaps in the next few hours there will be no remembrance of the past and no hope for the future that might have been. All the works of man will be consumed in the great fire out of which he was created, but perhaps at the heart of the burning light into which he has thrust his world there is a heart that cares more for him than he has ever cared for himself.

The clock stands at 10 minutes to midnight. The printers in the newspaper office wait with two alternative headlines ready for the presses: "World Saved" and "World Doomed," as Stenning concludes:

> And if there is a future for man, insensitive as he is, proud and defiant in his pursuit of power, let him resolve to live it lovingly, for he knows well how to do so. Then he may say once more, "truly, the light is sweet, and what a pleasant thing it is for the eyes to see the sun."

As Guest's camera pans in towards the cross atop St Paul's Cathedral, the distinctly Dickensian tone of Stenning's voice-over echoes the rhythm and intent of Dirk Bogarde's final lines in *A Tale of Two Cities* (dir. Ralph Thomas, 1958). The audience, meanwhile, is left to decide if the religious symbolism implies that God will prevail or if the image profoundly ironic?

Filmed three years later, Roger Corman's adaptation of Poe's *The Masque of the Red Death* is somewhat closer to the spirit of Benatar's view, in which death is portrayed as a liberator, even though extinction is avoided due to the casual mercy of the various figures of death which wander the world. The Red Death sends a message to the villagers who are oppressed by Prince Prospero (Vincent Price), "The day of your deliverance is at hand," but he does not mean that it is only Prospero who will ultimately die. In fact, all but six shall die, for the deliverance he offers from life's meaningless suffering is death itself.

Prospero attempts to escape the plague and death by locking himself up in his castle and worshipping the Devil, but there is no stopping the Red Death and his differently colored colleagues who all have much more work to do: "One hundred thousand perished at my passing this last night," says one. "Ten thousand sleep where I walked. I am very tired," says another. Finally: "The weariness of those to whom we bring rest burdens you."

Prospero symbolizes the restless striving of the Will, which Schopenhauer compares to "an unquenchable thirst."

> The basis of all willing, however, is need, lack, and hence pain. If, on the other hand, it lacks objects of willing, because it is at once deprived of them again by too easy a satisfaction, a fearful emptiness and boredom come over it; in other words, its being and its existence itself become an intolerable burden for it.[23]

Only death can bring to an end the restless suffering of the Will. While humanity carries on at the end of the film, despite the demise of so many, the masque of life is not endorsed. Before the infiltration of the Red Death, Prospero's castle has been the scene of humiliation, cynicism, torture, and murder, which show no signs of departure while humanity continues to exist. Death is indifferent to Prospero's cruelties and crimes, even though it might be tempting to consider Death's appearance as a punishment for them. Prospero is no different from anyone else, and the Red Death is truly democratic in his single, solemn duty.

War films, of course, are inescapably involved with portrayals of death, often in the context of heroism rather than of annihilation. The sexual element in violence, to which Freud referred in "The Ego and the Id" has however been explored in films such as *Once Before I Die* (dir. John Derek, 1966) as well as *Apocalypse Now!* The former is interesting solely because in one scene, Ursula Andress, as Alex, takes pity on John Derek's virginal soldier and has sex with him while other men in his regiment delight in attacking a Japanese tank, phallic pistols at the ready. Coppola's film, on the other hand, takes as one of its literary sources Michael Herr's volume of reportage, *Dispatches*, in which phrases such as "That's pure sex," with regard to the action of helicopter gunships, and "I love the smell of Napalm in the morning. ... It smells like Victory," suggest a strong correlation between the "ecstasy" of combat and the "petite mort" of orgasm. Coppola makes this quite clear when these lines are combined with the graphic and frankly erotic imagery of the film's battle scenes. These men are in love with annihilation, with weaponry and with sex. That Coppola begins his film with The Doors singing "This Is the End" epitomizes the power of Freud's death instinct more than any other war film, just as the shots of a padre holding a communion and intoning the Lord's Prayer during scenes of utter mayhem and carnage bring the Marat/Sade's opinion that "Man's a mad animal" strikingly up to date. (The cow that is airlifted over this padre against a blood red sky seems also to suggest the flying statue of Christ, which a helicopter hoists blasphemously over Rome at the beginning of Fellini's *La Dolce Vita* [1960].) Sade himself had anticipated these aspects of the psyche much earlier, in 1797, when his magnum opus *Juliette* first appeared. Decades before the investigations of Schopenhauer and Nietzsche, let alone Freud, into our psycho-sexual motivations, *Juliette* cut straight to the bone, correctly identifying the relationship between crime and sexual desire. The sexual impulse, which is the root of our actions, is fundamentally *anarchic*, and the history of civilization is really only the catalogue of our various attempts to reconcile ourselves with what so many have found unpalatable about our true nature. Religions attempt to demonize such impulses, whereas the Nazis were at least very honest in their approach to the truths Sade revealed to us. That the consequences of the implementation of these truths was so horrific does nothing to affect the impulses themselves. Sade writes, "There's not a woman on earth who'd ever have had cause to complain of my services if I'd been sure of being able to kill her afterwards,"[24] a line that was to be echoed on several occasions by Sean Connery's James Bond.

If killing other people in war is a crime (a still contentious question), Sade foreshadows the imagery of Michael Herr: "Very true it is," he writes, "to this I bear witness, that crime is a delectable thing; very certain it is that the flame it darts through our whole being is what sets alight the torch of lust, that it requires but the thought of crime to hurl us into a lubricious ferment."[25]

Similarly, while researching the background for *Dr. Strangelove*, Stanley Kubrick overheard Herman Kahn say to a group of war planners, "Gentlemen, you do not have a war plan. You have a Wargasm!" The Cold War turned the conventional war film towards more globally apocalyptic scenarios. *Dr. Strangelove* (1964), which significantly failed to win an Oscar against George Cukor's *My Fair Lady* (satire of such disturbing hilarity was no doubt considered to be too close to the bone), posits the complete annihilation of humanity as a Sadean black comedy. The policy of Mutually Assured Destruction (M.A.D.) along with the concept of a Doomsday Machine, leads to the film's final shots of nuclear explosions accompanied by Vera Lynn singing "We'll Meet Again."

The same subject was treated more realistically, without the black comedy in *Fail Safe*, directed in the same year by Sidney Lumet, though this film ends with a rapid montage of New Yorkers going about their business unaware that a nuclear bomb is on its way to annihilate them. Filmed in a completely different way, Lumet concentrates on intense, claustrophobic close-ups, but powerful though it is, the insane absurdity of nuclear conflict seems better suited to a satirical approach, much as the existential predicament of humanity is best served by the almost musical hall comedy which informs Samuel Beckett's play, *Waiting for Godot*.

Two years later, as part of its sci-fi series *Out of the Unknown*, the BBC screened J.B. Priestley's adaptation of Mordecai Roshwald's 1959 novel *Level Seven* (dir. Rudolph Cartier). The title refers to an underground bunker, 4,500 feet below the surface of the Earth. The higher levels are reserved for civilians, politicians, scientist and the military. In the manner of Georg Kaiser's expressionist *Gas* trilogy plays (1917, 1918 and 1920), the characters in level seven played by Keith Buckley and David Collings have no names. Instead they are referred to as X127 and X117, and their function is to fire the missiles that are destroying human civilization high above them. When victory is finally announced by Anthony Bate's General, it is discovered that everyone above ground is dead and the planet has been made uninhabitable by radiation. All X127 and X117 and their associates can do is await their end in the light of a report from those who have ventured up to the surface:

> There's nothing to see here, but twisted metal and radioactive dust. Nothing, no birds are singing. No flowers growing, no trees, no fields. No men, no women, no children. Bare burnt earth, tortured metal, murderous dust. Nothing to see; nothing to hope for; nothing to love.

Such a state of affairs is obviously horrific, but it does not disqualify Benatar's advocacy of extinction, which, on his terms, would achieve the avoidance of harm, which existence unavoidably imposes of each one of us. Benatar insists "human life contains much more pain (and other negative things) than people realize. Evaluatively, I have endorsed the asymmetry of pleasure and pain and suggested that whereas life's pleasures do not make life worth starting, life's pains of make life not worth starting."

> Given how much suffering occurs every minutes, there is very good reason to think that there will be much more suffering before sentient life comes to an end, although I cannot predict with any certainty just how much more suffering there will be. All things being equal, the longer sentient life continues the more suffering there will be. However, there is an optimistic spin on my view. ... Humanity and other sentient life

will eventually come to an end. For those who judge the demise of humanity to be a bad thing, the prediction that this is what will occur is a pessimistic one. By contrast, combining my evaluation that it would be better if there were no more people with the prediction that there will come a time when there will be no more people yields an optimistic assessment. Things are bad now, but they will not always be bad.[26]

However, the annihilation of civilization through nuclear war does not necessarily mean the annihilation of mankind as a species, as *Planet of the Apes* so sensationally demonstrates (after a nuclear war, apes have mutated into the master species and humanity has become enslaved). The sequel, *Beneath the Planet of the Apes* (dir. Ted Post, 1970) does indeed bring annihilation when a doomsday nuclear weapon destroys the planet. Paul Dehn's screenplay ends with a sepulchral voice-over: "In one of the countless billions of galaxies in the universe lies a medium-sized star, and one of its satellites, a green and insignificant planet, is now dead." The screen fades to white and devastating silence accompanies the final roll of credits. The film seems to usher in the chilly 1970s, the flower power of the previous decade fading fast. Douglas Trumbull's *Silent Running* (1972) laments the destruction of earth's flora, samples of which have been assembled on another Ark, but which the astronaut in charge, Freeman Lowell (Bruce Dern), is ordered to destroy by what remains of human government back on earth. But Lowell refuses, blowing up his own ship instead, but saving the geodesic greenhouse domes, which are left in the care of an appealing robot with a watering can, which is hardly an endorsement of Benatar's brave and uncompromising view.

This leads me to Srđan Spasojević's *A Serbian Film* (2010) and Lars Von Trier's *Melancholia* (2011). The former is a summation of what this book has been about. The latter, while being ostensibly concerned with the literal end of the world, is really a study in a particular state of mind. *A Serbian Film* reveals its meaning in the title, for this compendium of bodily horrors is an allegory of what happened in Serbia during the Bosnian war in the 1990s. Nothing that happens in this much-censured film is as appalling as what happened in that war, and therefore every act of violence in it is "justified" by historical reality. To be shocked by *A Serbian Film* merely indicates that one has not fully acknowledged those realities, and its ultimate nihilism is surely the logical consequence of those circumstances. Neither is any of the extreme sexual violence on display here new: Sade had explored it all in the 18th century in *120 Days of Sodom* and *Juliette*. In Spasojević's film, a rather charming middle-aged porn star called Milos (Srdjan "Zika" Todorovic), agrees to make a different kind of porno movie to help support his family, to whom we are introduced at the outset when we are shown images of his own even more delightful son watching one of his father's old movies on video, and here is where the main outrage against the film is surely focused, for it is the juxtaposition of children against adult sexual depravity that touches the raw nerve of contemporary sensibilities. In a world jaded by corruption, obsessed by pedophilia, sated by its own capitalist excess and disillusioned by its political failures, children have become the last depository of optimism, the illusory image of an innocence, which, as I have demonstrated, never really existed in the first place. After the tired and necessarily repetitive clichés of pornography which provide the foreplay of *A Serbian Film* (fellatio, sodomy, etc.) Spasojević has a young girl watch (and seemingly enjoy) such goings on, spiced up by the threat of violence (Milos is held by the neck by a black-clad armed guard). Only the presence of the girl makes these scenes in any way out of the ordinary, while the later scenes, in which a newborn baby is raped and Milos rapes a woman while decapitating her, are in fact straight out of Sade. With regard to the former, Sade, in *120 Days of Sodom,* has one of his characters (Duclos) enjoy "watching a woman bear a child; he murders it immediately it emerges from the womb and within full view of the mother, and does do while feigning to caress it."[27] With regard to the latter, Sade describes just such an erotic decapitation in *Juliette*:

> "Proceed, proceed," said Saint-Fond, well lodged in her ass, "but go softly, you've no idea the repercussions all this is having my nervous system. Bend this way a little, Delcour, so that I can warm your member while you work. Juliette, pay your respects to Delcour's ass, worship it; he's become a god in my consideration. And bring the mother's ass inside my reach. I want to kiss it while I have her daughter murdered...."
>
> "Ah, I savor crime, I do indeed," he exclaimed, uttering many incoherent oaths. "I adore crime, it bewitches me."
>
> Delcour cuts with exquisite slowness.... Cloris is deathly pale, half in a swoon, he averts his horror-filled gaze. Julie's beautiful head falls at last, like a rose that finally yields to the unflagging north wind.[28]

Sade's is not being entirely satirical here, though he is certainly that as well, his point being that humanity is not and never will be innocent as charged by idealists. In his bitter response to the optimistic idealism of Jean-Jacques Rousseau, Sade is concerned only with the truth, no matter how disconcerting that truth may be, and in the final analysis, the voracious violence of the sexual instinct cancels out any possibility of inherent innocence or "goodness." Sex obliterates morality in its irrational and voluptuous appetite, and it is so closely related to violence that it is the perfect metaphor for war in which atrocity and eroticism have always been so intimately connected. During the Bosnian War, its wounds still unresolved, many of its principle protagonists still unpunished (though war-criminal Slobodan Praljak famously committed suicide during his trial by swallowing poison in the witness box), up to 20,000 women were raped, while 100,000 people were killed. Sex is violence and violence is sex. Faced with such a reality, it is not at all surprising that *A Serbian Film* should end with the suicide of Milos and his family, a single bullet serving all three of them as they lie on their bed. But even then the horror is not over, as the two black-clad guards return with their cameras, and the mysterious bald-headed man we saw at the outset, the sinister but unexplained *éminence gris* behind the whole affair, returns to instruct one of the guards to "begin with the little boy" as the guard prepares to unzip his flies.

Melancholia seems to be a very different kind of film. There is no porn and no sexual violence, though it all starts with a wedding and a degree of psychological violence, which suggests the "truths" Spasojević deals with more graphically. Superficially, *Melancholia* is related to the science fiction film *When Worlds Collide* (dir. Rudolph Maté, 1951), in which a planet crashes into the Earth, thus destroying it, but *When Worlds Collide* promotes the salvation of humanity, charting the creation of a kind of rocket-powered Noah's Ark, which transports selected humans to a new planet and a new destiny. (The planet chosen appears already to have a civilization resembling that of Ancient Egypt, prompting one to wonder if these colonials will cause as much trouble in their new world as their ancestors caused throughout human history back on Earth.)

The immense planet that eventually crashes into the Earth at the end of von Trier's film is appropriately called Melancholia, but it is really a metaphor for the melancholic state of mind of Justine (Kirsten Dunst), who, in turn, represents von Trier's own pessimistic worldview. "The Earth is evil," Justine insists to her more optimistic sister, Claire (Charlotte Gainsbourg). "We don't need to grieve for it. Nobody will miss it. All I know is, life on earth is evil." She also believes that "life is only on earth—and not for long." Her instinct and insight tell her that we are alone in the universe and, therefore, in universal terms, utterly irrelevant. Justine is named after the eponymous heroine on Sade's novel, *Justine,* which is appropriate as both Dunst's Justine and Sade's Justine find themselves in a world where virtue—indeed any meaning or value—is cancelled out by the uncompromising reality of the situations in which they find themselves. Unlike Sade's Juliette, Sade's Justine exudes virtue, but the world continually reminds her that it is as meaningless as its opposite. Dunst's Justine is not virtuous, but she reflects Sade's view that it makes no difference in the final analysis if one is virtuous or not. We will die whether we are or whether we're not. The insight of pessimism has the advantage of investing the person who shares it with acceptance and therefore greater tranquility of spirit. Gainsbourg's Claire has, in von Trier's view, "something to lose"—a child, and a more optimistic investment in life. She represents what von Trier calls "the sane, normal human being." Consequently, she finds death more difficult to comes to term with than Justine, but Justine, through her depressive insight into the reality of life, has, in Wagner's words when describing the character of Wotan in the Ring Cycle, "risen to the tragic height of willing his own destruction." (Wotan having wrestled with power and mastery, "fatherhood," empire and victory, eventually realizes the futility of everything he has done. All Wotan now wants is "Das Ende"— the end.

> Fahre denn hin, herrische Pracht,
> göttlichen Prunkes prahlende Schmach!
> Zusammenbreche, was ich gebaut!
> Auf geb ich mein Werk; nur eines will ich noch:
> das Ende, das Ende!
>
> [Away, then with lordly splendor,
> divine pomp and shameful boasting!
> Let it fall to pieces, all that I built.
> I give up my work. Only one thing I want know:
> the end, the end!])

The destruction of the world at the end of *Melancholia* is really a cause for celebration, facilitating, as it does, a release from delusion. (Wagner named his villa in Bayreuth "Wahnfried"—"peace from delusion.") Von Trier's finale is therefore an expression of our subconscious desire to return to that state from which we came, and it is therefore highly appropriate that he uses (possibly to the extent of over-using) the Prelude to Wagner's *Tristan und Isolde*, which in many ways (though not all) is a musical response to Schopenhauer's philosophical negation of existence. *Tristan* expresses that endless yearning, that striving and pain, which forever seeks a resolution in boredom. Technically speaking, the music of *Tristan* is an apotheosis of the suspension (the suspension of one of the notes of a concord over another concordant but unrelated chord, thus resulting in a discord). The resulting musical tension provided Wagner with an apt musical symbol of Schopenhauer's philosophy of yearning. Only in dissolution, resolution into pure nothingness, can such yearning be assuaged. Indeed, Schopenhauer goes further than symbolizing this state than Wagner's equation of it with "Nirvana":

> We then look with deep and painful yearning at that state, beside which the miserable and desperate nature of our own appears in the clearest light by the contrast. Yet this consideration is the only one that can permanently console us, when, on the one hand, we have recognized incurable suffering and endless misery as essential to the phenomenon of the will, to the world, and on the other see the world melt away with the abolished will, and retain before us only empty nothingness. In this way ... we have to banish the dark impression of that nothingness, which as the final goal hovers behind all virtue and holiness, and which we fear as children fear darkness. We must not even evade it, as the Indians do, by myths and meaningless words, such as reabsorption in Brahman, or the Nirvana of the Buddhists. On the contrary, we freely acknowledge that what remains after the complete abolition of the will is, for all who are still full of the will, assuredly nothing. But also conversely, to those in whom the will has turned and denied itself, this very real world of course with all its suns and galaxies, is—nothing.[29]

Melancholia is a profoundly Romantic film: a conflation of Wagnerian yearning, and Schopenhauerian pessimism that moves far beyond Freud's pleasure principle. During an infamous press conference at the Cannes Film Festival, Von Trier unwisely equated himself with the Romantic catastrophe that was Hitler, who languished in his bunker as the world was destroyed around him. Such a comparison immediately caused outrage, incorrectly implying that he was a Nazi sympathizer; he did not mean that he was anti-Semitic or a Nazi, but rather a personality that was in sympathy with a German Romantic outlook, out of which Hitler emerged.

Far more like Hitler is the character of Hugo Drax in the James bond film, *Moonraker* (dir. Lewis Gilbert, 1979). Drax's dark dream is to create a purified master-race of perfect humans, and his means of achieving this is to poison humanity by means of a deadly orchid. He releases these in transparent globes from his space station forming "a necklace of death about the earth. Fifty globes, each releasing its nerve gas over a designated area. Each capable of killing one hundred million people. The human race, as you know it, will cease to exist. Then, a rebirth—a new world."

Like most tyrants, Drax is an optimist, and it is well known that optimists with beliefs usually cause more misery and devastation than any amount of

Fire and brimstone. Christopher Lee as Dracula in *The Satanic Rites of Dracula* (dir. Alan Gibson, 1973).

doubting pessimists. (Cioran concurs, finding "more comfort, more hope even in the weary emperor [Marcus Aurelius] than in the thundering prophet [Nietzsche's Zarathustra]."[30]) For all his technologically delivered destruction, Drax does not wish for "das Ende" at all—rather a new beginning, which will inevitably bring more suffering, though in a different guise.

Count Dracula, in Hammer's last film about him, *The Satanic Rites of Dracula*, offers an equally drastic but less "optimistic" apocalypse. His plan is similarly to exterminate humanity with a poisonous bacillus, even though this will have consequences for himself. In the company of secret agent, Peter Torrence (William Franklin) and policeman Inspector Murray (Michael Coles), Peter Cushing's Professor Van Helsing, offers an explanation for this apparently irrational act:

> **TORRENCE:** But Dracula would eventually end up with a totally barren earth.
> **MURRAY:** With only dead and diseased bodies to feed on surely even the vampire himself would perish.
> **VAN HELSING:** Perhaps deep in his subconscious that is what he really wants: An end to it all. He is a cursed immortal, existing on violence, fear and dread; but supposing—just supposing—he yearns for final peace. What then? He'd want to bring down the whole universe with him: The ultimate revenge.

This is what Christopher Lee's Count Dracula describes as "release." "In the days to come, you will pray for death," he snarls, having described his plan for Armageddon by means of a plague bacillus. Intriguingly, Sade had imagined much the same thing in *Juliette*: "Were I king, Juliette," says the libertine Noirceuil, "were I sovereign lord of this world, supreme here, my supreme sovereign pleasure would be to walk about with killing henchmen in my train, to massacre instantly whatever displeased my very sensitive glance....I'd tread the full length and breadth of my domain everywhere upon a carpet of corpses, and I'd be happy; I'd wade across an infinite scene of destruction, and to the sea of blood wherein my feet would steep I'd add my flowing seed."[31] Peter Cushing's Van Helsing, describes Count Dracula's plan in similar terms: "Supposing," he says, "—just supposing, he yearns for final peace. What then? He'd want to bring down the whole universe with him. The ultimate revenge: Thousands dying of the plague and like the Shadow of Death itself one figure scything its way through the terror and anguish. Count Dracula. It is the Biblical prophecy of Armageddon."

In the final scenes of the film, we see Dracula staring into the middle distance. Christopher Lee then invests the word "release" with an immense yearning for oblivion. It is one of his most powerful screen moments, and a truly Schopenhaurian one. Indeed, the premise of Don Houghton's script for this most philosophically interesting of Hammer's vampire films, is Schopenhaurian through and through. Nietzsche had identified such negation as representing a kind of revenge on life:

> To say it again, this depressive and contagious instinct thwarts those instincts bent on preserving and enhancing the value of life: both as a multiplier of misery and as a conservator of everything miserable it is one of the chief instruments for the advancement of decadence—pity persuades to nothingness! ... One does not say "nothingness": one says "the Beyond"; or "God"; or "true life"; or Nirvana, redemption, blessedness.[32]

Horror films, it would seem, tend more toward Schopenhauer than to Nietzsche, which was certainly the case with Herzog's *Nosferatu*. In one scene towards the end of the film, set in the town square of Delft where the film was partly shot, Herzog creates an unforgettable image of the ultimately absurd and grotesque nature of life below the veneer of bourgeois respectability and social optimism. Amid the disarray in the square, which is littered with furniture and misplaced objects, a sheep wanders in the distance. Smoke from impromptu bonfires drifts across the screen, while a pig walks behind the figure of an elderly lady fast asleep in a chair. Herzog then cuts to a long shot of the square from higher up, giving us a panorama of this vision of the end of the world. Lucy wanders through disparate figures: a cowled monk praying before a coffin, young men and women dancing, a man playing a Waldhorn, another man leaps onto a goat, while rats gather beneath a table at which elegantly dressed bourgeois townsfolk eat, drink and attempt to be merry, knowing that tomorrow they will die.

The courage to embrace one's own inevitable demise in the face of equally inevitable defeat has also been represented in film, though admittedly with less frequency that the triumph over adversity, which has always been the more conventional way to bring a film to its end. The end of *Dr. Strangelove* is a case in point, in which cowboy actor Slim Pickens as Major T.J. "King" Kong strides a falling atom bomb like a rodeo rider, waving his Stetson in jubilation. At the end of *Richard III* (dir. Richard Longcrain, 1996), Ian McKellen's Richard falls to his fiery death smiling gleefully directly at the camera, his hand raised in a welcoming salute, while Al Jolson sings "I'm Sitting on Top of the World." In spirit, this jubilant defiance against the conspiracy of the living, has much in common with the Norwegian novelist Knut Hamsun's 1892 novel *Mysteries*, in which the leading character, Nagel, carries around with him a phial of what is apparently Prussic Acid. For him, it represents a reassuring escape route should life become unendurable. In fact, the phial serves a purely symbolic purpose for him; it does not contain Prussic Acid (the liquid is harmless water), but that is hardly the point:

> What would it be like to be floating around up there among the planets, feeling the tails of the comets brushing against one's forehead? What a tiny speck the earth was, and how insignificant its inhabitants—Norway had two million bumpkins supported by mortgages and bank loans. What was the point of living, anyway? you fight your way ahead with blood and sweat for a few miserable years, only to turn into dust! Nagel put his head in his hands. He would finally get out of it all—end it! Yes, by God,

he wouldn't falter! He felt euphoric at the idea of having this escape hatch in reserve. Tears of rapture came into his eyes, and the intense emotion made his breathing heavy.[33]

The freedom Nagel feels in the face of death actually makes him happy, somewhat like Richard III and Major Kong.

Death as release from suffering and the limitations of the physical is also shared by many of the cinema's classic monsters. "To be die, to be really dead," muses Bela Lugosi's Dracula, "that must be glorious." We have already encountered the death wish of Christopher Lee's Count in *The Satanic Rites of Dracula,* and Hammer increasingly emphasized the Biblical imagery of their vampire anti-hero. Hammer's Dracula was a kind of Satan, whose various deaths parody Christ's crucifixion (the cross is fatal to both in different ways). After drowning in the sequel, *Dracula: Prince of Darkness* (dir. Terence Fisher, 1966), the Count weeps tears of blood after being impaled on a crucifix in *Dracula Has Risen from the Grave,* before being overcome by Christian iconography in *Taste the Blood of Dracula.* In *Scars of Dracula* (dir. Roy Ward Baker, 1970), divine intervention causes death by a thunderbolt, while holy water dispatches him in *Dracula A.D. 1972.* Finally, a crown of thorns adorns the dying vampire's head in *The Satanic Rites of Dracula.* All these deaths, by echoing Christ's passion, bring with them a sense of redemption, which Stoker had implied all along in his original description of the Count's death: "I shall be glad as long as I live," writes Mina Harker, "that even in that moment of final dissolution, there was in the face a look of peace, such as I never could have imagined might have rested there."[34] But this redemption is not resurrection and the life to come: It is release from existence. "Requiescat in pace ultima" as we read on a gravestone in *Dracula A.D. 1972*: "Rest in Final Peace."

Similarly, the various cinematic demises of Frankenstein's creatures bring with them a sense of relief that what has been so unfortunately animated is now fortunately returned to the inert matter whence it came. "We belong dead," shouts Karloff's monster in *The Bride of Frankenstein,* before blowing himself up along with his creator. Hammer also blew up their various creatures but emphasized the sense of dissolution by twice plunging them into a vat of acid (in *The Curse of Frankenstein* and *The Horror of Frankenstein* [dir. Jimmy Sangster, 1970]). The desire to Rest in Peace, mentioned on so many human tombstones, is, of course, "in sure and certain hope of the resurrection to eternal life through our Lord Jesus Christ," but there also exists a more secular transfiguration, derived from German Romanticism, in which Death leads to the peace of complete oblivion, a consummation devoutly to be wished by the creatures themselves if not their creator.

Epilogue: Consolation

"They give birth astride of a grave, the light gleams an instant, then it's night once more."

—Samuel Beckett[1]

If the terrors of the flesh are insistent and pervasive; they are also absurd. In an existence so wholly dependent upon the unpredictable and uncertain realities of the body, absurdity inevitably underlies all our actions and reactions. That master of the absurd, Eugène Ionesco, regarded life as a prison, and if we believe that consciousness is somehow independent of the body, we may well regard the body as a prison, from which only death can release us.

Stephen King, referred to this idea of Ionescu's when discussing *The Mist* with its director Frank Darabont on the DVD release of this film, referring to Ionescu's anti-fascist play *Rhinoceros*. Ionescu wrote absurdist dramas, which occupy that often contradictory space between comedy and tragedy, either of which can easily turn into the other, and the same thing can happen in horror movies.

Some years ago, the film composer John du Prez, who provided the soundtrack scores for many of the Monty Python films and *A Fish Called Wanda* (dir. Charles Crichton, 1988), recounted the following anecdote to me:

> Terry Jones once played me a Buster Keaton sequence. I think it's where his house gets destroyed by a hurricane, and he's running around, the hurricane's destroyed his home and there's debris rushing around everywhere, and the normal way of scoring this is to get a seven piece trad. jazz band and just steam through like a train, as they say in the trade. You just have this kind of background wash of jolly music. He played me the slow movement of an Albinoni oboe concerto against this footage, and it was a wonderful insight, because, all the clichés about Chaplin and the pathos of the little clown—it's all there. Comedy is terribly sad. I could never score a horror movie because I just find it so funny. I just crack up. I can never take any of it seriously. I

cannot suspend my disbelief, whereas ... even in *A Fish Called Wanda*: John Cleese's character is terribly sad. He's got a hopeless marriage. He's frustrated by everything, and it's not until the worm turns right at the very end and that he gets his balls, as an American critic once put, that his life journey got anywhere. Comedy is a very serious business as they say![2]

Our anxiety with the corporeal is frequently exorcised in cartoon comedies. MGM's *Tom and Jerry* films are astonishingly violent and transformative. Bodies are mutilated, dismembered, crushed, exploded, burnt and slaughtered with gay abandon, often magically to reconstitute themselves. Bodies are indestructible in cartoon films, fulfilling our wish for permanence or at least resurrection. The frankly appalling things that happen in these films were once considered to be rendered harmless because of such impossibly rectifications. Nowadays, the powers of political correctness are more censorious, and consequently attempt to deny the realities of life and death in the name of child protection. *Tom and Jerry* cartoons are no longer deemed suitable for children. (The perceived anti-social consequences of *Tom and Jerry* have been much more helpfully satirized by *The Simpsons*' "Itchy and Scratchy.")

Of course, *Tom and Jerry* was never originally intended for children, but in diverting the child gaze from such metamorphoses, contemporary opinion demonstrates a degree of neurosis in the face of reality. I repeat what Benatar has to say on the subject: "It is curious that while good people go to great lengths to spare their children from suffering, few of them seem to notice that the one (and only) guaranteed way to prevent all the suffering of their children is not to bring those children into existence in the first place."[3]

Cartoon films also explore the urge that underlies our will to procreate—the Will to Live itself. Nowhere is comedy more unexpectedly serious than during the eternally optimistic escapades of Wile E. Coyote in the Warner Brothers' Roadrunner cartoons. Wile's optimism is an inverse reflection of humanity's relationship with Schopenhauer's ideas about the Will—its restlessness and our inevitable frustration. The Roadrunner can just as easily be seen as an embodiment of the Will itself, inspiring desire and forever eluding us, whereas Wile's optimism always fails him.

In one Roadrunner cartoon, Wile E. paints a continuation of a mountain road on a canvas, hoping his elusive victim will burst through it and fall to his death down the ravine on the other side, but no sooner has he erected his trap than Roadrunner appears and runs into and along the false perspective (demonstrating in the process the illusory nature of reality and the fallibility of our senses.) A truck then appears along the same perspective and flattens Wile, who is standing in the middle of the road, perplexed and outraged. He then decides to try out the illusion himself but ("Oh no!" the dust from his heels spells out forlornly) he plunges into the chasm intended for Roadrunner. We are all crashing into reality and are similarly perplexed by the consequences.

Roadrunner is an instructive illustration of the restless and impeccable nature of the Will, which causes our yearning for Buñuel's obscure objects of desire and the inevitable suffering these bring. No one can defeat the Will, Wile E. Coyote being no exception. The Will insistently goads us, torments us, tantalizes us, and ultimately defeats us, no matter how ingenious or complicated out plans to do so may be. Wile is continually by his increasingly complex schemes to capture and defeat the Will (Roadrunner). Ironically, only our and his ultimate defeat in death can release us from the scourge of the Will.

The lack of dialogue the Roadrunner films aids their abstract and almost mythic grandeur. Music, as Schopenhauer argues so convincingly, is the most perfect expression of the Will, and the musical scores of the Roadrunner films not only mimic the action but also invest that action with the power and fluidity of the Will itself. There is no need for words in this almost metaphysical struggle between Vorstellung (Wile E.) and Wille (Roadrunner). Just as we can never *know* the Will—only feel its *effects*—so too can Wile E. Coyote only feel the effect of Roadrunner, who, being uncatchable, is equally unknowable.

The *Tom and Jerry* films, similarly voiceless for the most part, can also be adopted by Schopenhauerian philosophy. Tom the cat, like Wile E. Coyote, is a victim of his desire for Jerry, the mouse, but Jerry, the more intellectual of the two, continually defeats his would-be nemesis. Only the circumstances of the basic conflict change in the various episodes. Desire leads to suffering and suffering leads to desire in every case, our laughter notwithstanding. Increasingly exasperated, Tom's determination to succeed is comic because so delusional. Like Wile E. Coyote and the painted road, he is continually hoisted on his own petard but cannot stop himself from so doing. We might begin each day fully aware of its futility, and may even intensely enjoy ourselves, just as Tom begins each adventure thinking he will triumph, which he never will. Consequently, much as we are impressed by Jerry's ability to escape and cause Tom to bring injury upon himself, our sympathies lie with Tom, who, like us, is a hopeless victim of the Will. Only in the reconstitution of their frequently flattened bodies does *Tom and Jerry* differ from life's essential reality, but in the violence of their innumerable immolations they are surely very true to reality.

Similarly, *Monty Python's Meaning of Life* reveals, in the end, that there is no meaning to life other than life itself. The moral message of this film is that we should not add to the harm already caused by birth and avoid needlessly increasing the already inevitable sufferings of the body, but that is about all there is as far as any meaning goes. Each of the sections of the film systematically demonstrates the inadvisability of being born and the concomitant corporeal, psychological and intellectual consequences of such an event. The first part shows us a baby being ruthlessly extracted from the womb before being introduced to the world with perfunctory brutality. Part Two exposes the brutality and absurdity of our induction into society at school. One shot set in a public-school chapel is particularly resonant. After satirizing the absurdities of religion in morning prayers ("Oh Lord, Ooo you are so big. So absolutely huge, Gosh, we're all really impressed down here I can tell you. Forgive us O Lord for this our dreadful toadying, but you're so strong and well, just so super. Amen"). John Clease, as the Headmaster, adds, as an afterthought, "Oh, and Jenkins: apparently your mother died this morning." The camera focuses briefly on the bewildered and distressed young Jenkins, before swiftly moving on. My own experience of a British public school reminds me of just how well-observed this kind of behavior is, as are the representations of school masters and their wives discussing private matters before a classroom of boys. Admittedly, the absurd pleasures of sex—the focus of the Will, according to Schopenhauer—which are graphically demonstrated in the Python film before a classroom of school boys, exceed my own memories of school, but the sadistic brutalities of rugby matches in the rain do not, especially the anima evinced by the Masters, who trample the boys into the mud during a particularly vicious contest.

Out of the mud of the scrum we move to the even muddier horrors of the trenches during the First World War, and war was indeed regarded very much as a game at the time, in much the same way that rugby is still defined by its adherents today as "war without weapons."

Later in the film, the relation between over-population and religious beliefs concerning the sanctity of life are also exposed and ridiculed in the song, "Every sperm is sacred." The vacuities of middle age have already been raised in the main title song ("For millions, this life is a sad veil of tears, sitting round with really nothing to say") and they return during a dialogue between two middle-aged Americans, played by Eric Idle and Michael Palin, who order not coffee and cakes but conversation cards instead. (They chose philosophy, but don't get very far ["Ooo. I never knew Schopenhauer was a philosopher." "Yea, he's the one who begins with an 's'?" "Do all philosophers have an 's' in them ... does that mean Selina Jones is a philosopher?"] and after a prolonged silence they call the waiter, complaining that "this conversation isn't very good.")

The possibility of improving our lot by the application of philosophy is again briefly addressed in the midst of a board meeting of "The Very Big Corporation of America" where, among the agenda of the things that there are left for this corporation to own, "The Meaning of Life" itself is discussed by Michael Palin's American business man:

> "I've had a team working on this over the past few weeks, and what we've come up with can be reduced to two fundamental concepts. One: people are not wearing enough hats. Two: matter is energy,"

at which point meaningful suspense music, suggesting a metaphysical seriousness, underscores his subsequent words:

> In the universe there are many energy fields which cannot normally perceive. Some energies have a spiritual source which act upon a person's soul. However, this soul does not exist, *ab initio,* as orthodox Christianity teaches: it has to be brought into existence by a process of guided self-observation. However, this is rarely achieved due to man's unique ability to be distracted from spiritual matters by everyday trivia.

All this has much in common with classic German Idealism—and its concepts of *Bildung* (self-cultivation) and *Wissenschaft* (learning). Peter Watson has succinctly explained these two terms as follows:

> *Wissenschaft* is the philosophical insight that there *is* unity between the Real and the Ideal. *Wissenchaft* is innate in all men but it is a growing thing, evolving and dynamic and so central to this was the concept of *Bildung,* also drawn from idealist philosophy—the process of becoming in an educative sense. Under this system, discovery—research—was a moral act as much as anything.[4]

"What was that about hats, again?" asks another board member of the Very Big Corporation of America, just before the supporting feature of the film surrealistically intrudes upon the action. Few comedy films have ever addressed philosophical issues so profoundly while simultaneously demonstrating the complete indifference to such matters by the majority of people.

Death in *the Meaning of Life* is presented as being no more meaningful than the vacuity of existence, heaven being depicted as an eternity of consumer opportunities set in a bland shopping mall. Everyone is just as bored in heaven as they were on Earth, and distraction (in the form of the lavish production number "It's Christmas in Heaven") is just as necessary to avert boredom among the blessed.

That all this is extremely funny in no way disqualifies the film's ultimate pessimism (though it is not a pessimism that denies the possibility of living a harmless and indeed an interesting life). The deeply ironic final song of *Monty Python's Life of Brian* (dir. Terry Jones, 1979) revels in what at first appears to be a deeply despairing message ("Life's a load of shit, when you look at it"), but in fact, *Brian* is an assault on the consequences of evangelism—of *imposing* meaning on others.

It has been lamented that post-modern man lacks convictions and has only opinions to replace them, but this is surely a more beneficial state of affairs than during those periods of history during which the convictions of faith have caused so much more unnecessary unhappiness and bodily horror. *The Life of Brian* advocates thinking for oneself—the purpose of philosophy itself, after all, being opposed to the submission of thought to ideology. The aim of all philosophy is to help us avoid bumping into the furniture as we negotiate the dimly illumined house of life. The Python film leaves Christ's teachings to speak for themselves, for *Brian* is not an attack on Christ but rather upon the subsequent uses to which his teachings have been subjected by the Pauls of this world, long after Christ's disappearance from the scene.

The very last laugh belongs to Samuel Beckett, whose existential tragi-comedy, *Waiting for Godot,* was filmed in 2001 by Michael Lindsay-Hogg, with Barry McGovern and Johnny Murphy as the tramps Vladimir and Estragon. Set, as Beckett indicated in his text, in a wasteland of rubble (the rubble of civilization?), a lone, leafless tree is the only landmark, suggesting the Biblical Tree of Knowledge and perhaps even Yggdrasil, on which Wotan hung himself to gain spiritual insight. Vladimir and Estragon also contemplate hanging themselves from it, but, like all their other plans, fail to do anything except talk about it. The play is all talk and no action. Famously, nothing happens, twice (in the sense that the play is divided into two acts.) *Waiting for Godot* is the most extreme dramatization of Schopenhauer's world-view, packed, as it is with one-liners, which sum up so much of his philosophy. "What if we repented ... our being born?" Estragon wonders, before Vladimir suggests a suicide attempt, his reference to genital erections, semen and mandrakes echoing the legend that the ejaculation of semen caused by asphyxiation caused mandrakes to grow at the foot of gallows. (This legend

Born astride the grave. Barry McGovern (left) and Johnny Murphy as Vladimir and Estragon in *Waiting for Godot* **(dir. Michael Lindsay-Hogg, 2001).**

had been exploited earlier by Hanns Heinz Ewers, in his 1911 novel, *Alraune*, later filmed on several occasions.) Sex, like eating merely passes the time, and we all have no option but to pass the time if we don't kill ourselves. Vladimir and Estragon are, as Schopenhauer would have fully comprehended, bored to death in the midst of the nothingness of existence.

With the arrival of Pozzo and his ironically named companion, Lucky, Beckett satirizes capitalism and its exploitation of the masses. Pozzo is a pompous bourgeois, who leads Lucky on a rope, abusing him and ordering him about in a merciless manner. But Pozzo's domination seems to give him no pleasure. "That's how it is on this bitch of an earth," he complains, adding, "In the meantime, nothing happens. ... I shall suffer. No doubt about that." And when Lucky is finally ordered to "think," having a thinking hat placed on his head, a stream of consciousness pours out, the repeated words and evocative symbols of which satirize the speculations of theology. "For reasons unknown," Lucky reiterates, repeating also "the skull, the skull," that lies beneath the flesh. Pozzo sums up our existence on earth as "birth astride the grave." When Lucky is also allowed to dance, Pozzo calls it "the scapegoat's agony. He thinks he's caught in a net," which, of course, he is. Godot never comes, but Vladimir and Estragon endlessly wait for his appearance. A boy appears, who tells them that Godot will come tomorrow. Lindsay-Hogg's film interpolates a line that is not in the original text: one of the tramps asks if the Boy is an angel, emphasizing his annunciatory role—except that he has nothing to annunciate. And just as we search for meaning we also search for happiness, but being happy makes no difference. "What do we do now, now that we're happy," Estragon asks, but earlier he also confessed to being unhappy. "Since when?" asks Vladimir. "I've forgotten," Estragon concedes.

"The best thing would be to kill me," says Estragon, but that doesn't happen either. Again, all they can do is talk, slightly changing Beckett's text in the process: "Last night we blathered about nothing in particular. That's been going on for centuries." And optimism alternates with pessimism. "Tomorrow, everything will be better. Remind me to bring a bit of rope tomorrow. Nothing is certain."

It is, of course, quite possible to lead a happy and constructive life while simultaneously remaining in fundamental agreement with Schopenhauer and Benatar, and the body horror films of Cronenberg. Love, life and laughter are not incompatible with their philosophies, while the Marquis de Sade was insistent that it was only through nihilism that we could attain complete freedom.

While we are here it is surely a duty to ourselves to make life as enjoyable and bearable as we can, but this does not make it any more meaningful in a metaphysical or even a moral sense. As Benatar puts it,

The fact that one enjoys one's life does not make one's existence better than non-existence, because if one had not come into existence there would have been nobody to have missed the joy of leading that life and thus the absence of joy would not be bad. Notice, by contrast, that it makes sense to regret having come into existence if one does not enjoy one's life. In this case, if one had not come into existence then no being would have suffered the life one leads. That is good, even though there would be nobody who would have enjoyed that good.[5]

Contrary to concerns about global warming and the threatened extinction of humanity, Benatar's view is that extinction should to be welcomed (though not, ideally, through violent means). In an overpopulated world of suffering, extinction is really the only answer to the endlessly repeating complaints and harm of humanity:

> Is the prospect of human extinction something to be regretted?' I shall answer that although the process of extinction may be regrettable, and although the prospect of human extinction may, in some ways be bad for us, it would be better, all things considered, if there were no more people (and indeed no more conscious life). A secondary question about extinction is whether, given the fact of future extinction, it would be better if this came earlier or later. Here I shall argue that although very imminent extinction would be worse for us, earlier extinction nonetheless would be better than later extinction. This is because earlier extinction guarantees against the significant harm of future lives that would otherwise be started.[6]

Benatar regards the view that it would be best if humans continued to exist for as long a possible "sentimental," and in this he is in agreement with the Marquis de Sade, who argues that "the total disappearance of mankind ... would grieve [Nature] very little, she would no more pause in her career than if the whole species of rabbits or chickens were suddenly to be wiped off the face of the earth,"[7]

Stranded, as we are, on a planet, which the song in *The Meaning of Life* describes as revolving at 900 miles an hour, we have created the idea of God to help us negotiate our predicament. The Pythons suggest we pray for intelligent life in outer space, as "there's bugger all down here on earth," but, on the contrary, it is our own intelligence that has caused the problem: We *know* we will die; animals do not. Art articulates the sufferings and terrors of the flesh but it does not necessarily make us any happier; for Schopenhauer, the pursuit of happiness is anyway irrelevant:

> There is only one inborn error, and that is the notion that we exist to be happy. It is inborn in us, because it coincides with our existence itself, and our whole being is only its paraphrase, indeed our body is its monogram. We are nothing more than the will-to-live, and the successive satisfaction of all our willing is what we think of through the concept of happiness.
>
> So long as we persist in this inborn error, and indeed even become confirmed in it through optimistic dogmas, the world seems to us full of contradictions. For at every step, in great things as in small, we are bound to experience that the world and life are

certainly not arranged for the purpose of containing a happy existence. ... The consideration of this then often proves to be very depressing, especially when life is already drawing to an end; hence the countenances of almost all elderly persons wear the expression of what is called *disappointment*.

...Suffering expresses itself clearly enough to the whole of human existence as its true destiny. Life is deeply steeped in suffering and cannot escape from it; our entrance into it takes place amid tears, at bottom its course is always tragic, and its end is even more so. ... In fact, suffering is the process of purification by which alone man is in most cases sanctified, in other words, led back from the path of error of the will-to-live.[8]

The cinema of body horror teaches us the same lesson.

Chapter Notes

Epigraph

1. Marquis de Sade (trans. Austryn Wainhouse), *Juliette,* New York: Grove Press, 1968, 385–386.

Introduction

1. Friedrich Nietzsche (trans. R. J. Hollingdale), *Thus Spake Zarathustra,* Harmondsworth: Penguin, 1969, 61.
2. Marquis de Sade (trans. Austryn Wainhouse), *Juliette,* New York: Grove Press, 1968, 44–45.
3. Arthur Schopenhauer (trans. R. J. Hollingdale), *Essays and Aphorisms,* Harmondsworth: Penguin, 1970, 47–48 ("On the Suffering of the World").
4. *David Cronenberg and the Cinema of the Extreme,* BBC 1997, https://www.youtube.com/watch?v=bJMq-T40K_A.
5. Dez Skinn (ed.), *Hammer's House of Horror,* No. 20, London: Top Sellers, May 1978, 20–21 ("Doctors of Death").
6. Ibid., 20.
7. Arthur Schopenhauer (trans. E.F.J Payne), *The World as Will and Representation,* Vol. 1, New York: Dover, 1969, 312.
8. Charles Dickens, *A Tale of Two Cities/A Christmas Carol* London: Hazell, Watson & Viney, no date, 357 ("A Christmas Carol").
9. Friedrich Nietzsche (trans. Douglas Smith), *On the Genealogy of Morals,* London: Penguin, 1996, 106.
10. Schopenhauer, *The World as Will and Representation,* Vol. 1, 170–171.
11. Ted Honderich, ed., *The Oxford Companion to Philosophy,* Oxford: Oxford University Press, 1995, 342 (Peter Singer's entry one G. W. F. Hegel).
12. Sigmund Freud (trans. James Strachey), *On Metapsychology,* Penguin, 1984, 322 ("Beyond the Pleasure Principle").
13. Carlos Clarens, *Horror Movies: An Illustrated Survey,* London: Secker & Warburg, 1968, 12.
14. David Benatar, *Better Never to Have Been: The Harm of Coming Into Existence,* Oxford: Oxford University Press, 2006, 6.
15. "Illness as Horror Movie, and Other Thoughts on Time, Disease, and Capitalism. Matthew Sharpe in Conversation with Anne Elizabeth Moore," https://lithub.com/illness-as-horror-movie-and-other-thoughts-on-time-disease-and-capitalism/.
16. Aristotle (trans. Anthony Kenny), *Poetics,* Oxford: Oxford University Press, 2013, 23.
17. Lotte H. Eisner (trans. Roger Greaves), *The Haunted Screen,* London: Thames and Hudson, 1969, 9.
18. Friedrich Nietzsche (trans. Walter Kaufmann), *The Birth of Tragedy and The Case of Wagner,* New York, Vintage,1967, 60 ("The Birth of Tragedy").
19. Clarens, *Horror Movies: An Illustrated Survey,* 9.
20. Marcus Aurelius (trans. George Long), *The Harvard Classics,* Danbury, Grolier Enterprises, 1980, 298 ("The Meditations of Marcus Aurelius").
21. Sophocles (trans. E. F. Watling), *King Oedipus,* Harmondsworth: Penguin, 1947, 68.
22. William Shakespeare (ed. W. J. Craig), *Complete Works,* Oxford: Oxford University Press, 1945, 83 ("Measure For Measure," Act III, scene 1).
23. Ibid., 867–868 ("Macbeth," Act V, scene 3).
24. Shakespeare, *Complete Works,* 886 ("Hamlet," Act III, scene 1).

25. Christopher Marlowe (ed. E. D. Pendry), *Complete Poems and Plays*, London: J. M. Dent, 1976, xxii–xxiii.
26. *Ibid.*, vii.
27. Sylvan Barnet, Morton Berman and William Burto (eds.), *Classic Theatre: The Humanities in Drama*, Boston: Little, Brown, 1975, 174 (John Webster, "The Duchess of Malfi," Act V, scene 2).
28. *Ibid.*, 167 (John Webster, "The Duchess of Malfi," Act IV, scene 2).
29. *Ibid.*, 168 (Webster, "The Duchess of Malfi," Act IV, scene 2).
30. Friedrich Nietzsche (trans. R. J. Hollingdale), *Thus Spoke Zarathustra*, Harmondsworth: Penguin 1969, 62.
31. Walt Whitman, *Leaves of Grass*, London: G. P. Putnam's Sons, 1897, 87–88 ("I Sing the Body Electric").

Chapter One

1. Charles Baudelaire, *Oeuvres Posthumes*, Paris: Société du Mercures de France, 1908, 49 ("l'amour ressemblait fort à une torture ou à une opération chirurgicale.").
2. Mary Shelley, *Frankenstein*, London: Dent, 1912, 48.
3. *Ibid.*
4. Marquis de Sade (trans. Austryn Wainhouse), *Juliette*, New York: Grove Press, 1968, 52.
5. Shelley, *Frankenstein*, 179.
6. Arthur Schopenhauer (trans. R. J. Hollingdale), *Essays and Aphorisms*, Harmondsworth: Penguin, 1970, 64 ("The Will to Live").
7. Arthur Schopenhauer (trans. E. F. J. Payne), *The World as Will and Representation*, Vol. 2, New York: Dover, 1969, 514.
8. Mary Shelley, *Frankenstein*, London: Dent, 1912, 50.
9. Schopenhauer, *Essays and Aphorisms*, 50 ("On the Suffering of the World").
10. *Ibid.*, 49 ("On the Suffering of the World").
11. E. M. Cioran (trans. Richard Howard), *The Trouble with Being Born*, New York: Arcade, 1976, 6.
12. Mary Shelley, *Frankenstein*, London: Dent, 1912, 166–167.
13. Christopher Bram, *Father of Frankenstein*, London: Penguin/Plume, 1996, 141.
14. *Ibid.*, 152.
15. Arthur Schopenhauer (trans. E.F.J Payne), *Parerga and Paralipomena: Short Philosophical Essays*, Vol. 2, Oxford: Clarendon Press, 1974, 316 ("Additional Remarks on the Doctrine of Affirmation and Denial of the Will-to-Live").
16. Bram Stoker, *Dracula*, London: Constable, 1904, 52.
17. Bram Stoker, "The Censorship of Fiction," *The Nineteenth Century*, Sept. 1908, 483 (http://www.bramstoker.org/pdf/nonfic/fiction.pdf).
18. Stoker, *Dracula*, 39.
19. Maurice Lever, *The New York Times Book Review*, quoted by Richard Davenport-Hines in "Doing Some Measuring Ahead of Time," *London Review of Books*, Vol. 23, No. 15, 9 August 2001, 16.
20. Walter Pater, *The Renaissance: Studies in Art and Poetry*, London: Folio Society, 2013, 87.
21. Marquis de Sade, *Juliette*, 64.
22. Roman Polanski, *Roman by Polanski*, London: Heinemann, 1984, 182.
23. *Ibid.*, 182.
24. *Ibid.*, 194.
25. Ivan Butler, *Horror in the Cinema* (Third Edition), London: Tantivy Press, 1979, 88.
26. Joan Lindsay, *Picnic at Hanging Rock*, Harmondsworth: Penguin, 1977, 211.

Chapter Two

1. Mary Shelley, *Frankenstein*, London: Dent, 1912, xii.
2. Gabriele D'Annunzio (trans. Georgina Harding), *L'Innocente (The Victim)*, Sawtry: Dedalus, 1991, 168–169.
3. *Ibid.*, 301–302.
4. Laurence Schifano (trans. William S. Byron), *Luchino Visconti: The Flames of Passion*, London: Collins, 1990, 413.
5. Mary Shelley, *Frankenstein*, London: Dent, 1912, 51.
6. Marquis de Sade (trans. Austryn Wainhouse), *Juliette*, New York: Grove Press, 1968, 396.
7. John Milton, *The Poetical Works of John Milton*, London: Frederick Warne, 1896, 340 ("Paradise Lost").
8. *To the Devil ... The Death Hammer* (dir. Marcus Hearn, 2002).
9. Dennis Wheatley, *To the Devil a Daughter*, Geneva: Heron, 1972, 218.
10. *Ibid.*, 219.

11. *To the Devil ... The Death of Hammer* (dir. Marcus Hearn, 2002).
12. David Benatar, *Better Never to Have Been: The Harm of Coming Into Existence*, Oxford: Clarendon Press, 2006, 6.
13. Henry James, *The Turn of the Screw and Other Stories*, Harmondsworth: Penguin, 1969, 13 ("The Turn of the Screw").
14. *Ibid.*, 11.
15. *Ibid.*, 45.
16. Henry James (ed. Leon Edel), *Literary Criticism. French Writers. Other European Writers*, New York: Library of America, 1984, 923 ("Gabriele D'Annunzio").
17. Gabrielle D'Annunzio (trans. Georgina Harding), *The Child of Pleasure*, Sawtry: Dedalus, 1991, 206.
18. R. M. Ballantyne, *The Coral Island*, London: Blackie & Son, no date, 29–30.
19. William Golding, *Lord of the Flies*, London: Guild Publishing, 1980, 12.
20. Thomas Mann (trans. H. T. Lowe-Porter), *The Magic Mountain*, London: Secker & Warburg, 1979, 494.
21. William Golding, *Lord of the Flies*, 128.
22. *Ibid.*, 107.
23. *Ibid.*, 225.
24. *Ibid.*, 160–161.
25. *Ibid.*, 154.
26. Anne Rice, *Interview with the Vampire*, London: Futura, 1977, 150.

Chapter Three

1. Peter Cushing in *Frankenstein and the Monster from Hell* (dir. Terence Fisher, 1974).
2. Marquis de Sade (trans. Austryn Wainhouse), *Juliette*, New York: Grove Press, 1987, 63.
3. Colin Spencer, *The Heretic's Feast: A History of Vegetarianism*, London: Fourth Estate, 1993, 307.
4. Adolf Hitler (trans. Norman Cameron and R.H. Stevens), *Hitler's Table Talk 1941–1944: His Private Conversations*, New York: Enigma Books, 2000, 572 (July 8, 1944).
5. *Ibid.*, 640 (August 20, 1944).
6. John Dryden (ed. John Sargeaunt), *The Poems of John Dryden*, Oxford: Oxford University Press, 1913, p. 496 (Translations from Ovid: "Of the Pythagorean Philosophy").
7. *Ibid.*, 497.
8. Roland Barthes (trans. Annette Lavers), *Mythologies*, London: Paladin, 1986, 62.
9. *Hammer—The Studio That Dripped Blood* (dir. David Thompson, 1987).
10. John Brosnan, *The Horror People*, London: St Martin's Press 1976, 115–16.
11. Werner Herzog (ed. Paul Cronin), *Herzog on Herzog*, New York: Faber and Faber, 2002, 218.
12. Edward Lloyd, *The String of Pearls*, Ware: Wordsworth, 2005, 26.
13. *Ibid.*, 27.
14. Karl Marx (ed. David McLellan), *Capital: An Abridged Edition*, Oxford, Oxford University Press, 1995, 119.
15. William Shakespeare (ed. W. J. Craig), *Complete Works*, Oxford: Oxford University Press, p. 761 ("Titus Andronicus," Act V, sceve 2).
16. S. Clarke Hulse, *Criticism*, Vol. XXI, No. 2, Detroit: Wayne State University, Spring 1979, 106–118 ("Wresting the Alphabet: Oratory and Action in 'Titus Andronicus'").
17. Bram Stoker, *Dracula: The Definitive Author's Cut*, Creation Books, 2005, 41.
18. James Orbesen, "Review: Anne Elizabeth Moore's Body Horror: Capitalism, Fear, Misogyny, Jokes," https://thirdcoastreview.com/2017/04/25/review-anne-elizabeth-moores-body-horror-capitalism-fear-misogyny-jokes/.
19. Marx, *Capital*, 149.
20. Colin Spencer, *The Heretic's Feast: A History of Vegetarianism*, 44.
21. *Ibid.*, 45.
22. Charles Darwin, *The Voyage of the "Beagle,"* Geneva: Edito Service S.A., 1968, 35.
23. *Ibid.*, 36–37.
24. André Pierre de Mandiargues (trans. J. Fletcher), *Portrait of an Englishman in His Chateau*, Sawtry: Dedalus, 1999, 45–46.
25. John Wyndham, *The Day of the Triffids*, London: BCA, 1981, 84.
26. H. G. Wells, "The Flowering of a Strange Orchid," http://www.online-literature.com/wellshg/2865/.
27. Geraldine Beare (ed.), *Adventure Stories from the "Strand,"* London: Folio Society, 1995, 55 ("The Purple Terror" by Fred M. White).
28. *Ibid.*, 64 ("The Purple Terror").
29. Thomas Mann (trans. Richard and Clara Winston), *Thomas Mann Diaries, 1918–1939*, London: Robin Clark, 1984,

248 (Entry for Tuesday, November 12, 1935: "I felt better once the feature started, a very good American thriller called *The Mummy*").
30. Thomas Mann (trans. H. T. Lowe-Porter), *Doctor Faustus: The Life of the German Composer Adrian Leverkühn as Told by a Friend*, London: Secker & Warburg, 1949, 18.
31. *Ibid.*, 19.
32. Wyndham, *The Day of the Triffids*, 22.
33. *Ibid.*, 57.
34. *Ibid.*, 35.
35. *Ibid.*, 170.
36. Arthur Schopenhauer (trans. E. F. J. Payne), *The World as Will and Representation*, Vol 1., New York: Dover, 1969, 147.
37. *Ibid.*, 148.

Chapter Four

1. Antony Easthope, *What a Man's Gotta Do*, London: Paladin Grafton Books, 1986, 36
2. *Ibid.*, 39–40.
3. *Ibid.*, 41.
4. https://www.vice.com/en_us/article/mvpkex/more-than-davids-daughter-an-interview-with-jennifer-lynch.
5. Charles Darwin, *The Voyage of the "Beagle,"* Geneva: Edito Service S.A., 1968, 27.
6. Lotte H. Eisner (trans. Roger Greaves), *The Haunted Screen*, London: Thames and Hudson, 1973, 145.
7. *Ibid.*, 106.
8. David J. Skal, *The Monster Show*, London: Plexus, 1993, 69.
9. Gaston Leroux, *The Phantom of the Opera*, London: Michael O'Mara, 1987, 115.
10. *Ibid.*, 113–114.
11. *Ibid.*, 113.
12. E. M. Cioran (trans. Richard Howard), *The Trouble with Being Born*, New York: Arcade, 1976, 36.
13. Gaston Leroux, *The Phantom of the Opera*, 198.
14. Jean Lorrain (trans. Francis Amery), *Monsieur de Phocas*, Sawtry: Dedalus, 1994, 105.
15. Cioran, *The Trouble with Being Born*, 22.
16. Leroux, *The Phantom of the Opera*, 115.
17. David Miller, *The Peter Cushing Companion*, London: Reynolds & Hearn, 2000, 116.
18. Arthur Schopenhauer (trans. E. F. J. Payne), *The World as Will and Representation*, Vol. 1, New York: Dover, 1969, 119–120.
19. Schopenhauer, *The World as Will and Representation*, Vol. 2, 24–25.
20. V. S. Ramachandran and Sandra Blakeslee, *Phantoms in the Brain*, London: Fourth Estate, 1999, 22.
21. *Ibid.*, 112.
22. *Ibid.*, 126.
23. See Sigmund Freud, "Medusa's Head," https://www.pep-web.org/document.php?id=se.018.0273a.
24. E. M. Cioran (trans. Richard Howard), *The Trouble with Being Born*, New York: Arcade, 1976, 222.
25. *Ibid.*, 207.
26. *Ibid.*, 218.
27. *Ibid.*, 222.
28. George Bernard Shaw, *The Complete Plays of Bernard Shaw*, London: Odhams Press, no date, 374 ("Man and Superman").
29. Robert Irwin, *The Arabian Nightmare*, Harmondsworth: Penguin/Viking, 1987, 96.
30. Sigmund Freud (trans. James Strachey), *The Penguin Freud Library, Vol. 11: "On Metapsychology,"* London: Penguin, 1984, 380–381 ("The Ego and the Id").
31. Arthur Koestler, *The Ghost in the Machine*, London: Hutchinson, 1976, 272.
32. *Ibid.*, 273.
33. *Ibid.*, 312.
34. Easthope, *What a Man's Gotta Do*, 111.

Chapter Five

1. "Illness as Horror Movie, and Other Thoughts on Time, Disease, and Capitalism. Matthew Sharpe in Conversation with Anne Elizabeth Moore," https://lithub.com/illness-as-horror-movie-and-other-thoughts-on-time-disease-and-capitalism/.

Chapter Six

1. Henry Beston, *The Outermost House*, Harmondsworth: Penguin, 1988, 25.
2. E. M. Cioran, *The Trouble with Being Born*, New York, Arcade, 1976, 68.
3. Franz Kafka (trans. Willa and Edwin Muir), *Metamorphosis and Other Stories*,

Harmondsworth: Penguin, 1961, 11 ("Metamorphosis").
4. Donald Spotto, *The Art of Alfred Hitchcock: Fifty Years of His Films*, London: Fourth Estate,1992, 330.
5. *Ibid.*, 337.
6. Arthur Schopenhauer (trans. E.F.J Payne), *The World as Will and Representation*, Vol. 1, New York: Dover, 1969, 313.
7. Alfred Hitchcock, https://www.youtube.com/watch?v=jmKdGY004Xc .
8. Benatar, *Better Never to Have Been*, 65.
9. Heinrich von Kleist (trans. David Constantine), *Selected Writings*, London: Dent, 1997, 416 ("The Puppet Theatre").
10. David J. Skal, *The Monster Show*, London: Plexus, 1993, 171.
11. Gustav Meyrink (trans. Maurice Rarity), *The Opal and Other Stories*, Sawtry: Dedalus, 1994, 109 ("Dr. Cinderella's Plants").
12. H. P. Lovecraft, *The Fiction: Complete and Unabridged*, New York: Barnes and Noble, 2008, 377 ("The Call of Cthulhu").
13. Oscar Wilde, *Stories*, London: Folio Society, 1993, 1–2 ("The Picture of Dorian Gray").
14. Lovecraft, *The Fiction: Complete and Unabridged*, 377 ("The Call of Cthulhu").
15. Fitz-James O'Brien, *The Fantastic Tales of Fitz-James O'Brien*, London: John Calder, 1977, 110 ("Seeing the World").
16. Jean Lorrain (trans. Francis Amery), *Monsieur de Phocas*, Sawtry: Dedalus, 1994, 179.

Chapter Seven

1. E. M. Cioran (trans. Richard Howard), *The Trouble with Being Born*, New York: Arcade, 1976, 54.
2. H. Rider Haggard, *She*, London: Collins, 1974, 297.
3. William Blake, *Songs of Innocence and of Experience*, London: Oxford University Press, 1970, plate 40.
4. Edgar Allan Poe, *The Complete Illustrated Stories and Poems of Edgar Allan Poe*, London: Chancellor Press, 1988, 561 ("The System of Dr. Tarr and Professor Fether").
5. *Ibid.*, 547 ("The System of Dr. Tarr and Professor Fether").
6. Arthur Schopenhauer (trans. E. F. J. Payne), *The World as Will and Representation*, Vol. 1, New York: Dover, 1969, 192.

7. Peter Weiss (trans. Geoffrey Skelton and Adrian Mitchell), *Marat*, London: Calder and Boyars, 1970, 32–33.
8. *Ibid.*, 40.
9. Cioran, *The Trouble with Being Born*, 48.
10. Werner Herzog (ed. Paul Cronin), *Herzog on Herzog*, London: Faber and Faber, 2002, 218.
11. *Ibid.*, 112.
12. *Ibid.*, 111.
13. *Ibid.*, 112.
14. *Ibid.*, 115.
15. Michael Newton, *Savage Girls and Wild Boys*, London: Faber and Faber 2002, 160.
16. Arthur Schopenhauer (trans. E. F. J. Payne), *The World as Will and Representation*, Vol. 1, New York: Dover, 1969, 193.
17. *Ibid.*, 193–194.
18. Herzog, *Herzog on Herzog*, 116.
19. *Ibid.*, 125.
20. Newton, *Savage Girls and Wild Boys*, 106.
21. *Ibid.*, 112–113.

Chapter Eight

1. E. M. Cioran (trans. Richard Howard), *The Trouble with Being Born*, New York: Arcade, 1976, 108.
2. Sigmund Freud (trans. James Strachey), *The Penguin Freud Library, Vol. 11: "On Metapsychology,"* London: Penguin, 1984, 322 ("Beyond the Pleasure Principle").
3. *Ibid.*, 380–381 ("The Ego and the Id").
4. *Ibid.*, 381 ("The Ego and the Id").
5. *Ibid.*, 385 ("The Ego and the Id").
6. Mircea Eliade, *From Primitives to Zen: A Thematic Sourcebook of the History of Religions*, London: Collins, 1979, 110 (from the "Rig Veda").
7. Richard Wagner (trans. Stewart Spencer), *Selected Letters of Richard Wagner*, London: Dent, 1987, 346 (Letter to Franz Liszt, 7 June 1855).
8. Arthur Schopenhauer (trans. R. J. Hollingdale), *Essays and Aphorisms*, Harmondsworth: Penguin, 1970, 48 ("On the Suffering of the World").
9. Lord Byron, *The Poetical Works of Lord Byron*, London: Virtue, 1860, 193 ("Darkness").
10. Mary Shelley, *The Last Man*, Lincoln: University of Nebraska Press, 1993, 337.

11. Peter Weiss (trans. Geoffrey Skelton and Adrian Mitchell), *Marat*, London: Calder and Boyars, 1970, 32.
12. *Ibid.*
13. David Benatar, *Better Never to Have Been: The Harm of Coming Into Existence*, Oxford: Oxford University Press, 2006, 195.
14. Karl Marx (ed. David McLellan), *Capital: An Abridged Edition*, Oxford, Oxford University Press, 1995, 149.
15. Richard Matheson, *I Am Legend*, London: Millennium/Orion, 1999, 26.
16. *Ibid.*, 94.
17. John Wakeman (ed.), *World Film Directors*, Vol. 1. New York: H. W. Wilson Company, 1987, p. 65 (Robin Wood quoted).
18. Richard Matheson, *I Am Legend*, 157.
19. David J. Skal, *The Monster Show: A Cultural History of Horror,* London: Plexus, 1993, 226.
20. Arthur Koestler, *The Ghost in the Machine*, London: Hutchinson, 1976, 321–322.
21. Percy Bysshe Shelley, *Essays and Letters*, London: Walter Scott, no date, 27 ("A Defense of Poetry").
22. John Milton, *The Poetical Works of John Milton,* London: Frederick Warne, 1896, 52 ("Paradise Lost").
23. Arthur Schopenhauer (trans. E. F. J. Payne), *The World as Will and Representation*, Vol. 1, New York: Dover, 1969, 312.
24. Marquis de Sade (trans. Austryn Wainhouse), *Juliette*, New York: Grove Press, 1968, 404.
25. *Ibid.*, 412.
26. Benatar, *Better Never to Have Been*, 208–209.
27. Marquis de Sade (trans. Austryn Wainhouse & Richard Seaver), *The 120 Days of Sodom and Other Writings,* New York: Grove Press, 1966, 638 ("The 120 Days of Sodom").
28. Marquis de Sade (trans. Austryn Wainhouse), *Juliette*, 332.
29. Schopenhauer, *The World as Will and Representation*, Vol. 1, 411–412.
30. Cioran, *The Trouble with Being Born*, 91.
31. Marquis de Sade, *Juliette*, 185.
32. Friedrich Nietzsche (trans. R. J. Hollingdale), *Twilight of the Idols and The Anti-Christ,* Harmondsworth: Penguin, 1968, 118 ("The Anti-Christ").
33. Knut Hamsun (trans. Gerry Bothmer), *Mysteries*, London: Souvenir Press, 1973, 63–64.
34. Bram Stoker, *Dracula*, London: Constable, 1904, 388.

Epilogue

1. Samuel Beckett, *Waiting for Godot*, London: Faber, 1965, 89.
2. John du Prez in conversation with the author.
3. David Benatar, *Better Never to Have Been: The Harm of Coming Into Existence,* Oxford: Oxford University Press, 2006, 6.
4. Peter Watson, *The German Genius: Europe's Third Renaissance, the Second Scientific Revolution and the Twentieth Century,* London: Simon & Schuster, 2010, 229.
5. David Benatar, *Better Never to Have Been*, Oxford: Oxford University Press, 2006, 58.
6. *Ibid.*, 164.
7. Marquis de Sade (trans. Austryn Wainhouse), *Juliette*, New York: Grove Press, 1987, 67.
8. Schopenhauer, *The World as Will and Representation*, Vol. 2, 634–636.

Bibliography

Aristotle (trans. Anthony Kenny), *Poetics*, Oxford: Oxford University Press, 2013.
Ballantyne, R. M., *The Coral Island*, London: Blackie & Son, no date.
Barnet, Sylvan, Morton Berman and William Burto, eds., *Classic Theatre: The Humanities in Drama*, Boston: Little, Brown, 1975.
Barthes, Roland (trans. Annette Lavers), *Mythologies*, London: Paladin, 1986.
Baudelaire, Charles, *Oeuvres Posthumes*, Paris: Société du Mercures de France, 1908.
Beare, Geraldine, ed., *Adventure Stories from the "Strand,"* London: Folio Society, 1995.
Beckett, Samuel, *Waiting for Godot*, London: Faber, 1965.
Benatar, David, *Better Never to Have Been: The Harm of Coming Into Existence*, Oxford: Oxford University Press, 2006.
Beston, Henry, *The Outermost House*, Harmondsworth: Penguin, 1988.
Blake, William, *Songs of Innocence and of Experience*, London: Oxford University Press, 1970.
Bram, Christopher, *Father of Frankenstein*, London: Penguin/Plume, 1996.
Brosnan, John, *The Horror People*, London: St. Martin's Press 1976.
Butler, Ivan, *Horror in the Cinema* (Third Edition), London: Tantivy Press, 1979.
Byron, Lord George Gordon, *The Poetical Works of Lord Byron*, London: Virtue, 1860.
Clarens, Carlos, *Horror Movies: An Illustrated Survey*, London: Secker & Warburg, 1968.
Cioran, E. M. (trans. Richard Howard), *The Trouble with Being Born*, New York: Arcade, 1976.
D'Annunzio, Gabrielle (trans. Georgina Harding), *The Child of Pleasure*, Sawtry: Dedalus, 1991.
D'Annunzio, Gabrielle (trans. Georgina Harding), *L'Innocente (The Victim)*, Sawtry: Dedalus, 1991.
Darwin, Charles, *The Voyage of the "Beagle,"* Geneva: Edito Service S.A., 1968.
Dryden, John (ed. John Sargeaunt), *The Poems of John Dryden*, Oxford: Oxford University Press, 1913.
Easthope, Antony, *What a Man's Gotta Do*, London: Paladin Grafton Books, 1986.
Eisner, Lotte H. (trans. Roger Greaves), *The Haunted Screen*, London: Thames and Hudson, 1969.
Eliade, Mircea, *From Primitives to Zen: A Thematic Sourcebook of the History of Religions*, London: Collins, 1979.
Fitz-James O'Brien, *The Fantastic Tales of Fitz-James O'Brien*, London: John Calder, 1977.
Freud, Sigmund, "Medusa's Head," https://www.pep-web.org/document.php?id=se.018.0273a
Freud, Sigmund (trans. James Strachey), *The Penguin Freud Library, Vol 11: "On Metapsychology,"* London: Penguin, 1984.
Golding, William, *Lord of the Flies*, London: Guild Publishing, 1980.
Haggard, H. Rider, *She*, London: Collins, 1974.
Hamsun, Knut (trans. Gerry Bothmer), *Mysteries*, London: Souvenir Press, 1973.
Herzog, Werner (ed. Paul Cronin), *Herzog on Herzog*, New York: Faber & Faber, 2002.
Hitler, Adolf (trans. Norman Cameron and R.H. Stevens), *Hitler's Table Talk 1941–1944: His Private Conversations*, New York: Enigma Books, 2000.

Honderich, Ted, ed., *The Oxford Companion to Philosophy*, Oxford: Oxford University Press, 1995.

Hulse, S. Clarke, *Criticism*, Vol. XXI, No. 2, Detroit: Wayne State University, Spring 1979.

Irwin, Robert, *The Arabian Nightmare*, Harmondsworth: Penguin/Viking, 1987.

James, Henry, *The Turn of the Screw and Other Stories*, Harmondsworth: Penguin, 1969,

James, Henry (ed. Leon Edel), *Literary Criticism. French Writers. Other European Writers*, New York: Library of America, 1984.

Kafka, Franz (trans. Willa and Edwin Muir), *Metamorphosis and Other Stories*, Harmondsworth: Penguin, 1961.

Kleist, Heinrich von (trans. David Constantine), *Selected Writings*, London: Dent, 1997.

Koestler, Arthur, *The Ghost in the Machine*, London: Hutchinson, 1976.

Leroux, Gaston, *The Phantom of the Opera*, London: Michael O'Mara, 1987.

Lindsay, Joan, *Picnic at Hanging Rock*, Harmondsworth: Penguin, 1977.

Lorrain, Jean (trans. Francis Amery), *Monsieur de Phocas*, Sawtry: Dedalus, 1994.

Lovecraft, H.P., *The Fiction: Complete and Unabridged*, New York: Barnes and Noble, 2008.

Mandiargues, André Pierre de (trans. J. Fletcher), *Portrait of an Englishman in his Chateau*, Sawtry: Dedalus, 1999.

Mann, Thomas (trans. H. T. Lowe-Porter), *Doctor Faustus: The Life of the German Composer Adrian Leverkühn as Told by a Friend*, London: Secker & Warburg, 1949.

Mann, Thomas (trans. H. T. Lowe-Porter), *The Magic Mountain*, London: Secker & Warburg, 1979.

Mann, Thomas (trans. Richard and Clara Winston), *Thomas Mann Diaries, 1918–1939*, London: Robin Clark, 1984.

Marlowe, Christopher (ed. E. D. Pendry), *Complete Poems and Plays*, London: J. M. Dent, 1976.

Marx, Karl (ed. David McLellan), *Capital: An Abridged Edition* Oxford, Oxford University Press, 1995.

Matheson, Richard, *I Am Legend*, London: Millennium/Orion, 1999.

Meyrink, Gustav (trans. Maurice Rarity), *The Opal (and Other Stories)*, Sawtry: Dedalus, 1994.

Miller, David, *The Peter Cushing Companion*, London: Reynolds & Hearn, 2000.

Milton, John, *The Poetical Works of John Milton*, London: Frederick Warne, 1896.

Newton, Michael, *Savage Girls and Wild Boys*, London: Faber & Faber 2002.

Nietzsche, Friedrich (trans. Douglas Smith), *On the Genealogy of Morals*, London: Penguin, 1996.

Nietzsche, Friedrich (trans. R. J. Hollingdale), *Thus Spake Zarathustra*, Harmondsworth: Penguin, 1969.

Nietzsche, Friedrich (trans. R. J. Hollingdale), *Twilight of the Idols and the Anti-Christ*, Harmondsworth: Penguin, 1968.

Nietzsche, Friedrich (trans. Walter Kaufmann), *The Birth of Tragedy and the Case of Wagner*, New York: Vintage, 1967.

Pater, Walter, *The Renaissance: Studies in Art and Poetry*, London: Folio Society, 2013.

Poe, Edgar Allan, *The Complete Illustrated Stories and Poems of Edgar Allan Poe*, London: Chancellor Press, 1988.

Polanski, Roman, *Roman by Polanski*, London: Heinemann, 1984.

Prest, Thomas, *The String of Pearls*, Ware: Wordsworth, 2005.

Ramachandran, V. S., and Sandra Blakeslee, *Phantoms in the Brain*, London: Fourth Estate, 1999.

Rice, Anne, *Interview With the Vampire*, London: Futura, 1977.

Sade, Donatien Alphonse François, Marquis de (trans. Austryn Wainhouse), *Juliette*, New York: Grove Press, 1968.

Sade, Donatien Alphonse François, Marquis de (trans. Austryn Wainhouse and Richard Seaver), *120 Days of Sodom and other writings*, New York: Grove Press, 1966.

Schifano, Laurence (trans. William S. Byron), *Luchino Visconti: The Flames of Passion*, London: Collins, 1990.

Schopenhauer, Arthur (trans. E.F.J. Payne), *Parerga and Paralipomena: Short Philosophical Essays*, Vol. 2, Oxford: Clarendon Press, 1974.

Schopenhauer, Arthur (trans. E.F.J. Payne), *The World as Will and Representation*, two volumes, New York: Dover, 1969.

Schopenhauer, Arthur (trans. R. J. Hollingdale), *Essays and Aphorisms*, Harmondsworth: Penguin, 1970.

Shakespeare, William (ed. W. J. Craig), *Complete Works*, Oxford: Oxford University Press, 1945.

Shaw, George Bernard, *The Complete Plays*

of Bernard Shaw, London: Odhams Press, no date.
Shelley, Mary, *Frankenstein*, London: Dent, 1912.
Shelley, Mary, *The Last Man*, Lincoln: University of Nebraska Press, 1993.
Shelley, Percy Bysshe, *Essays and Letters*, London: Walter Scott, no date.
Skal, David J., *The Monster Show*, London: Plexus, 1993.
Skinn, Dez, ed., *Hammer's House of Horror*, No. 20, London: Top Sellers, May 1978.
Sophocles (trans. E. F. Watling), *King Oedipus*, Harmondsworth: Penguin, 1947.
Spencer, Colin, *The Heretic's Feast: A History of Vegetarianism*, London: Fourth Estate, 1993.
Spotto, Donald, *The Art of Alfred Hitchcock: Fifty Years of His Films*, London: Fourth Estate, 1992.
Stoker, Bram, "The Censorship of Fiction," *The Nineteenth Century*, Sept. 1908, 483. http://www.bramstoker.org/pdf/nonfic/fiction.pdf.
Stoker, Bram, *Dracula*, London: Constable, 1904.
Stoker, Bram, *Dracula: The Definitive Author's Cut*, Creation Books, 2005.
Wagner, Richard (trans. Stewart Spencer), *Selected Letters of Richard Wagner*, London: Dent, 1987.
Wakeman, John, ed., *World Film Directors*, Vol. 1. New York: H. W. Wilson Company, 1987.
Watson, Peter, *The German Genius: Europe's Third Reniassance, The Second Scientific Revolution and the Twentieth Century*, London: Simon & Schuster, 2010.
Weiss, Peter (trans. Geoffrey Skelton and Adrian Mitchell), *Marat*, London: Calder and Boyars, 1970.
Wells, H. G., "The Flowering of a Strange Orchid." http://www.online-literature.com/wellshg/2865/.
Wheatley, Dennis, *To the Devil a Daughter*, Geneva: Heron, 1972.
Whitman, Walt, *Leaves of Grass*, London: G. P. Putnam's Sons, 1897.
Wilde, Oscar, *Stories*, London: Folio Society, 1993.
Wyndham, John, *The Day of the Triffids*, London: BCA, 1981.

Websites

Alfred Hitchcock, https://www.youtube.com/watch?v=jmKdGY004Xc.
David Cronenberg and the Cinema of the Extreme, BBC 1997, https://www.youtube.com/watch?v=bJMq-T40K_A.
"Illness as Horror Movie, and Other Thoughts on Time, Disease, and Capitalism. Matthew Sharpe in Conversation with Anne Elizabeth Moore," https://lithub.com/illness-as-horror-movie-and-other-thoughts-on-time-disease-and-capitalism/.
James Orbesen, "Review: Anne Elizabeth Moore's Body Horror: Capitalism, Fear, Misogyny, Jokes," https://thirdcoastreview.com/2017/04/25/review-anne-elizabeth-moores-body-horror-capitalism-fear-misogyny-jokes/.

Index

Numbers in **_bold italics_** indicate pages with illustrations

Abbott and Costello Meet Frankenstein (dir. Barton) 95
The Abominable Dr. Phibes (dir. Fuest) 11, 85
Adjani, Isabelle 103
The Adventures of Sherlock Holmes (dir. Werker) 74
Ainley, Anthony 30
Albinoni, Tomaso 162
Alice in Wonderland (Carroll) 50
Alien (dir. Scott) 22, 25, 33
Alraune (Ewers) 167
"The Ambiguity of Henry James" (Wilson) 39
An American Werewolf in London (dir. Landis) 114, **_115_**
"Ancient Sorceries" (Blackwood) 115
Andersson, Harriet 87, 88
Andress, Ursula 127, 151
Andrews, Dana 93
Andrews, Harry 10, **_10_**
Angulo, Álex 51
Ankers, Evelyn 113
Antonioni, Michelangelo 145
Apocalypse Now! (dir. Coppola) 140, 151, 152
The Arabian Nightmare (Irwin) 97
Aristotle 6
Asquith, Robin 95
Asylum (dir. Baker) 130, 132
Atkins, Eileen 32
Attenborough, Sir David 76
Atwill, Lionel 56, 85
Augustine, St. 36
Aurelius, Marcus 7, 159
The Awakening (dir. Newell) 26
Ayres, Lew 90

Bach, J.S. 78, 82
Badham, John 55, 129
Baker, Roy Ward 46, 56, 100, 130, 161
Balch, Anthony 95
Ballantyne, R.M. 42
Band, Albert 111
Bannen, Ian 104
Baquero, Ivana 50
Barthes, Roland 56

Barton, Charles 95
Barton Fink (dir. Ethan and Joel Coen) 96–97
Bate, Anthony 153
Bates, Ralph 31, 100
Baudelaire, Charles 15
The Bay (dir. Levinson) 107
The Beast with Five Fingers (dir. Florey) 78, 82
Beckett, Samuel 153, 161, 167, 168
Bedlam (dir. Robson) 131–132
Beethoven, Ludwig van 61, 107
Before I Hang (dir. Grinde) 98
La belle et la bête (dir. Cocteau) 113
Benatar, David 5, 8, 36, 106, 109, 117, 142–143, 149, 151, 153–154, 163, 168–169
Beneath the Planet of the Apes (dir. Post) 154
Bergman, Ingmar 87–89
Bernard, James 12
Bernds, Edward 111
Beston, Henry 111
Beswick, Martine 100
"Beyond the Pleasure Principle" (Freud) 5, 98, 140
The Birds (dir. Hitchcock) 76, 116–118
Birthistle, Eva 38
"The Black Cat" (Poe) 132
The Black Cat (dir. Ulmer) 147
Black Friday (dir. Lubin) 91
Blackman, Honor 33, 109
Blackmer, Sidney 28
Blackwood, Algernon 66, 115
Blake, William 30, 129
Bleak Moments (dir. Leigh) 58
The Blob (dir. Yeaworth & Doughton) 66
The Blood Beast Terror (dir. Sewell) 111
Blood for Dracula (dir. Morrissey) 56
Blood from the Mummy's Tomb (dir. Holt) 26, 78
Blood on Satan's Claw (dir. Haggard) 29–30, 31
Blotch, Dorothy 65
Bogarde, Dirk 61, 150
Booth, Anthony 87
Bosch, Hieronymus 36
Bowie, Les 34
Bowker, Judy 129

181

182 Index

Boxing Helena (dir. Jennifer Chambers Lynch) 80–81
Boyle, Danny 106
The Boys from Brazil (dir. Schaffner) 93
Bram, Christopher 17
Branagh, Kenneth 15, 19
Brassneur, Pierre 85
Braxton, Hank 107
Breck, Kathleen 93, **94**
Brennan, Michael **105**
The Bride of Frankenstein (dir. Whale) 17, 161
The Brood (dir. Cronenberg) 28, 29
Brook, Peter **43**, 44, 132, **133**
Brooks, Mel 112
Browne, Coral 10
Browning, Logan 70
Browning, Tod 25, 55, 81, 118, **118**, 119, 122
Bryans, John 48
Buckley, Keith 153
Bujold, Geneviève 125
Bulger, Jamie 28, 29, 30
Bulwer-Lytton, Sir Edward (Lord Lytton) 95
Buñuel, Luis 86, 125, 164
Burke, Raymond John 54
Burns, Marilyn 61, **62**
Burns, Mark 129
Burton, Tim 58, 59
Butler, Ivan 23
Byron, Lord George Gordon 141

Cabin Fever (dir. Zariwny) 108–109
The Cabinet of Dr. Caligari (dir. Wiene) 130
"The Call of Cthulhu" (Lovecraft) 122
Callow, Simon 67
Calthrop, Donald 98
Cammell, Donald 22
The Campaign for Nuclear Disarmament 150
Capernaum (dir. Labaki) 49
Capital (Marx) 62, 143
Capote, Truman 39, 42
Cardiff, Jack 76, 120, **121**, 122
Carlson, Larry 91
Caro, Marc 63
Carpenter, John 122
Carradine, John 102
Carriers (dir. Àlex & David Pastor) 106, 109
Carry On Screaming (dir. Thomas) 85
Carson, John 143
Cartier, Rudolf 153
Casanova, Giacomo 132, 135
"The Cask of Amontillado" (Poe) 132
Cat People (dir. Tourneur) 115
Cellier, Frank 98
"The Censorship of Fiction" (Stoker) 20
Cet obscur objet du désir (dir. Buñuel) 125
Chamberlain, Richard 25
Chambers, Marilyn 53, 81
Chaney, Lon, Jr. 21, 83, **84**, 85, 95, 112
Chaplin, Charles 162
Chapman, Graham 31

Chemical Peel (dir. Braxton) 107
Chemical Wedding (dir. Doyle) 67–68
Un chien Andalou (dir. Buñuel) 86 m;
Children of the Corn (dir. Kiersch) 49, 76
Children of the Corn (King) 49
Children of the Damned (dir. Leader) 91
"Children of the Full Moon" (dir. Clegg) 47
Chirico, Giorgio de 145
Christie, Julie 21, 22
Cioran, E.M. 16, 84, 85, 95, 111, 127, 134, 140, 159
Clarens, Carlos 5, 7
Claydon, George 32
Clayton, Jack 38, 39, 41, 42
Clease, John 31, 70, **71**, 163, 165
Clegg, Tom 47
Clive, Colin 16
Cocteau, Jean 113
Coen, Ethan 96, 97
Coen, Joel 96, 97
Cohen, Larry 18–19, **18**, 27, 31, 95
Coles, Michael 159
Collings, David 128, 153
Collins, Joan 31
Collins, Wilkie 132
Condemned (dir. Gesner) 107–108
Condon, Bill 17
Connery, Sean 152
Connolly, Ella 37
Connor, Kevin 4
Conrad, Joseph 44
Constantine, Michael 55
Contagion (dir. Soderbergh) 106–107
Contracted (dir. England) 107, 112
Coote, Robert 10
Coppola, Francis Ford 140, 151–152
The Coral Island (Ballantyne) 42
Corman, Roger 26, 71, 103, 124, 151
Corruption (dir. Hartford-Davis) 87, 89, 93–94
Cossins, James 62
Costello, Lou 95
Count Dracula (dir. Saville) 129
Countess Dracula (dir. Sasdy) 22
Crabtree, Arthur 92, **93**
Craig, Wendy 65
The Crazies (dir. Romero) 104, 107, 109–110, 144
Creley, Jack 4
Crichton, Charles 162
Cries and Whispers (dir. Bergman) 87–89
Cronenberg, David 2, 4, **21**, 22, 28, 29, 37, 52–53, 54, 70, 81, 87, 91, 95, 111, **113**, 114, 125, 129, 147, 168
Crowley, Aleister 67, 68
Cruise, Tom 67
Cukor, George 152
The Curse of Frankenstein (dir. Fisher) 12, 94, 120, 161
The Curse of the Fly (dir. Sharp) 112

Index   183

The Curse of the Werewolf (dir. Fisher) 32, 46–47
Curtiz, Michael 56, 85
Cushing, Peter 18, 48, 51, 64, 87, 89, 93, 97, 104, 111, 115, 159
Cymbeline (Shakespeare) 10

Damiens, Robert-François 132, 135
The Damned (dir. Losey) 46
The Damned (dir. Visconti) 61
Daniels, Jennifer 53
D'Annunzio, Gabrielle 27, 40
Dante 96
Darabont, Frank 66, 67, 162
"Darkness" (Byron) 141–142
Darwin, Charles 25, 66–67, 81, 82
Davies, Robin 30
Davis, Bette 46, 65
Davis, Frank 18
Davis, Geena 112
Davis, Gerry 104
Davis, Leigh 107
Dawn of the Dead (dir. Romero) 144, **144**
Day, Robert 127
The Day the Earth Caught Fire (dir. Guest) 149–150
The Day the Earth Stood Still (dir. Wise) 149
The Day of the Triffids (dir. Sekely) 74
The Day of the Triffids (Wyndham) 72, 74–76
Dead Ringers (dir. Cronenberg) 125–126
Death Line (dir. Sherman) 62
Dehn, Paul 154
Delicatessen (dir. Caro & Jeunet) 63–64
Demon Seed (dir. Cammell) 22–23
Denberg, Susan 94
Deneuve, Catherine 23
Depp, Johnny 58
Derek, John 151
Dern, Bruce 154
The Devils (dir. Russell) 128, 134–135
Diana, Princess 52
Dickens, Charles 3, 94
Dido and Aeneas (Purcell) 93
Diffring, Anton 127
Disintegration (dir. McLeod) 128
Disney, Walt 73
Dispatches (Herr) 152
Dix, William 46, 65
"Dr. Cinderella's Plants" (Meyrinck) 121
Doctor Faustus (Mann) 72
Doctor Faustus (Marlowe) 11–12, 96
Dr. Jekyll and Mr. Hyde (Stevenson) 91, 98
Dr. Jekyll and Sister Hyde (dir. Baker) 100
Dr. Phibes Rises Again (dir. Fuest) 11, 85, 109
Dr. Renault's Secret (dir. Lachman) 111
Dr. Strangelove (dir. Kubrick) 148, 152–153, 160
Dr. Terror's House of Horrors (dir. Francis) 75–76
Doctor Who (TV series) 74, 104
Doctor X (dir. Curtiz) 56

La Dolce Vita (dir. Fellini) 152
Donner, Richard 32, 35
Donovan's Brain (dir. Feist) 90
Don't Look Now (dir. Roeg) 20–21, 29, 31
Doomwatch (dir. Sasdy) 104, **105**
Doomwatch (TV series) 104, 105, 106
The Doors 152
Dors, Diana 47
Doughten, Russell 66
Doyle, Patrick 67
Dracula (dir. Badham) 55
Dracula (dir. Browning) 25, 143
Dracula (Stoker) 19–20, 57, 60–61, 129
Dracula A.D. 1972 (dir. Gibson), 22, 33, 46, 161
Dracula Has Risen from the Grave (dir. Francis) 24, 161
Dracula: Prince of Darkness (dir. Fisher) 161
Dracula's Dog see *Zoltan, Hound of Dracula*
Dragonwyk (dir. Mankiewicz) 74
Drefus, Jean-Claude 63
Dryden, John 53
The Duchess of Malfi (Webster) 12–13
Duffell, Peter 47–48
Duffer, Matt 109
Duffer, Ross 109
Duncan, Isadora 108
Dunne, Griffin 114, **115**
Dunning, George 73
Dunst, Kisten 47, 156
Dürer, Albrecht 36
Dvorsky, Peter 53
Dworet, Laurence 106

The Earth Dies Screaming (dir. Fisher) 143
Easthope, Antony 78–79, 99
Eaton, Shirley 132
Eck, Johnny **118**
L'eclisse (dir. Antonioni) 145
Eggar, Samantha 28
"The Ego and the Id" (Freud) 98–99, 140, 151
Eisner, Lotte H. 6.83
Emge, David **144**
Emmerich, Roland 107
L'enfant sauvage (dir. Truffaut) 138
England, Eric 107, 112
The Enigma of Kaspar Hauser (dir. Herzog) 135–138, **136**, 139
Eraserhead (dir. David Lynch) 34, **35**, 54, 58–59, 64, 67, 69
Evans, Clifford 103
Ewers, Hanns Heinz 73, 167
Exorcist (dir. Friedkin) 36

Fail Safe (dir. Lumet) 153
Fantasia (dir. Jackson, et al) 73
Father of Frankenstein (Bram) 17
The Fearless Vampire Killers (dir. Polanski) 100
Feist, Felix E. 90
Fellini, Federico 116, 152
Fenn, Sherilyn 80

Index

Ferreri, Marco 54
Fiander, Lewis 100
Fiend Without a Face (dir. Crabtree) 92–93, **92**
A Fish Called Wanda (dir. Crichton) 162, 163
Fisher, Terence 12, 32, 46, 47, 57, 64, 66, 89, 94, 100, 105, 114, 127, 127, 143, 161
Fleischer, Richard 61
Florey, Robert 25, 78
"The Flowering of a Strange Orchid" (Wells) 72
The Fly (dir. Cronenberg) 70, 111, **113**, 114, 129
The Fly (dir. Neumann) 111, 129
Forbes, Brian 63
Forbidden Planet (dir. Wilcox) 92, 93, 98
Forman, Miloš 132
Fox, Sidney 25
Francis, Freddie 24, 75, 76, 104, 109
Franco, Francisco 49
Franju, Georges 85–86, **86**, 87
Frankel, Cyril 46, 104
Frankenhooker (dir. Henenlotter) 100–101
Frankenstein (dir. Whale) 16, 80, 123
Frankenstein (Shelley) 15, 16, 17, 19, 26, 28, 32, 33, 79, 93, 100, 114, 141, 142
Frankenstein Created Woman (dir. Fisher) 94, 98
Frankenstein Must Be Destroyed (dir. Fisher) 64, 97, 98
Frankenstein: The True Story (dir. Smight) 17–18
Franklin, John 49
Franklin, William 159
Franks, Chloe 47–48
Frazer, Sir James 49
Freaks (dir. Browning) 55, 81, 118–119, **118**, 120, 122
Freeman, Morgan 106
Freud, Sigmund 5, 65, 98, 140, 151, 152, 158
Freund, Karl 72
The Frozen Dead (dir. Leder) 93, **94**
Full Metal Jacket (dir. Kubrick) 44

Gains, Courtney 49
Gainsbourg, Charlotte 156
Gas trilogy (Kaiser) 153
Geeson, Judy 23, 104, **105**
Geissendörfer, Hans W. 147
Gesner, Eli Morgan 107, 108
Geyser, Morgan 30
The Ghoul (dir. Francis) 104
Gibson, Alan 22, 46, 102, **158**
Giger, H.R. 33
Gilbert and George 68
Gilbert, Lewis 158
Gilbert, Philip **94**
Gillen, Aiden 38
Gilliam, Terry **71**
Gilling, John 92, 111
Gilmore, Peter 4
Gods and Monsters (dir. Condon) 17

Goethe, Johann Wolfgang von 137
Goldblum, Jeff 70, 112, **113**
The Golden Bough (Frazer) 49
Goldfinger (dir. Hamilton) 132
Golding, William 42–44
Goldsmith, Jerry 49
Golightly, Gage 109
Gonzalez, Joseph 101
Goodman, John 97
Gorak, Chris 106
The Gorgon (dir. Fisher) 89
Gothard, Michael 80
Gothic (dir. Russell) 81
Gough, Michael 83, 95
Graham, Michael 112
Grainer, Ron 31
La Grande bouffes (dir. Ferreri) 54
Grandier, Urbain 134–135
Grimm Brothers 65
Grinde, Nick 98
Guest, Val 103, 149, 150
Gwynne, Fred 36
Gwynne, Michael 97

Haggard, H. Rider 127
Haggard, Piers 29, 30
Halperin, Victor 143
Hamilton, Guy 132
Hamilton, Linda 49
Hamlet (dir. Olivier) 59
Hamlet (Shakespeare) 9, 68
Hammer House of Horror (TV series) 47, 63
Hampton, Paul **21**
Hamsun, Knut 160
The Hands of Orlac (dir. Wiene) 82–83
Hands of the Ripper (dir. Sasdy) 22, 46
Hannibal (dir. Scott) 64
Hardy, Robin 104
Harry, Debbie 53
Hartford-Davis, Robert 87
Hatton, Rondo 104
Hawkins, Jack 10
Hayden, Linda 30
Hearst, Lydia 107
Hedren, Tippi 116
Hegel, G.W.F. 4
Heijningen, Matthija van 122, 123
Hendry, Ian 10
Henenlotter, Frank 100, 101
Henry VI: Part One (Shakespeare) 10
Héroux, Denis 115
Herr, Michael 152
Herzog, Werner 57, 64, 103, 135–138, **136**, 139, 160
Hessler, Gordon 80, 81
Heston, Charlton 26, 61, 144
Hickox, Douglas 9, **10**, **60**
Hidden (dir. Matt & Ross Duffer) 109
Hillcoat, John 64
Hindle, Art 28

Index

Hines, Cindy 28
His Dark Materials trilogy (Pullman) 119
Hitchcock, Alfred 22, 76, 115–118
Hitler, Adolf 33, 53, 61, 74, 82, 86, 93, 147, 158
Hodgson, Leyland 131
Hoffman, Dustin 106
Hoffman, Heinrich 30
Hoffmann, E.T.A. 30, 83
Holland, Tom 54
Holt, Seth 26, 46
Hooper, Tobe 47, 61, *62*
Hopkins, Anthony 63
Hopper, Edward 117
Hordern, Sir Michael 9
Horror Hospital (dir. Balch) 94–95
The Horror of Frankenstein (dir. Sangster) 161
Houghton, Don 159
House, Billy 131
House of Dracula (dir. Kenton) 102
The House That Dripped Blood (dir. Duffell) 47–48
Hughes, Miko 36
Hulse, S. Clarke 59
Human Centipede films (dir. Six) 69–70
Hurt, John 25, 33

I Am Legend (dir. Lawrence) 144–147
I Am Legend (Matheson) 143
I, Daniel Blake (dir. Loach) 58
I Don't Want to Be Born (dir. Sasdy) 31–33, 35
I Walked with a Zombie (dir. Tourneur) 49
Idle, Eric 165
Independence Day (dir. Emmerich) 107
L'Innocente (D'Annunzio) 27
L'Innocente (dir. Visconti) 27
The Innocents (dir. Clayton) 38–42
Inseminoid (dir. Warren) 23
Interview with the Vampire (dir. Jordan) 47
Interview with the Vampire (Rice) 47
The Invasion of the Body Snatchers (dir. Siegal) 103
Ionescu, Eugène 162
Irons, Jeremy 125
Ironside, Michael 91
Irwin, Robert 97
Isherwood, Christopher 17
The Island of Lost Souls (dir. Kenton) 119–120
Island of Terror (dir. Fisher) 66, 127, 105
Itard, Jean Marc Gaspard 138
It's Alive (dir. Cohen) 18–19, *18*, 31–32, 95

Jackson, Glenda 24–25
Jacobs, Paula 63
James, Henry 38, 39, 40
Jenkins, Megs 40
Jeunet, Jean-Pierre 63
The Jewel of Seven Stars (Stoker) 26
Joan of Arc 136
Jolson, Al 160
Jonathan (dir. Geissendörfer) 147

Jones, Freddie 57, 58, 97, 103
Jones, Selina 165
Jones, Terry 31, *71*, 162, 166
Jordan, Neil 47
Josephson, Erland 88
Judd, Edward 149
Julien, Rupert 83, *84*, 85
Juliette (de Sade) 1, 22, 152, 154, 155, 159
Julius Caesar (Shakespeare) 9
Justine (de Sade) 156

Kafka, Franz 112
Kahn, Herman 152
Kaiser, Georg 153
Kant, Immanuel 3, 89
Karloff, Boris 17, 18, 79, 91, 97, 98, 123, 128, 131, 147, 161
Keating, David 19, 37
Keaton, Buster 162
Keats, John 38
Kemp, Jeremy 75
Kenton, Erle C. 102, 119
Kerr, Deborah 38
Kerwin, Lance 47
Key, Janet 33
Kier, Udo 56
Kiersch, Fritz 49, 76
King, George 57
King, Stephen 36, 49, 54, 55, 66, 162
King Kong (dir. Cooper & Schoedsack) 25
King Lear (Shakespeare) 10
King Oedipus (Sophocles) 7
King's Row (dir. Wood) 91
Kinski, Klaus 103
Kinski, Nastassja 33
Kirchin, Basil. 77
Kiss of the Vampire (dir. Sharp) 53, 102
Kleist, Heinrich von 119, 137
Klinger, Max 82
Knowles, Patric 113
Knox, Alexander 46
Knudsen, Eric 30
Koestler, Arthur 99, 148
Kramer, Stanley 142
Krauss, Werner 130
Krumm, Paul Albert 147
Kubrick, Stanley 30, 43, 73, 97, 148, 152
Kydd, Sam 127

Labaki, Nadine 49
Lacey, Catherine 134
Lachman, Harry 111
Lack, Steven 91
Ladd, David 62
Lambert, Mary 36
Lanchester, Elsa 17, 120
Landis, John 114, *115*
Langelaan, George 112
Langella, Frank 130
Langen, Glenn 74

186 Index

Laser, Dieter 69, 70
The Last Man (Shelley) 141, 142
The Last Man on Earth (dir. Ragona & Salkow) 142, 144, 145, *146*
Laughton, Charles 119, 120
Laurinz, James 100
Lautner, Peyton 30
Leader, Anton 91
Leder, Herbert J. 93, *94*
Lee, Anna 131
Lee, Bernard 75
Lee, Christopher 24, 34, 48, 62, 80, 102, 132, *158*, 159, 161
Le Fanu, Sheridan 132
Legend of the Werewolf (dir. Francis) 109
Leigh, Mike 58
Leonardo da Vinci 78
Leppard, Raymond 44
Leroux, Gaston 11, 83, 84
"Level Seven" (dir. Cartier) 153
"Level Seven" (Roshwald) 153
Lever, Maurice 20
Levi-Strauss, Claude 51
Levinson, Barry 107
Lewton, Val 49, 115, 131, 132
Lievsay, Skip 96
Lindfors, Viveca 46
Lindsay, Joan 24
Lindsay-Hogg, Michael 167, *167*, 168
Liotta, Ray 64
Liszt, Franz 128, 141
Lisztomania (dir. Russell) 128
Little Shop of Horrors (dir. Oz) 122
Lloyd, Danny 30
Lloyd, Edward 57
Lloyd, Sue 87
Loach, Ken 58
Loder, John 98
Lom, Herbert 83
Longcrain, Richard 160
López, Sergi 50
Lord of the Flies (dir. Brook) *43*, 44–45
Lord of the Flies (Golding) 42–43, 45, 49
The Lord of the Rings (Tolkien) 48
Lorrain, Jean 84, 125
Losey, Joseph 46
Louis XV 132
Lovecraft, H.P. 120, 122, 123, 124, 125
Lowe, Arthur 10
Lubin, Arthur 91
Lugosi, Bela 25, 113, 143, 147, 161
Lumet, Sidney 153
Lynch, David 34, *35*, 58, 64
Lynch, Jennifer Chambers 80, 81
Lynn, Vera 153

Macbeth (Shakespeare) 8–9
Magee, Patrick 132
The Magic Mountain (Mann) 43
Mahler (dir. Russell) 128

Malthus, Thomas Robert 61
Man and Superman (Shaw) 96
The Man Who Changed His Mind (dir. Stevenson) 97–98
The Man Who Could Cheat Death (dir. Fisher) 127
"The Man Whom the Trees Loved" (Blackwood) 66
Mandiargues, André Pieyre de 68
Maniac Cop (dir. Cohen) 19
Mankiewicz, Joseph L. 74
Mann, Daniel 68
Mann, Thomas 43, 73, 121
Maraschal, Launce *92*
Marat, Jean-Paul 132
Marat/Sade (Weiss) 132–134, *133*, 135, 152
Marlowe, Christopher 11, 96
Marx, Karl 58, 62
Mary Shelley's Frankenstein (dir. Branagh) 15, 19
Mason, Hilary 31
The Masque of the Red Death (dir. Corman) 103, 151
Massey, Daniel 56
Maté, Rudolph 156
Matheson, Richard 143–147
McCabe, Ruth 37
McCartney, Paul 31
McEnvoy, Anne Marie 49
McGovern, Barry 167, *167*
McKellen, Sir Ian 160
McKern, Leo 149
McLeod, Roger 128
Measure for Measure (Shakespeare) 8
Melancholia (dir. von Trier) 154, 156–158
The Merchant of Venice (Shakespeare) 10
Metamorphoses (Ovid) 53
"Metamorphosis" (Kafka) 112
Meyerbeer, Giacomo 85
Meyrinck, Gustav 121
Michelangelo 68
Migicovsky, Alan 22
Milland, Ray 71
Milton, John 114, 148–149
Les Misérables (Schönberg & Boublil) 58
The Mist (dir. Darabont) 66, 67, 77, 162
The Mist (King) 66
Monsieur de Phocas (Lorrain) 84, 125
Monty Python's Life of Brian (dir. Jones) 166–167
Monty Python's Meaning of Life (dir. Jones) 31, 70, *71*, 164–166, 169
Moonraker (dir. Gilbert) 158
Moore, Anne Elizabeth 5–6, 62, 102
Moritzen, Henning 88
Morley, Robert 10, 59, *60*
Morrissey, Paul 56
Mostell, Zero 112
Mozart, Wolfgang Amadeus 82
Mullen, Patty 100

The Mummy (dir. Freund) 72
Murders in the Rue Morgue (dir. Florey) 25
Murnau, F.W. 72, 147
Murphy, Johnny 167, **167**
The Music Lovers (dir. Russell) 24–25, 128
Mussolini, Benito 145, 146
The Mutations (dir. Cardiff) 76–77, 120–122, **121**
My Fair Lady (dir. Cukor) 152
Mysteries (Hamsun) 160–161
The Mysteries of Udolpho (Radcliffe) 12
Mystery and Imagination (TV series) 57
The Mystery of the Wax Museum (dir. Curtiz) 85

Naish, J. Carrol 111
Nance, Jack 34
The Nanny (dir. Holt) 46, 65–66
The Nazis ¾ A Warning from History (TV series) (dir. Rees) 147–148
Nelligan, Kate 130
Neumann, Kurt 111
Newell, Mike 26
Newton, Michael 138
Nicholas, Paul 128
Nietzsche, Friedrich 1–2, 3, 7, 13, 95, 130, 152, 159, 160
The Night of the Living Dead (dir. Romero) 144
Nosferatu (dir. Murnau) 72–73, 147
Nosferatu: Phantom der Nacht (dir. Herzog) 103, 160
Nyby, Christian 122, 123

O'Brien, Fitz-James 124
Ogilvy, Ian 134
Oland, Werner 73
Olivier, Sir Laurence 59
The Omega Man (dir. Sagal) 92, 142, 144, 147
The Omen (dir. Donner) 32, 33, 35, 49, 94
On the Beach (dir. Kramer) 142, 143
On the Beach (Shute) 142
Once Before I Die (dir. Derek) 151
One Flew Over the Cuckoo's Nest (dir. Forman) 132
120 Days of Sodom (de Sade), 68, 154, 155
Orbesen, James 62
Ouspenskaya, Maria 113
Out of the Unknown (TV series) 153
Outbreak (dir. Petersen) 106
Ovid 53–54
Owen, Chris 66
Oz, Frank 122

Palin, Michael 165
Palk, Anna **94**
Pandemic (dir. Suits) 109–110
Pan's Labyrinth (dir. del Toro) 49–51
Paradise Lost (Milton) 32, 113, 148–149
Parker, Kim 93

Passonlini, Pier Paolo 68
Pastor, Àlex 106
Pastor, David 106
Pater, Walter 20
Pearce, Jaqueline 111
Pearson, Richard 63
Peck, Gregory 36
Pedler, Kit 104
Pendry, E.D. 11–12
Penn, Dylan 108
The Perfection (dir. Shepard) 70–71
Pet Semetary (dir. Lambert) 36
Pet Semetary (King) 36
Petersen, Wolfgang 106
Petrie, Susan 22
The Phantom of the Opera (dir. Julien) 83, **84**, 85
The Phantom of the Opera (Leroux) 11, 83–85
Il Piacerel (D'Annunzio) 40
Pickens, Slim 160
Picnic at Hanging Rock (dir. Weir) 24
Pidgeon, Walter 93
Pine, Chris 106
Pitt, Brad 47
Pitt, Ingrid 22
Plague of the Zombies (dir. Gilling) 91, 143
Planet of the Apes (dir. Schaffner) 116, 154
Playing for Time (dir. Mann) 68
Pleasence, Donald 31, 55, 62, 76–77, 122, 130
Pleshette, Suzanne 116
Poe, Edgar Allan 12, 26, 130, 132, 133, 151
Polanski, Roman 23–24, 27–28, 100
Pollock, Jackson 108
Pool, Robert Roy 106
Portrait of an Englishman in His Chateau (Mandiargues) 68–69
Post, Ted 154
Powell, Robert 128, 132
Praljak, Slobodan 155
The Premature Burial (dir. Corman) 71
Prez, John du 162
Price, Dennis 9
Price, Vincent 9, **10**, 11, 26, 59, **60**, 74, 80, 85, **146**, 151
Priestley, J.B. 153
The Private Life of Plants (TV series) 76
The Producers (dir. Brooks) 112
Psycho (dir. Hitchcock) 22, 107, 116, 117
Puccini, Giacomo 81
Pullman, Philip 119
"The Puppet Theater" (Kleist) 119
Purcell, Henry 93
"The Purple Terror" (White) 72
Pythagoras 53, 64

The Quatermass Experiment (dir. Guest) 103–104, 120
Quatermass 2 (dir. Guest), 103

188 Index

Rabid (dir. Cronenberg) 22, 53, 81–82, 95
Radcliffe, Ann 12
Radian, Prince 81, *118*
Ragona, Ubaldo 142, 145, *146*
Rains, Claude 112
Ramachandran, V. S. 90
Raw Meat see *Death Line*
Reagan, Nancy 91
Reagan, Ronald 36, 58, 91
Redgrave, Michael 40
Redgrave, Vanessa 68, 134
Reed, Oliver 29, 114, 134
Rees, Laurence 148
Reeves, Kynaston 93
Reeves, Michael 134
Reid, Milton 109
Reiniger, Scott H. *144*
Reinl, Harald 78
Rennie, Michael 149
The Reptile (dir. Gilling) 111
Repulsion (dir. Polanski) 23–24
Reski, Waltraud 147
Return of the Fly (dir. Bernds) 111
The Revenge of Frankenstein (dir. Fisher) 56–57, 94, 97, 98
Rhinoceros (Ionescu) 162
Rice, Anne 47
Richard II (dir. Longcrain) 160
Richard III (Shakespeare) 10
Richelieu, Cardinal 134, 135
Ridges, Stanley 91
Rigg, Diana *10*
Right at Your Door (dir. Gorak) 106
Rilla, Wolf 28, *29*
The Road (dir. Hillcoat) 64
Roadrunner cartoons 163–164
Robert, Rachel 24
Robinson, Edward G. 61
Robson, Mark 131, 132
Roeg, Nicolas 20
Romeo and Juliet (Shakespeare) 10
Romero, George A. 88, 104, 107, 144, *144*
The Rose and the Key (Le Fanu) 132
Rosemary's Baby (dir. Polanski) 27–28
Roshwald, Mordecai 153
Rousseau, Jean-Jacques 138, 139, 155
Russell, Elizabeth 115
Russell, Ken 24–25, 81, 128, 134–135

Sade, Marquis de 1–2, 15, 20, 22, 31–32, 52, 68, 130, 132, 133, 142, 149, 152, 153, 154, 155, 156, 159, 168, 169
Sagal, Boris 92
'Salem's Lot (dir. Hooper) 47
Salkow, Sidney 145, *146*
Salo (dir. Passolini) 68
"The Sandman" (Hoffmann) 30
Sands, Julian 80, 81
Sangster, Jimmy 56, 161
Sarazin, Michael 17

Sasdy, Peter 22, 31, 33, 35, 46, 104, *105*
The Satanic Rites of Dracula (dir. Gibson) 102, 103, 106, *158*, 159, 161
Savage, Brad 47
Savory, Gerald 129
Scanners (dir. Cronenberg) 91
Scars of Dracula (dir. Baker) 161
Schaffner, Franklin, J. 93, 116
Schiffano, Laurence 27
Die Schlangengrube und das Pendel (dir. Reinl) 78, 133
Schleinstein, Bruno *136*
Schoenhals, Albrecht 61
Schönberg, Claude Michel 58
Schopenhauer, Arthur 1–2, 3, 5, 8, 15–16, 19, 77, 89, 91, 114, 116–117, 130, 131, 137, 140, 141, 151, 152, 157, 158, 159, 160, 163, 164, 165, 167, 168–169
Schubert, Franz 48
Schulman, Ariel 109
Scob, Édith 85, 86
Scott, Ridley 22, 64
Scream and Scream Again (dir. Hessler) 80, 81, 91
"Seeing the World" (O'Brien) 124
Sekely, Steve 74
Seltzer, David 35
A Serbian Film (dir. Spasojević) 154–156
Sewell, Vernon 111
Shakespeare, William 8, 10, 11, 59
Sharp, Don 53, 112
Shaw, George Bernard 96
She (dir. Day) 127
Shelley, Mary 15, 16, 17, 26, 32, 33, 79, 80, 114, 139, 141, 142
Shelley, Percy Bysshe 81, 148
Shepard, Richard 70
Shepherd, Jack 129
Sherman, Gary 62
The Shining (dir. Kubrick) 30–31, 97
Shivers (dir. Cronenberg) 2, *21*, 22, 52, 54
Shute, Neville 142
Siegal, Don 103
Siegfried (Wagner) 95
Silent Running (dir. Trumbull) 154
Silver, Joe 52
The Simpsons (TV series) 163
Simon, Simone 115
Singer, Peter 4, 61
Six, Tom 69, 70
Skal, David J. 83, 147
Slaughter, Tod 57, 58
Slender Man (dir. White) 37, 66
Smith, Will 144
So the Witch Won't Eat Me (Blotch) 65
Society (dir. Yuzna) 63
Soderbergh, Steven 106
Sondheim, Stephen 58
Songs of Innocence and Experience (Blake) 30
Sophocles 7

Index

The Sorcerers (dir. Reeves) 134
Soylent Green (dir. Fleischer) 61, 63
Spall, Timothy 19
Spasojević, Srđan 154–155, 156
Spencer, Colin 64
Spotto, Donald 116
Star Wars (dir. Lucas) 36
Steele, Barbara 22
The Stepford Wives (dir. Forbes) 63
Stevens, Martin 38
Stevenson, Robert 97
Stoker, Bram 19–20, 26, 57, 60–61, 129, 161
Strewelpeter (Hoffman) 30
Suits, John 109
Summers, Montague 34
Survivors (TV series) 104–105
Sutherland, Donald 21, 106
Sweeney Todd (dir. Burton) 58, 59
The Sweeney Todd Demon Barber of Fleet Street (dir. King) 57
Syberberg, Hans-Jürgen 148
Sykes, Peter 33
Sylwan, Kari 88
"The System of Doctor Tarr and Professor Fether" (Poe) 130

A Tale of Two Cities (Dickens) 94
A Tale of Two Cities (dir. Thomas) 151
Tales of Terror (dir. Corman) 26–27
Tandy, Jessica 117
Taste the Blood of Dracula (dir. Sasdy) 46, 161
Taylor, Rod 116
Tchaikovsky, Pyotr 25, 73, 128
Telezynska, Isabella 33
Tennyson, Alfred Lord 67
The Texas Chain Saw Massacre (dir. Hooper) 61–62, **62**
Thackeray, William Makepeace 101
Thatcher, Margaret 58
Theatre of Blood (dir. Hickox) 9–10, **10**, 11, 59, **60**
Thesiger, Ernest 17
The Thing (dir. Carpenter) 122 124
The Thing (dir. Nyby) 122, 123, 124
The Thing (dir. van Heijningen) 122, 123, 124–125
Thinner (dir. Holland) 54–55
Thinner (King) 54
"The Thirteenth Reunion" (dir. Sasdy) 56, 63, 64
Thomas, Gerald 85
Thomas, Ralph 151
Thompson, Marshall 92
Thompson, Robert 29
Thulin, Ingrid 88
Titus Andronicus (Shakespeare) 59
To the Devil a Daughter (dir. Sykes) 33–34, 35, 109
To the Devil a Daughter (Wheatley) 33–34
Todorovic, Srdjan "Zika," 154

Tom and Jerry cartoons 135, 163, 164
Toro, Guillermo del 49–50
The Torture Chamber of Dr. Sadism (dir. Reinl) see *Die Schlangengrube und das Pendel*
Tourneur, Jacques 115
Townsend, Najarra 107
Trier, Lars von 154, 156, 157, 158
Tristan und Isolde (Wagner) 157
Troilus and Cressida (Shakespeare) 10
The Trouble with Being Born (Cioran) 85
Truffaut, François 138–139
Trumbull, Douglas 154
Turandot (Puccini) 81
"The Turn of the Screw" (James) 38–39
Turturro, John 96
Twain, Mark 108
28 Days Later (dir. Boyle), 106
2001¾A Space Odyssey (dir. Kubrick), 73

Ullmann, Liv 88
Ulmer, Edgar G. 147
The Uncanny (dir. Héroux) 115–116

The Vampire Lovers (dir. Baker) 46, 100
Vanity Fair (Thackeray) 101
Vault of Horror (dir. Baker) 56
Veidt, Conrad 82, 83, 130
Venables, Jon 29
Ventham, Wanda 111
Verdú, Maribel 50
Vernon, Glenn 131
Videodrome (dir. Cronenberg) 2, 4, 37, 53, 91
Village of the Damned (dir. Rilla) 28, **29**, 38
Villiers, James 65
Viral (dir. Ariel Schulman and Henry Joost) 109
Visconti, Luchino 27, 61
Voyage of the "Beagle" (Darwin) 66–67

Wagner, Richard 95, 128, 141, 156–157, 158
Waiting for Godot (Beckett) 153, 167
Waiting for Godot (dir. Lindsay-Hogg) 167–168, **167**
Wakewood (dir. Keating) 19, 37–38, 66
Walker, Jonathan 124
Walker, Stuart 73
Walter, Justin 46
Warlords of Atlantis (dir. Connor) 4
Warner, David 36, 94
Warren, Norman J. 23
Watson, Peter 166
Webster, John 12
Weier, Anissa 30
Weir, Peter 24
Weiss, Peter 132, 133, 142
Wells, H.G. 72, 119
The Werewolf of London (dir. Walker) 73, 122
Werker, Alfred 74
Whale, James 16–17, 79, 80

Wheatley, Dennis 33, 34
When Worlds Collide (dir. Maté) 156
White, Fred M. 72
White, Sylvan 37
White Zombie (dir. Halperin) 143
Whiting, Leonard 17
Whitman, Walt 13
The Wicker Man (dir. Hardy) 104
Widmark, Richard 33
Wiene, Robert 82, 83, 130
Wilcox, Fred M. 92
Wilde, Oscar 4, 122
Williams, Kenneth 85
Willman, Noel 53
Wilson, Alison 70
Wilson, Edmund 39
Wise, Robert 149
The Witches (dir. Frankel) 46, 104
Wolf, Hugo 128
The Wolf Man (dir. Waggner) 112–114
The Woman in White (Collins) 132
Wood, Sam 91

Woods, James 2
Woodwood, Edward 104
Wordsworth, Richard 57, 103, 120
The World as Will and Representation (Schopenhauer) 15–16
Wray, Fay 85
Wray, John 56
Wyndham, John 71, 74, 76
Wyngarde, Peter 39

X—The Man with X-Ray Eyes (dir. Corman) 124

Yeaworth, Irvin 66
Yellow Submarine (dir. Dunning) 73
Les Yeux sans Visage (dir. Franju) 85–87, **86**
Yuzna, Brian 63

Zariwny, Travis 108
Zerbe, Anthony 147
Zoltan, Hound of Dracula (dir. Band) 111
Zucco, George 74, 111

www.ingramcontent.com/pod-product-compliance
Lightning Source LLC
Chambersburg PA
CBHW020837020526
44114CB00040B/1242